2001 Suppleme
to
IMMIGRATION AND CITIZENSHIP:
PROCESS AND POLICY
Fourth Edition

By

Thomas Alexander Aleinikoff
Professor of Law
Georgetown University Law Center

David A. Martin
Henry L. & Grace Doherty Professor of Law
University of Virginia

Hiroshi Motomura
Nicholas Doman Professor of International Law
President's Teaching Scholar
University of Colorado School of Law

AMERICAN CASEBOOK SERIES®

WEST GROUP

A THOMSON COMPANY

ST. PAUL, MINN., 2001

American Casebook Series, and the West Group symbol are registered trademarks used herein under license.

COPYRIGHT © 2001 By WEST GROUP
                      610 Opperman Drive
                      P.O. Box 64526
                      St. Paul, MN 55164–0526
                      1–800–328–9352

ISBN 0–314–25950–3

 TEXT IS PRINTED ON 10% POST CONSUMER RECYCLED PAPER

Preface

The immigration and citizenship laws of the United States apply a bit differently now from when the fourth edition of *Immigration and Citizenship: Process and Policy* was published in 1998. No statutory changes as significant as the Illegal Immigration Reform and Immigrant Responsibility Act of 1996 (IIRIRA) have occurred, nor indeed any as significant as the immigration amendments contained in that year's Anti-terrorism and Effective Death Penalty Act (AEDPA). But Congress decidedly has not been quiet. The tone and trend of most of these smaller-scale initiatives stand in marked contrast to the restrictive 1996 enactments. They generally take the form of measures either freeing selected groups from specified restrictions (as in the 1998 Haitian Refugee Immigration Fairness Act or the 2000 Legal Immigrant Family Equity Act) or extending selected benefits on more generous terms (for example, exempting certain disabled applicants from the naturalization oath requirement or extending citizenship almost automatically to children adopted by U.S. citizens). Congress also created several new nonimmigrant visa categories and eased restrictions on business-related immigration as the economy boomed.

Significant developments in the case law have also taken place. Predictably, we now have decisions construing several of the key provisions adopted by IIRIRA or AEDPA—sometimes settling the meaning and other times reflecting sharp differences of view among the federal courts. Administrative and judicial decisions have begun to wrestle systematically with the application of the asylum provisions to claims by women fleeing domestic abuse. The summer of 2001 also brought three highly important immigration decisions from the U.S. Supreme Court, settling long-fought battles over the interpretation of a few of the 1996 amendments, but also bearing major insights into how the Constitution is to apply henceforth to immigration and citizenship questions.

These developments, and many others of smaller scope, are presented or summarized in this Supplement. Each entry is keyed to the corresponding page of the Casebook. Some are truly supplemental to the material we presented in 1998; other segments here are meant to replace sections of the Casebook. The entry heading should make clear which we intended. Abbreviations and technical matters of form and citation follow the conventions in the opening pages of the Casebook. In particular, we have uniformly changed statutory citations to use the numbering system of the Immigration and Nationality Act (INA), rather than the numbers from 8 U.S.C. And we have sometimes dropped citations and footnotes from cases without explicitly indicating such omissions.

We would like to thank Grace Hyun Im, University of Virginia School of Law, class of 2003, for diligent editorial and research assistance in the preparation of both this Supplement and the 2001 Statutory Supplement.

Because we expect to publish a fifth edition of the Casebook in 2003, comments and suggestions are welcome and may be sent to any of the authors.

ALEX ALEINIKOFF
DAVID MARTIN
HIROSHI MOTOMURA

July 5, 2001

Summary of Contents

Preface...iii

Summary of Contents..iii

Table of Authorities vi

Chapter One: Citizenship 1

Chapter Two: Foundations of the Immigration Power 20

Chapter Three: Federal Agencies and Courts 22

Chapter Four: Admissions: Categories and Procedures.......................25

Chapter Five: Constitutional Protection of Aliens After Admission 47

Chapter Six: Unauthorized Migrants in the United States....................57

Chapter Seven: Deportability and Relief From Removal 59

Chapter Eight: Removal Procedures 96

Chapter Nine: Refugees and Political Asylum 161

Table of Authorities

CASES

Abankwah v. INS, 185 F.3d 18 (2d Cir.1999) 205
Abdulai v. Ashcroft, 239 F.3d 542 (3d Cir.2001) 207
Aguirre-Cervantes v. INS, 242 F.3d 1169 (9th Cir.2001) 176, 200
Ali v. Reno, 237 F.3d 591 (6th Cir.2001) 200, 205
Alikhani v. Fasano, 70 F.Supp.2d 1124 (S.D.Cal.1999) 120
Alwaday v. Beebe, 43 F.Supp.2d 1130 (D.Or. 1999) 108
American Immigration Lawyers Association v. Reno, 18 F.Supp.2d 38
  (D.D.C. 1998) 105
American Immigration Lawyers Association v. Reno, 199 F.3d 1352
  (D.C.Cir.2000) 105
Amoakowaa v. Reno, 94 F.Supp.2d 903 (N.D.Ill.2000) 48
Avramenkov v. INS, 99 F.Supp.2d 210 (D.Conn.2000); 120
Barrera-Echavarria v. Rison, 44 F.3d 1441 (9th Cir.) (en banc), cert. denied,
  516 U.S. 976, 116 S.Ct. 479, 133 L.Ed.2d 407 (1995) 120
Califano v. Sanders, 430 U.S. 99, 97 S.Ct. 980, 51 L.Ed.2d 192 (1977) 171
Castro-Cortez v. INS, 239 F.3d 1037 (9th Cir.2001) 105
Chevron U.S.A. Inc. v. Natural Resources Defense Council, Inc., 467 U.S.
  837, 104 S.Ct. 2778, 81 L.Ed.2d 694 (1984) 203
City of Chicago v. Shalala, 189 F.3d 598 (7th Cir.1999), cert. denied, 529
  U.S. 1036, 120 S.Ct. 1530, 146 L.Ed.2d 345 (2000) 52
Cordon-Garcia v. INS, 204 F.3d 985 (9th Cir.2000) 206
Danh v. Demore, 59 F.Supp.2d 994 (N.D.Cal. 1999) 120
Diallo v. INS, 232 F.3d 279 (2d Cir.2000) 206
Drakes v. Zimski, 240 F.3d 246 (3d Cir.2000) 88
Florida Power & Light Co. v. Lorion, 470 U.S. 729, 105 S.Ct. 1598, 84
  L.Ed.2d 643 (1985) 170
González ex rel. González v. Reno, 212 F.3d 1338 (11th Cir.2000),
  affirming 86 F.Supp.2d 1167 (S.D.Fla.2000), rehearing and rehearing en
  banc denied with opinion, 215 F.3d 1243 (11th Cir.2000), cert. denied,
  530 U.S. 1270, 120 S.Ct. 2737, 147 L.Ed.2d 1001 (2000) 201
Gorbach v. Reno, 219 F.3d 1087 (9th Cir.2000) (en banc) 19
Guerrero-Perez v. INS, — F.3d — , 2001 WL 747384 (July 2, 2001) 88
Guerrero-Perez v. INS, 242 F.3d 737 (2001) 87
Henderson v. INS, 157 F.3d 106 (2d Cir.1998), cert. denied, 526 U.S. 1004,
  119 S.Ct. 1141, 143 L.Ed.2d 209 (1999). 69
Hernandez-Montiel v. INS, 225 F.3d 1084 (9th Cir.2000) 176
Humanitarian Law Project v. Reno, 205 F.3d 1130 (9th Cir.2000), cert.
  denied, 121 S.Ct. 1226, 149 L.Ed.2d 136 (2001) 43
In re Resendiz, 25 Cal.4th 230, 19 P.3d 1171, 105 Cal.Rptr.2d 431 (2001) 89
INS v. Aguirre-Aguirre, 526 U.S. 415, 119 S.Ct. 1439, 143 L.Ed.2d 590
  (1999) 202
INS v. St. Cyr, 121 S.Ct. 2271 (2001) 69, 89, 90, 142

Jankowski v. INS, 138 F.Supp.2d 269 (D.Conn.2001) 103
Kataria v. INS, 232 F.3d 1107 (9th Cir.2000) 207
Kiareldeen v. Reno, 71 F.Supp.2d 402 (D.N.J. 1999) 105
Kim v. Schiltgen, 1999 U.S. Dist. LEXIS 12511 (N.D.Cal. 1999), appeal
    pending.. 111
Ladha v. INS, 215 F.3d 889 (9th Cir.2000) 207
Lara-Ruiz v. INS, 241 F.3d 934 (7th Cir.2001) 102
Mart v. Beebe, 94 F.Supp.2d 1120 (D.Or.2000) 48
Matter of Arguelles-Campos, Int.Dec. 3399 (BIA 1999) 89
Matter of Cordova, Int.Dec. 3408 (BIA 1999) 89
Matter of Crammond, 23 I&N Dec. 9 (BIA 2001) 71
Matter of C-V-T-, Int.Dec. 3342 (BIA 1998) 102
Matter of C-Y-Z-, Int.Dec. 3319 (BIA 1997) 176
Matter of Ho, Int.Dec. 3362 (Assoc. Comm'r 1998). 37
Matter of Hsiung, Int.Dec. 3361 (Assoc. Comm'r 1998) 37
Matter of Izumii, Int.Dec. 3360 (Assoc. Comm'r 1998) 37
Matter of K-V-D-, Int.Dec. 3422 (BIA 1999) (en banc) 88
Matter of Lopez-Meza, Int.Dec. 3423 (BIA 1999) 70
Matter of L-S-, Int.Dec. 3386 (BIA 1999) 204
Matter of Marin, 16 I&N Dec. 581 (BIA 1978) 102
Matter of M-D-, Int.Dec. 3339 (BIA 1998) 206
Matter of Michel, Int.Dec. 3335 (BIA 1998) 102
Matter of Monreal-Aguinaga, 23 I&N Dec. 56 (BIA 2001) (en banc) 91
Matter of New York State Dept. of Transportation (NYSDOT), Int.Dec.
    3363 (Assoc. Comm'r 1998) 35
Matter of Perez, Int.Dec. 3389 (BIA 1999) (en banc) 91
Matter of Puente-Salazar, Int.Dec. 3412 (BIA 1999) (en banc) 88
Matter of R-A-, Int.Dec. 3403 (BIA 1999) (en banc) 177, 178, 198
Matter of S-A-, Int.Dec. 3433 (BIA 2000) 177, 195
Matter of S-M-J-, Int.Dec. 3303 (BIA 1997) 206
Matter of Soffici, Int.Dec. 3359 (Assoc. Comm'r 1998); 37
Matter of S-S-, Int.Dec. 3374 (BIA 1999) 204
Matter of S-V-, Int.Dec. 3430 (BIA 2000) 205
Matter of Tijam, Int.Dec. 3372 (BIA 1998) 103
Matter of Torres-Varela, 23 I&N Dec. 78 (BIA 2001) 70
Mayers v. INS, 175 F.3d 1289 (11th Cir.1999). 170
Mustata v. United States Dept of Justice, 179 F.3d 1017 (6th Cir.1999) 169
Najjar v. Reno, 97 F.Supp.2d 1329 (S.D.Fla. 2000) 106
National Council of Resistance of Iran v. Department of State, 251 F.3d 192
    (D.C.Cir.2001) 45
Nguyen v. INS, 121 S.Ct. 2053 (2001) 1, 29, 31
Parra v. Perryman, 172 F.3d 954 (7th Cir.1999) 109
People's Mojahedin Organization of Iran v. United States Department of
    State, 182 F.3d 17 (D.C.Cir.1999), cert. denied, 529 U.S. 1104, 120 S.Ct.
    1846, 146 L.Ed. 788 (2000) 42, 45
R.L. Investment Partners v. INS, 86 F.Supp.2d 1014 (D.Haw.2000) 37

Reno v. American-Arab Anti-Discrimination Committee, 525 U.S. 471, 119 S.Ct. 936, 142 L.Ed.2d 940 (1999) 65, 156

Reno v. Flores, 507 U.S. 292, 113 S.Ct. 1439, 123 L.Ed.2d 1 (1993) 108

Reyes v. Underdown, 73 F.Supp.2d 653 (W.D.La.1999) 120

Rosales-Garcia v. Holland, 238 F.3d 704 (6th Cir.2001) 121

Shaughnessy v. United States ex rel. Mezei, 345 U.S. 206, 73 S.Ct. 625, 97 L.Ed. 956 (1953) 121

Sidhu v. INS, 220 F.3d 1085 (9th Cir.2000) 207

Skidmore v. Swift & Co., 323 U.S. 134, 65 S.Ct. 161, 89 L.Ed. 124 (1944) 31

Song v. INS, 82 F.Supp.2d 1121 (C.D.Cal. 2000) 103

Tapia Garcia v. INS, 237 F.3d 1216 (10th Cir.2001) 88

United States v. Benitez-Villafuerte, 186 F.3d 651 (5th Cir.1999), cert. denied, 528 U.S. 1097, 120 S.Ct. 838, 145 L.Ed. 2d 704 (2000) 107

United States v. Chapa-Garza, 243 F.3d 921 (5th Cir.2001) 88

United States v. Hinojosa-Lopez, 130 F.2d 691 (5th Cir.1997) 88

United States v. Marin-Navarette, 244 F.3d 1284 (11th Cir.2001) 88

United States v. Mead Corp., 121 S.Ct. 2164 (2001) 31

Van Eeton v. Beebe, 49 F.Supp.2d 1186 (D.Or. 1999) 120

Zadvydas v. Davis, 121 S.Ct. 2491 (2001) 122

BOOKS AND ARTICLES

Akram, *Scheherezade Meets Kafka: Two Dozen Sordid Tales of Ideological Exclusion*, 14 Geo. Immig. L.J. 51 (1999) 107

Aleinikoff, T.A., and D. Klusmeyer, eds., Citizenship Today: Global Perspectives and Practices (2001) 1

Aleinikoff, T.A., and D. Klusmeyer, eds., From Migrants to Citizens: Membership in a Changing World (2000) 1

Aleinikoff, *The Green Card Solution,* The American Prospect, Dec. 20, 1999 39

An Investigation of the Immigration and Naturalization Service's Citizenship USA Initiative, http://www.usdoj.gov/oig/igspercr1.htm. 18

Andreas, P., Border Games: Policing the U.S.-Mexico Divide (2000) 63

Bennett, *The Unconstitutionality of Nonuniform Immigration Consequences of "Aggravated Felony" Convictions*, 74 N.Y.U. L. Rev. 1696 (1999) 89

Bleichmar, *Deportation as Punishment: A Historical Analysis of the British Practice of Banishment and Its Impact on Modern Constitutional Law*, 14 Geo. Immig. L.J. 115 (1999) 21

Branigin & Farah, *Asylum Seeker is Impostor, INS Says: Woman's Plea Had Powerful Support*, Wash. Post, Dec. 20, 2000 205

Burkemper, *The Impact of The IIRIRA's Unlawful Presence and Overstay Provisions on Temporary Workers*, 76 Interp.Rel. 1749 (1999) 42

Camarota, *The Slowing Progress of Immigrants: An Examination of Income, Home Ownership, and Citizenship, 1970-2000*, Center for Immigration Studies Backgrounder, Mar. 2001 26

Carnegie Endowment for Int'l Peace, Mexico-U.S. Migration: A Shared Responsibility (2001) 38

Census Finds Immigrants Blending in Faster, Easier, U.S.A. Today, Dec. 27, 2000 26

Chin, *Segregation's Last Stronghold: Race, Discrimination and the Constitutional Law of Immigration*, 46 UCLA L. Rev. 1 (1998) 22

Cohn & Roche, *Indentured Servants for High-Tech Trade*, Baltimore Sun, Feb. 21, 2000 41

Cole, *Damage Control? A Comment on Professor Neuman's Reading of* Reno v. AADC, 14 Geo. Immig. L.J. 347 (2000) 69

Donnelly, *Indefinitely Temporary: Senate Boost to High-Tech Guest Workers Will Block Green Cards,* Center for Immigration Studies Backgrounder, Mar. 2000 40

Espenoza, *No Relief for the Weary: VAWA Relief Denied for Battered Immigrants Lost in the Intersections*, 83 Marquette L. Rev. 163 (1999) 30

Frenzen, *National Security and Procedural Fairness: Secret Evidence and the Immigration Laws*, 76 Interp.Rel. 1677 (1999) 107

General Counsel Criticizes Immigrant Investor Arrangements, Sparking Controversy, 75 Interp.Rel. 323 (1998) 37

Gilbert, *Family Violence and U.S. Immigration Law: New Developments*, Immigration Briefings, Mar. 2001 30, 200

Table of Authorities

Hathaway, *International Refugee Law: The Michigan Guidelines on the Internal Protection Alternative*, 21 Mich. J. Int'l L. 131 (1999) ... 175

Here Come the Kosovars, Refugee Reports, May 1999 ... 173

Holley, *Bad Hosts*, Legal Times, Apr. 9, 2001 ... 39

Immigration and Naturalization Service, Monthly Statistical Report First Quarter Ending December 2000 (Jan. 31, 2001) ... 63

Immigration and Naturalization Service, Monthly Statistical Report, September 2000 FY Year End Report (Oct. 31, 2000) ... 63

INS Fact Sheet, *Changes to the H-1B Program,* 77 Interp.Rel. 1732 (2000) ... 41

INS Office of Policy and Planning, Annual Report, Legal Immigration, Fiscal Year 1998, July 1999 ... 27, 28

INS Provides Important Clarification on Public Charge Standards for Immigrants Receiving Public Benefits, 76 Interp.Rel. 843 (1999) ... 47

INS Reports to Congress on the EB–5 Investor Visa Program, 76 Interp.Rel. 595 (1998) ... 37

Jacklin, *The Haitian Refugee Immigration Fairness Act ("HRIFA")*, Immigration Briefings, Sept. 1999 ... 209

Joaquin & Cancilla, *Protecting Immigrants and the Community: A New Approach to Public Charge Determinations*, 76 Interp.Rel. 885 (1999) ... 47

Johnson, *Race Matters: Immigration Law and Policy Scholarship, Law in the Ivory Tower, and the Legal Indifference of the Race Critique*, U. Ill. L. Rev. 525 (2000) ... 22

Joint Statement of the US-Mexico High Level Working Group on Migration, April 4, 2001 ... 38

Kanstroom, *Deportation, Social Control, and Punishment: Some Thoughts About Why Hard Laws Make Bad Cases*, 113 Harv. L. Rev. 1889 (2000) ... 69, 107

Kirschten, *Labor: Immigrants Without Immigration,* National Journal, Feb. 10, 2001 ... 39

Klasko, *American Competitiveness in the 21st Century: H-1Bs and Much More,* 77 Interp.Rel. 1689 (2000) ... 28, 34, 41

Labor, H-1B, Migration News, July 2001 ... 41

Legomsky, *Fear and Loathing in Congress and the Courts: Immigration and Judicial Review*, 78 Tex. L. Rev. 1615 (2000) ... 156

Maclean, *The Labor Certification Process*, in 1 Immigration and Nationality Law Handbook, 2000-01 Edition, 377, 390-91 (AILA 2000) ... 32

Martin, Mandel, Cheng Fan Kwok *and Other Unappealing Cases: The Next Frontier of Immigration Reform*, 27 Va. J. Int'l L. 803, 809 (1987) ... 170

Martin, *New Rules on Dual Nationality for a Democratizing Globe: Between Rejection and Embrace*, 14. Geo. Immig. L.J. 1 (1999) ... 19

Martin, *On Counterintuitive Consequences and Choosing the Right Control Group: A Defense of* Reno v. AADC, 14 Geo. Immig. L.J. 363 (2000) ... 69

Martin, P., *Guest Worker Programs for the 21st Century,* Center for Immigration Studies Backgrounder, Apr. 2000 ... 39

Martin, S., Schoenholtz, & Meyers, *Temporary Protection: Towards a New Regional and Domestic Framework.* 12 Geo. Immig. L.J. 543 (1998) ... 209

Martin, *Two Cheers for Expedited Removal Under the New Immigration Laws*, 40 Va. J. Int'l L. 673 (2000) ... 104

Martin, *Waiting for Solutions*, Legal Times, May 28, 2001   49

Matloff, *High-Tech Cheap Labor,* Wash. Post, Sept. 12, 2000   40

Matloff, *This Program Exploits Programers,* Newsday, Dec. 22, 2000   40

McDonnell, *Prop. 187 Talks Offered Davis Few Choices*, L.A. Times, July 30, 1999   64

Morawetz, *Understanding the Impact of the 1996 Deportation Laws and the Limited Scope of Proposed Reforms*, 113 Harv. L. Rev. 1938 (2000)   20, 70

Motomura, *Judicial Review in Immigration Cases After* AADC: *Lessons From Civil Procedure*, 14 Geo. Immig. L.J. 385 (2000)   170

Motomura, *The Year is 2020: Looking Back on the Elián González Case (A Fantasy)*, 77 Interp.Rel. 853 (2000)   202

Musalo & Knight, *Gender-Based Asylum: An Analysis of Recent Trends*, 77 Interp.Rel. 1533 (2000)   177

Musalo et al., *The Expedited Removal Study: Report on the First Three Years of Implementation of Expedited Removal*, <http://www.uchastings.edu/ers/reports/2000/2000%20Report.pdf>(2000)   104

Neuman, *Federal Courts Issues in Immigration Law*, 76 Tex. L. Rev. 1661 (2000)   156

Neuman, *Jurisdiction and the Rule of Law After the 1996 Immigration Act*, 113 Harv. L. Rev. 1963 (2000)   156

Neuman, *Terrorism, Selective Deportation and the First Amendment after* Reno v. AADC, 14 Geo. Immig. L.J. 313 (2000)   68

Nugent, *Strengthening Access to Justice: Prehearing Rights Presentations for Detained Respondents*, 76 Interp.Rel. 1077 (1999)   104

Papademetriou, D., & M. Heppel, Balancing Acts: Toward a Fair Bargain on Seasonal Agricultural Workers (Int'l Migration Series: Carnegie Endowment for Int'l Peace, 1999)   39

Papademetriou, D., T.A. Aleinikoff, & D. Meyers, *Reorganizing the U.S. Immigration Function: Toward a New Framework for Accountability* (1998)   24

Pauw, *A New Look at Deportation As Punishment: Why At Least Some of the Constitution's Criminal Procedure Protections Must Apply*, 52 Admin. L. Rev. 305 (2000)   21, 108

Population, States Briefs, Migration News, Sept. 2000   26

Romero, *The Congruence Principle Applied: Rethinking Equal Protection Review in Federal Alienage Classifications After* Adarand Constructors, Inc. v. Pena, 76 Or. L. Rev. 425 (1997)   21

Rosser, Note, *The National Interest Waiver of IMMACT 90,* 14 Geo. Immig. L.J. 165 (1999)   35

Saito, *Alien and Non-Alien Alike: Citizenship, "Foreignness," and Racial Hierarchy in American Law*, 76 Or. L. Rev. 261 (1997)   21

Schmitt, *Abuses are Cited in Trade of Money for U.S. Residence,* N.Y.Times, Apr. 13, 1998   37

Schrag, P.G., A Well-Founded Fear: The Congressional Battle to Save Political Asylum in America (2000)   174

Silverman & Joaquin, *NACARA for Guatemalans, Salvadorans and Former Soviet Bloc Nationals: An Update*, 76 Interp.Rel. 1141 (1999)   207

Stanton, *Changing Paradigms for Labor Certification: New Strategies, Opportunities, and Risks*, Immigration Briefings, Sept. 1997   32

U.S. Census Bureau, *The Foreign-Born Population in the United States,* Current Population Reports, Mar. 2000 (issued Jan. 2001)   26

U.S. Department of State, Bureau of Consular Affairs, Visa Bulletin   29

Waxman, *New York State Department of Transportation: National Interest Waivers One Year Down the Road*, 76 Interp.Rel. 1641 (1999)   35

Weiss, *Employment-based (EB) Immigration at the Millennium: An Examination of the Immigration Act of 1990, Its Aftermath, and The American Competitiveness in the Twenty First Century Act*, Immigration Briefings, Dec. 2000   33

Wheeler, *Affidavit of Support: The Ten Most Common Mistakes*, 5 Bender's Imm. Bulletin 125 (2000)   47

Wheeler, *Affidavit of Support: The Year in Review*, 4 Bender's Imm. Bulletin 97 (1999)   47

Wishnie, *Laboratories of Bigotry?: Devolution of the Immigration Power, Equal Protection, and Federalism*, 76 N.Y.U. L. Rev. 493 (2001)   61

Yale-Loehr, *Beating the Bar: Avoiding, Delaying or Remedying Unlawful Presence*, 3 Bender's Imm. Bulletin 779 (1998)   42

Zitner, *Immigrant Tally Doubles in Census Count: U.S. has twice as many undocumented workers as estimated*, L.A. Times, Mar. 10, 2001   63

Chapter One: Citizenship

9: The Concept of Citizenship (add new note 4)

4. For comparative studies of citizenship law and policy, *see* T.A. Aleinikoff and D. Klusmeyer, eds., From Migrants to Citizens: Membership in a Changing World (2000); T.A. Aleinikoff and D. Klusmeyer, eds., Citizenship Today: Global Perspectives and Practices (2001).

29-43: Gender Discrimination and Jus Sanguinis (delete *Miller v. Albright* and notes 1, 2, and 3 on page 43, and add)

NGUYEN v. INS
Supreme Court of the United States, 2001.
121 S.Ct. 2053.

JUSTICE KENNEDY delivered the opinion of the Court.

This case presents a question not resolved by a majority of the Court in a case before us three Terms ago. *See Miller v. Albright,* 523 U.S. 420 (1998). INA § 309 governs the acquisition of United States citizenship by persons born to one United States citizen parent and one noncitizen parent when the parents are unmarried and the child is born outside of the United States or its possessions. The statute imposes different requirements for the child's acquisition of citizenship depending upon whether the citizen parent is the mother or the father. The question before us is whether the statutory distinction is consistent with the equal protection guarantee embedded in the Due Process Clause of the Fifth Amendment.

I

Petitioner Tuan Ahn Nguyen was born in Saigon, Vietnam, on September 11, 1969, to copetitioner Joseph Boulais and a Vietnamese citizen. Boulais and Nguyen's mother were not married. Boulais always has been a citizen of the United States, and he was in Vietnam under the employ of a corporation. After he and Nguyen's mother ended their relationship, Nguyen lived for a time with the family of Boulais' new Vietnamese girlfriend. In June 1975, Nguyen, then almost six years of age, came to the United States. He became a lawful permanent resident and was raised in Texas by Boulais.

In 1992, when Nguyen was 22, he pleaded guilty in a Texas state court to two counts of sexual assault on a child. He was sentenced to eight years in prison on each count. Three years later, the United States Immigration and Naturalization Service (INS) initiated deportation proceedings against Nguyen as an alien who had been convicted of two crimes involving moral turpitude, as well as an aggravated felony. *See* INA § 237(a)(2)(A)(ii) and (iii). Though later he would change his position and argue he was a United States citizen, Nguyen testified at his deportation hearing that he was a citizen of Vietnam. The Immigration Judge found him deportable.

Nguyen appealed to the Board of Immigration of Appeals and, in 1998, while the matter was pending, his father obtained an order of parentage from a state court, based on DNA testing. By this time, Nguyen was 28 years old. The

1

Board dismissed Nguyen's appeal, rejecting his claim to United States citizenship because he had failed to establish compliance with INA § 309(a), which sets forth the requirements for one who was born out of wedlock and abroad to a citizen father and a noncitizen mother.

Nguyen and Boulais appealed to the Court of Appeals for the Fifth Circuit, arguing that § 309 violates equal protection by providing different rules for attainment of citizenship by children born abroad and out of wedlock depending upon whether the one parent with American citizenship is the mother or the father. The court rejected the constitutional challenge to §309(a). 208 F.3d 528, 535 (2000).

The constitutionality of the distinction between unwed fathers and mothers was argued in *Miller,* but a majority of the Court did not resolve the issue. Four Justices, in two different opinions, rejected the challenge to the gender-based distinction, two finding the statute consistent with the Fifth Amendment, *see* 523 U.S., at 423 (opinion of Stevens, J., joined by Rehnquist, C.J.), and two concluding that the court could not confer citizenship as a remedy even if the statute violated equal protection, *see id.,* at 452 (Scalia, J., joined by Thomas, J., concurring in judgment). Three Justices reached a contrary result, and would have found the statute violative of equal protection. *Id.,* at 460 (Ginsburg J., joined by Souter and Breyer, JJ., dissenting); *id.,* at 471 (Breyer, J., joined by Souter and Ginsburg, JJ., dissenting). Finally, two Justices did not reach the issue as to the father, having determined that the child, the only petitioner in *Miller,* lacked standing to raise the equal protection rights of his father. *Id.,* at 445 (O'Connor, J., joined by Kennedy, J., concurring in judgment).

* * *

II

The general requirement for acquisition of citizenship by a child born outside the United States and its outlying possessions and to parents who are married, one of whom is a citizen and the other of whom is an alien, is set forth in INA § 301(g). The statute provides that the child is also a citizen if, before the birth, the citizen parent had been physically present in the United States for a total of five years, at least two of which were after the parent turned 14 years of age.

As to an individual born under the same circumstances, save that the parents are unwed, § 309(a) sets forth the following requirements where the father is the citizen parent and the mother is an alien:

(1) a blood relationship between the person and the father is established by clear and convincing evidence,

(2) the father had the nationality of the United States at the time of the person's birth,

(3) the father (unless deceased) has agreed in writing to provide financial support for the person until the person reaches the age of 18 years, and

(4) while the person is under the age of 18 years—

(A) the person is legitimated under the law of the person's residence or domicile,

2

> (B) the father acknowledges paternity of the person in writing under oath, or
>
> (C) the paternity of the person is established by adjudication of a competent court.

In addition, § 309(a) incorporates by reference, as to the citizen parent, the residency requirement of § 301(g).

When the citizen parent of the child born abroad and out of wedlock is the child's mother, the requirements for the transmittal of citizenship are described in § 309(c):

> (c) Notwithstanding the provision of subsection (a) of this section, a person born, after December 23, 1952, outside the United States and out of wedlock shall be held to have acquired at birth the nationality status of his mother, if the mother had the nationality of the United States at the time of such person's birth, and if the mother had previously been physically present in the United States or one of its outlying possessions for a continuous period of one year.

Section 309(a) thus imposes a set of requirements on the children of citizen fathers born abroad and out of wedlock to a noncitizen mother that are not imposed under like circumstances when the citizen parent is the mother. All concede the requirements of §§ 309(a)(3) and (a)(4), relating to a citizen father's acknowledgment of a child while he is under 18, were not satisfied in this case. We need not discuss § 309(a)(3), however. It was added in 1986, after Nguyen's birth; and Nguyen falls within a transitional rule which allows him to elect application of either the current version of the statute, or the pre-1986 version, which contained no parallel to § 309(a)(3). *See* Immigration and Nationality Act Amendments of 1986, 100 Stat. 3655; note following 8 U.S.C. § 1409; *Miller, supra,* at 426, n.3, 432 (opinion of Stevens, J.). And in any event, our ruling respecting § 309(a)(4) is dispositive of the case. As an individual seeking citizenship under § 309(a) must meet all of its preconditions, the failure to satisfy § 309(a)(4) renders Nguyen ineligible for citizenship.

III

For a gender-based classification to withstand equal protection scrutiny, it must be established "'at least that the [challenged] classification serves "important governmental objectives and that the discriminatory means employed" are "substantially related to the achievement of those objectives."'" *United States* v. *Virginia,* 518 U.S. 515, 533 (1996) (quoting *Mississippi Univ. for Women* v. *Hogan,* 458 U.S. 718, 724 (1982) in turn quoting *Wengler* v. *Druggists Mut. Ins. Co.,* 446 U.S. 142, 150 (1980)). For reasons to follow, we conclude § 309 satisfies this standard. Given that determination, we need not decide whether some lesser degree of scrutiny pertains because the statute implicates Congress' immigration and naturalization power. *See Miller,* 523 U.S., at 434, n.11 (explaining that the statute must be subjected to a standard more deferential to the congressional exercise of the immigration and naturalization power, but that "[e]ven if . . . the heightened scrutiny that normally governs gender discrimination claims applied in this context," the statute would be sustained (citations omitted)).

Before considering the important governmental interests advanced by the statute, two observations concerning the operation of the provision are in order. First, a citizen mother expecting a child and living abroad has the right to re-enter the United States so the child can be born here and be a 14th Amendment citizen. From one perspective, then, the statute simply ensures equivalence between two expectant mothers who are citizens abroad if one chooses to reenter for the child's birth and the other chooses not to return, or does not have the means to do so. This equivalence is not a factor if the single citizen parent living abroad is the father. For, unlike the unmarried mother, the unmarried father as a general rule cannot control where the child will be born.

Second, although § 309(a)(4) requires certain conduct to occur before the child of a citizen father, born out of wedlock and abroad, reaches 18 years of age, it imposes no limitations on when an individual who qualifies under the statute can claim citizenship. The statutory treatment of citizenship is identical in this respect whether the citizen parent is the mother or the father. A person born to a citizen parent of either gender may assert citizenship, assuming compliance with statutory preconditions, regardless of his or her age. And while the conditions necessary for a citizen mother to transmit citizenship under § 309(c) exist at birth, citizen fathers and/or their children have 18 years to satisfy the requirements of § 309(a)(4).

The statutory distinction relevant in this case, then, is that § 309(a)(4) requires one of three affirmative steps to be taken if the citizen parent is the father, but not if the citizen parent is the mother: legitimation; a declaration of paternity under oath by the father; or a court order of paternity. Congress' decision to impose requirements on unmarried fathers that differ from those on unmarried mothers is based on the significant difference between their respective relationships to the potential citizen at the time of birth. Specifically, the imposition of the requirement for a paternal relationship, but not a maternal one, is justified by two important governmental objectives. We discuss each in turn.

A

The first governmental interest to be served is the importance of assuring that a biological parent-child relationship exists. In the case of the mother, the relation is verifiable from the birth itself. The mother's status is documented in most instances by the birth certificate or hospital records and the witnesses who attest to her having given birth.

In the case of the father, the uncontestable fact is that he need not be present at the birth. If he is present, furthermore, that circumstance is not incontrovertible proof of fatherhood. Fathers and mothers are not similarly situated with regard to the proof of biological parenthood. The imposition of a different set of rules for making that legal determination with respect to fathers and mothers is neither surprising nor troublesome from a constitutional perspective. Section 309(a)(4)'s provision of three options for a father seeking to establish paternity—legitimation, paternity oath, and court order of paternity—is designed to ensure an acceptable documentation of paternity.

Petitioners argue that the requirement of § 309(a)(1), that a father provide clear and convincing evidence of parentage, is sufficient to achieve the end of establishing paternity, given the sophistication of modern DNA tests. Brief for Petitioners 21-24. Section 309(a)(1) does not actually mandate a DNA test, however. The Constitution, moreover, does not require that Congress elect one particular mechanism from among many possible methods of establishing paternity, even if that mechanism arguably might be the most scientifically advanced method. With respect to DNA testing, the expense, reliability, and availability of such testing in various parts of the world may have been of particular concern to Congress. The requirement of § 309(a)(4) represents a reasonable conclusion by the legislature that the satisfaction of one of several alternatives will suffice to establish the blood link between father and child required as a predicate to the child's acquisition of citizenship. Given the proof of motherhood that is inherent in birth itself, it is unremarkable that Congress did not require the same affirmative steps of mothers.

Finally, to require Congress to speak without reference to the gender of the parent with regard to its objective of ensuring a blood tie between parent and child would be to insist on a hollow neutrality. As Justice Stevens pointed out in *Miller,* Congress could have required both mothers and fathers to prove parenthood within 30 days or, for that matter, 18 years, of the child's birth. 523 U.S., at 436. Given that the mother is always present at birth, but that the father need not be, the facially neutral rule would sometimes require fathers to take additional affirmative steps which would not be required of mothers, whose names will appear on the birth certificate as a result of their presence at the birth, and who will have the benefit of witnesses to the birth to call upon. The issue is not the use of gender specific terms instead of neutral ones. Just as neutral terms can mask discrimination that is unlawful, gender specific terms can mark a permissible distinction. The equal protection question is whether the distinction is lawful. Here, the use of gender specific terms takes into account a biological difference between the parents. The differential treatment is inherent in a sensible statutory scheme, given the unique relationship of the mother to the event of birth.

B

1

The second important governmental interest furthered in a substantial manner by § 309(a)(4) is the determination to ensure that the child and the citizen parent have some demonstrated opportunity or potential to develop not just a relationship that is recognized, as a formal matter, by the law, but one that consists of the real, everyday ties that provide a connection between child and citizen parent and, in turn, the United States. In the case of a citizen mother and a child born overseas, the opportunity for a meaningful relationship between citizen parent and child inheres in the very event of birth, an event so often critical to our constitutional and statutory understandings of citizenship. The mother knows that the child is in being and is hers and has an initial point of contact with him. There is at least an opportunity for mother and child to develop a real, meaningful relationship.

The same opportunity does not result from the event of birth, as a matter of biological inevitability, in the case of the unwed father. Given the 9-month interval between conception and birth, it is not always certain that a father will know that a child was conceived, nor is it always clear that even the mother will be sure of the father's identity. This fact takes on particular significance in the case of a child born overseas and out of wedlock. One concern in this context has always been with young people, men for the most part, who are on duty with the Armed Forces in foreign countries. *See* Department of Defense, Selected Manpower Statistics 48, 74 (1999) (reporting that in 1969, the year in which Nguyen was born, there were 3,458,072 active duty military personnel, 39,506 of whom were female); Department of Defense, Selected Manpower Statistics 29 (1970) (noting that 1,041,094 military personnel were stationed in foreign countries in 1969); Department of Defense, Selected Manpower Statistics 49, 76 (1999) (reporting that in 1999 there were 1,385,703 active duty military personnel, 200,287 of whom were female); *id.,* at 33 (noting that 252,763 military personnel were stationed in foreign countries in 1999).

When we turn to the conditions which prevail today, we find that the passage of time has produced additional and even more substantial grounds to justify the statutory distinction. The ease of travel and the willingness of Americans to visit foreign countries have resulted in numbers of trips abroad that must be of real concern when we contemplate the prospect of accepting petitioners' argument, which would mandate, contrary to Congress' wishes, citizenship by male parentage subject to no condition save the father's previous length of residence in this country. In 1999 alone, Americans made almost 25 million trips abroad, excluding trips to Canada and Mexico. *See* U.S. Dept. of Commerce, 1999 Profile of U.S. Travelers to Overseas Destinations 1 (Oct. 2000). Visits to Canada and Mexico add to this figure almost 34 million additional visits. *See* U.S. Dept. of Commerce, U.S. Resident Travel to Overseas Countries, Historical Visitation 1989-1999, p.1 (Oct. 2000). And the average American overseas traveler spent 15.1 nights out of the United States in 1999. 1999 Profile of U.S. Travelers to Overseas Destinations, *supra,* at 4.

Principles of equal protection do not require Congress to ignore this reality. To the contrary, these facts demonstrate the critical importance of the Government's interest in ensuring some opportunity for a tie between citizen father and foreign born child which is a reasonable substitute for the opportunity manifest between mother and child at the time of birth. Indeed, especially in light of the number of Americans who take short sojourns abroad, the prospect that a father might not even know of the conception is a realistic possibility. Even if a father knows of the fact of conception, moreover, it does not follow that he will be present at the birth of the child. Thus, unlike the case of the mother, there is no assurance that the father and his biological child will ever meet. Without an initial point of contact with the child by a father who knows the child is his own, there is no opportunity for father and child to begin a relationship. Section 309 takes the unremarkable step of ensuring that such an opportunity, inherent in the event of birth as to the mother-child relationship, exists between father and child before citizenship is conferred upon the latter.

The importance of the governmental interest at issue here is too profound to be satisfied merely by conducting a DNA test. The fact of paternity can be established even without the father's knowledge, not to say his presence. Paternity can be established by taking DNA samples even from a few strands of hair, years after the birth. *See* Federal Judicial Center, Reference Manual on Scientific Evidence 497 (2d ed. 2000). Yet scientific proof of biological paternity does nothing, by itself, to ensure contact between father and child during the child's minority.

Congress is well within its authority in refusing, absent proof of at least the opportunity for the development of a relationship between citizen parent and child, to commit this country to embracing a child as a citizen entitled as of birth to the full protection of the United States, to the absolute right to enter its borders, and to full participation in the political process. If citizenship is to be conferred by the unwitting means petitioners urge, so that its acquisition abroad bears little relation to the realities of the child's own ties and allegiances, it is for Congress, not this Court, to make that determination. Congress has not taken that path but has instead chosen, by means of § 309, to ensure in the case of father and child the opportunity for a relationship to develop, an opportunity which the event of birth itself provides for the mother and child. It should be unobjectionable for Congress to require some evidence of a minimal opportunity for the development of a relationship with the child in terms the male can fulfill.

* * *

Petitioners and their *amici* argue in addition that, rather than fulfilling an important governmental interest, § 309 merely embodies a gender-based stereotype. Although the above discussion should illustrate that, contrary to petitioners' assertions, § 309 addresses an undeniable difference in the circumstance of the parents at the time a child is born, it should be noted, furthermore, that the difference does not result from some stereotype, defined as a frame of mind resulting from irrational or uncritical analysis. There is nothing irrational or improper in the recognition that at the moment of birth—a critical event in the statutory scheme and in the whole tradition of citizenship law—the mother's knowledge of the child and the fact of parenthood have been established in a way not guaranteed in the case of the unwed father. This is not a stereotype. *See Virginia,* 518 U.S., at 533 ("The heightened review standard our precedent establishes does not make sex a proscribed classification. . . . Physical differences between men and women . . . are enduring.")

2

Having concluded that facilitation of a relationship between parent and child is an important governmental interest, the question remains whether the means Congress chose to further its objective—the imposition of certain additional requirements upon an unwed father—substantially relate to that end. Under this test, the means Congress adopted must be sustained.

First, it should be unsurprising that Congress decided to require that an opportunity for a parent-child relationship occur during the formative years of the child's minority. In furtherance of the desire to ensure some tie between this country and one who seeks citizenship, various other statutory provisions concerning citizenship and naturalization require some act linking the child to the United States to occur before the child reaches 18 years of age. *See, e.g.,* INA § 320 (child born abroad to one citizen parent and one noncitizen parent shall become a citizen if, *inter alia*, the noncitizen parent is naturalized before the child reaches 18 years of age and the child begins to reside in the United States before he or she turns 18); § 321 (imposing same conditions in the case of a child born abroad to two alien parents who are naturalized).

Second, petitioners argue that § 309(a)(4) is not effective. In particular, petitioners assert that, although a mother will know of her child's birth, "knowledge that one is a parent, no matter how it is acquired, does not guarantee a relationship with one's child." Brief for Petitioners 16. They thus maintain that the imposition of the additional requirements of § 309(a)(4) only on the children of citizen fathers must reflect a stereotype that women are more likely than men to actually establish a relationship with their children. *Id.* at 17.

This line of argument misconceives the nature of both the governmental interest at issue and the manner in which we examine statutes alleged to violate equal protection. As to the former, Congress would of course be entitled to advance the interest of ensuring an actual, meaningful relationship in every case before citizenship is conferred. Or Congress could excuse compliance with the formal requirements when an actual father-child relationship is proved. It did neither here, perhaps because of the subjectivity, intrusiveness, and difficulties of proof that might attend an inquiry into any particular bond or tie. Instead, Congress enacted an easily administered scheme to promote the different but still substantial interest of ensuring at least an opportunity for a parent-child relationship to develop. Petitioners' argument confuses the means and ends of the equal protection inquiry; § 309(a)(4) should not be invalidated because Congress elected to advance an interest that is less demanding to satisfy than some other alternative.

Even if one conceives of the interest Congress pursues as the establishment of a real, practical relationship of considerable substance between parent and child in every case, as opposed simply to ensuring the potential for the relationship to begin, petitioners' misconception of the nature of the equal protection inquiry is fatal to their argument. A statute meets the equal protection standard we here apply so long as it is """"substantially related to the achievement of"""" the governmental objective in question. *Virginia, supra,* at 533 (quoting *Hogan,* 458 U.S., at 724 (in turn quoting *Wengler,* 446 U.S., at 150)). It is almost axiomatic that a policy which seeks to foster the opportunity for meaningful parent-child bonds to develop has a close and substantial bearing on the governmental interest in the actual formation of that bond. None of our gender-based classification equal protection cases have required that the statute under consideration must be capable of achieving its ultimate objective in every instance.

In this difficult context of conferring citizenship on vast numbers of persons, the means adopted by Congress are in substantial furtherance of important governmental objectives. The fit between the means and the important end is "exceedingly persuasive." *See Virginia*, 518 U.S., at 533. We have explained that an "exceedingly persuasive justification" is established "by showing at least that the classification serves 'important governmental objectives and that the discriminatory means employed' are 'substantially related to the achievement of those objectives.'" *Hogan, supra*, at 724 (citations omitted). Section 309 meets this standard.

C

In analyzing § 309(a)(4), we are mindful that the obligation it imposes with respect to the acquisition of citizenship by the child of a citizen father is minimal. This circumstance shows that Congress has not erected inordinate and unnecessary hurdles to the conferral of citizenship on the children of citizen fathers in furthering its important objectives. Only the least onerous of the three options provided for in § 309(a)(4) must be satisfied. If the child has been legitimated under the law of the relevant jurisdiction, that will be the end of the matter. *See* § 309(a)(4)(A). In the alternative, a father who has not legitimated his child by formal means need only make a written acknowledgement of paternity under oath in order to transmit citizenship to his child, hardly a substantial burden. *See* § 309(a)(4)(B). Or, the father could choose to obtain a court order of paternity. *See* § 309(a)(4)(C). The statute can be satisfied on the day of birth, or the next day, or for the next 18 years. In this case, the unfortunate, even tragic, circumstance is that Boulais did not pursue, or perhaps did not know of, these simple steps and alternatives. Any omission, however, does not nullify the statutory scheme.

Section 309(a), moreover, is not the sole means by which the child of a citizen father can attain citizenship. An individual who fails to comply with § 309(a), but who has substantial ties to the United States, can seek citizenship in his or her own right, rather than via reliance on ties to a citizen parent. *See, e.g.,* INA §§ 312, 316. This option now may be foreclosed to Nguyen, but any bar is due to the serious nature of his criminal offenses not to an equal protection denial or to any supposed rigidity or harshness in the citizenship laws.

IV

* * *

* * * [In light of our holding that there is no equal protection violation,] we need not assess the implications of statements in our earlier cases regarding the wide deference afforded to Congress in the exercise of its immigration and naturalization power. *See, e.g., Fiallo v. Bell,* 430 U.S. 787, 792-793, and n.4 (1977) (quoting *Galvan v. Press,* 347 U.S. 522, 531 (1954)); 430 U.S., at 792 (quoting *Oceanic Steam Nav. Co. v. Stranahan,* 214 U.S. 320, 339 (1909)). These arguments would have to be considered, however, were it to be determined that § 309 did not withstand conventional equal protection scrutiny.

V

To fail to acknowledge even our most basic biological differences—such as the fact that a mother must be present at birth but the father need not be—risks making the guarantee of equal protection superficial, and so disserving it. Mechanistic classification of all our differences as stereotypes would operate to obscure those misconceptions and prejudices that are real. The distinction embodied in the statutory scheme here at issue is not marked by misconception and prejudice, nor does it show disrespect for either class. The difference between men and women in relation to the birth process is a real one, and the principle of equal protection does not forbid Congress to address the problem at hand in a manner specific to each gender.

The judgment of the Court of Appeals is

Affirmed.

JUSTICE SCALIA, with whom JUSTICE THOMAS joins, concurring.

I remain of the view that the Court lacks power to provide relief of the sort requested in this suit—namely, conferral of citizenship on a basis other than that prescribed by Congress. *See Miller* v. *Albright,* 523 U.S. 420, 452 (1998) (Scalia, J., concurring in judgment). A majority of the Justices in *Miller* having concluded otherwise, *see id.*, at 423 (opinion of Stevens, J., joined by Rehnquist, C. J.); *id.*, at 460 (Ginsburg, J., joined by Souter and Breyer, JJ., dissenting); *id.*, at 471 (Breyer, J., joined by Souter and Ginsburg, JJ., dissenting); and a majority of the Court today proceeding on the same assumption; I think it appropriate for me to reach the merits of petitioners' equal protection claims. I join the opinion of the Court.

JUSTICE O'CONNOR, with whom JUSTICE SOUTER, JUSTICE GINSBURG, and JUSTICE BREYER join, dissenting.

* * *

II

* * *

A

According to the Court, "[t]he first governmental interest to be served is the importance of assuring that a biological parent-child relationship exists." The majority does not elaborate on the importance of this interest, which presumably lies in preventing fraudulent conveyances of citizenship. Nor does the majority demonstrate that this is one of the actual purposes of § 309(a)(4). Assuming that Congress actually had this purpose in mind in enacting parts of § 309(a)(4), the INS does not appear to rely on this interest in its effort to sustain § 309(a)(4)'s sex-based classification. In light of the reviewing court's duty to "determine whether the proffered justification is 'exceedingly persuasive,'" *Virginia,* 518 U.S., at 533, this disparity between the majority's defense of the statute and the INS' proffered justifications is striking, to say the least.

The gravest defect in the Court's reliance on this interest, however, is the insufficiency of the fit between § 309(a)(4)'s discriminatory means and the asserted end. Section 309(c) imposes no particular burden of proof on mothers wishing to convey citizenship to their children. By contrast, § 309(a)(1), which petitioners do not challenge before this Court, requires that "a blood relationship between the person and the father [be] established by clear and convincing evidence." Atop § 309(a)(1), § 309(a)(4) requires legitimation, an acknowledgment of paternity in writing under oath, or an adjudication of paternity before the child reaches the age of 18. It is difficult to see what § 309(a)(4) accomplishes in furtherance of "assuring that a biological parent-child relationship exists," that § 309(a)(1) does not achieve on its own. The virtual certainty of a biological link that modern DNA testing affords reinforces the sufficiency of § 309(a)(1).

It is also difficult to see how § 309(a)(4)'s limitation of the time allowed for obtaining proof of paternity substantially furthers the assurance of a blood relationship. Modern DNA testing, in addition to providing accuracy unmatched by other methods of establishing a biological link, essentially negates the evidentiary significance of the passage of time. Moreover, the application of § 309(a)(1)'s "clear and convincing evidence" requirement can account for any effect that the passage of time has on the quality of the evidence.

The Court criticizes petitioners' reliance on the availability and sophistication of modern DNA tests, but appears to misconceive the relevance of such tests. No one argues that § 309(a)(1) mandates a DNA test. Legitimation or an adjudication of paternity, *see* §§ 309(a)(4)(A), (C), may well satisfy the "clear and convincing" standard of § 309(a)(1). (Satisfaction of § 309(a)(4) by a written acknowledgment of paternity under oath, *see* § 309(a)(4)(B), would seem to do little, if anything, to advance the assurance of a blood relationship, further stretching the means-end fit in this context). Likewise, petitioners' argument does not depend on the idea that one particular method of establishing paternity is constitutionally required. Petitioners' argument rests instead on the fact that, if the goal is to obtain proof of paternity, the existence of a statutory provision governing such proof, coupled with the efficacy and availability of modern technology, is highly relevant to the sufficiency of the tailoring between § 309(a)(4)'s sex-based classification and the asserted end. Because § 309(a)(4) adds little to the work that §309(a)(1) does on its own, it is difficult to say that § 309(a)(4) "substantially furthers" an important governmental interest.

The majority concedes that Congress could achieve the goal of assuring a biological parent-child relationship in a sex-neutral fashion, but then, in a surprising turn, dismisses the availability of sex-neutral alternatives as irrelevant. As the Court suggests, "Congress could have required both mothers and fathers to prove parenthood within 30 days or, for that matter, 18 years, of the child's birth." Indeed, whether one conceives the majority's asserted interest as assuring the existence of a biological parent-child relationship, or as ensuring acceptable documentation of that relationship, a number of sex-neutral arrangements—including the one that the majority offers—would better serve that end. As the majority seems implicitly to acknowledge at one point, a mother will not always have formal legal documentation of birth because a birth certificate may not issue or may subsequently be lost. Conversely, a father's name may well appear on a birth certificate. While it is doubtless true that a mother's blood relation to a child is uniquely "verifiable from the birth itself" to those present at birth, the majority has not shown that a mother's birth relation is uniquely verifiable *by the INS,* much less that any greater verifiability warrants a sex-based, rather than a sex-neutral, statute.

In our prior cases, the existence of comparable or superior sex-neutral alternatives has been a powerful reason to reject a sex-based classification. The majority, however, turns this principle on its head by denigrating as "hollow" the very neutrality that the law requires. While the majority trumpets the availability of superior sex-neutral alternatives as confirmation of § 309(a)(4)'s validity, our precedents demonstrate that this fact is a decided strike *against* the law. Far from being "hollow," the avoidance of gratuitous sex-based distinctions is the hallmark of equal protection.

* * *

B

The Court states that "[t]he second important governmental interest furthered in a substantial manner by § 309(a)(4) is the determination to ensure that the child and the citizen parent have some demonstrated opportunity or potential to develop not just a relationship that is recognized, as a formal matter, by the law, but one that consists of the real, everyday ties that provide a connection between child and citizen parent and, in turn, the United States." The Court again fails to demonstrate that this was Congress' actual purpose in enacting § 309(a)(4). The majority's focus on "some demonstrated opportunity or potential to develop . . . real, everyday ties," in fact appears to be the type of hypothesized rationale that is insufficient under heightened scrutiny.

The INS asserts the governmental interest of "ensuring that children who are born abroad out of wedlock have, during their minority, attained a sufficiently recognized or formal relationship to their United States citizen parent—and thus to the United States—to justify the conferral of citizenship upon them." Brief for Respondent 11. The majority's asserted end, at best, is a simultaneously watered-down and beefed-up version of this interest asserted by the INS. The majority's rendition is weaker than the INS' in that it emphasizes the "opportunity or potential to develop" a relationship rather than the actual relationship about which the INS claims Congress was concerned. The majority's version is also stronger in that it goes past the formal relationship apparently desired by the INS to "real, everyday ties."

Assuming, as the majority does, that Congress was actually concerned about ensuring a "demonstrated opportunity" for a relationship, it is questionable whether such an opportunity qualifies as an "important" governmental interest apart from the existence of an actual relationship. By focusing on "opportunity" rather than reality, the majority presumably improves the chances of a sufficient means-end fit. But in doing so, it dilutes significantly the weight of the interest. It is difficult to see how, in this citizenship-conferral context, anyone profits from a "demonstrated opportunity" for a relationship in the absence of the fruition of an actual tie. Children who have an "opportunity" for such a tie with a parent, of course, may never develop an actual relationship with that parent. If a child grows up in a foreign country without any postbirth contact with the citizen parent, then the child's never-realized "opportunity" for a relationship with the citizen seems singularly irrelevant to the appropriateness of granting citizenship to that child. Likewise, where there is an actual relationship, it is the actual relationship that does all the work in rendering appropriate a grant of citizenship, regardless of when and how the opportunity for that relationship arose.

Accepting for the moment the majority's focus on "opportunity," the attempt to justify § 309(a)(4) in these terms is still deficient. Even if it is important "to require that an opportunity for a parent-child relationship occur during the formative years of the child's minority," it is difficult to see how the requirement that *proof* of such opportunity be obtained before the child turns 18 substantially furthers the asserted interest. As the facts of this case demonstrate, it is entirely possible that a father and child will have the opportunity to develop a relationship and in fact will develop a relationship without obtaining the proof of the opportunity during the child's minority. After his parents' relationship had ended, petitioner Nguyen lived with the family of his father's new girlfriend. In 1975, before his sixth birthday, Nguyen came to the United States, where he was reared by his father, petitioner Boulais. In 1997, a DNA test showed a 99.98% probability of paternity, and, in 1998, Boulais obtained an order of parentage from a Texas court.

* * *

Moreover, available sex-neutral alternatives would at least replicate, and could easily exceed, whatever fit there is between § 309(a)(4)'s discriminatory means and the majority's asserted end. According to the Court, § 309(a)(4) is designed to ensure that fathers and children have the same "opportunity which the event of birth itself provides for the mother and child." Even assuming that this is so, Congress could simply substitute for § 309(a)(4) a requirement that the parent be present at birth or have knowledge of birth. Congress could at least allow proof of such presence or knowledge to be one way of demonstrating an opportunity for a relationship. Under the present law, the statute on its face accords different treatment to a mother who is by nature present at birth and a father who is by choice present at birth even though those two individuals are similarly situated with respect to the "opportunity" for a relationship. The mother can transmit her citizenship at birth, but the father cannot do so in the absence of at least one other affirmative act. The different statutory treatment is solely on account of the sex of the similarly situated individuals. This type of treatment is patently inconsistent with the promise of equal protection of the laws.

Indeed, the idea that a mother's presence at birth supplies adequate assurance of an opportunity to develop a relationship while a father's presence at birth does not would appear to rest only on an overbroad sex-based generalization. A mother may not have an opportunity for a relationship if the child is removed from his or her mother on account of alleged abuse or neglect, or if the child and mother are separated by tragedy, such as disaster or war, of the sort apparently present in this case. There is no reason, other than stereotype, to say that fathers who are present at birth lack an opportunity for a relationship on similar terms. The "[p]hysical differences between men and women," *Virginia,* 518 U.S., at 533, therefore do not justify § 309(a)(4)'s discrimination.

The majority later ratchets up the interest, for the sake of argument, to "the establishment of a real, practical relationship of considerable substance between parent and child in every case, as opposed simply to ensuring the potential for the relationship to begin." But the majority then dismisses the distinction between opportunity and reality as immaterial to the inquiry in this case. The majority rests its analysis of the means-end fit largely on the following proposition: "It is almost axiomatic that a policy which seeks to foster the opportunity for meaningful parent-child bonds to develop has a close and substantial bearing on the governmental interest in the actual formation of that bond." A bare assertion of what is allegedly "almost axiomatic," however, is no substitute for the "demanding" burden of justification borne by the defender of the classification. *Virginia, supra,* at 533.

Moreover, the Court's reasoning hardly conforms to the tailoring requirement of heightened scrutiny. The fact that a discriminatory policy embodies the good intention of "seek[ing] to foster" the opportunity for something beneficial to happen is of little relevance in itself to whether the policy substantially furthers the desired occurrence. Whether the classification indeed "has a close and substantial bearing" on the actual occurrence of the preferred result depends on facts and circumstances and must be proved by the classification's defender. Far from being a virtual axiom, the relationship between the intent to foster an opportunity and the fruition of the desired effect is merely a contingent proposition. The majority's sweeping claim is no surrogate for the careful application of heightened scrutiny to a particular classification.

The question that then remains is the sufficiency of the fit between §309(a)(4)'s discriminatory means and the goal of "establish[ing] . . . a real, practical relationship of considerable substance." If Congress wishes to advance this end, it could easily do so by employing a sex-neutral classification that is a far "more germane bas[i]s of classification" than sex, *Craig* [*v. Boren,* 429 U.S. 190, 198 (1976)]. For example, Congress could require some degree of regular contact between the child and the citizen parent over a period of time.

The majority again raises this possibility of the use of sex-neutral means only to dismiss it as irrelevant. The Court admits that "Congress could excuse compliance with the formal requirements when an actual father-child relationship is proved," but speculates that Congress did not do so "perhaps because of the subjectivity, intrusiveness, and difficulties of proof that might attend an inquiry into any particular bond or tie." We have repeatedly rejected efforts to justify sex-based classifications on the ground of administrative convenience. There is no reason to think that this is a case where administrative convenience concerns are so powerful that they would justify the sex-based discrimination, especially where the use of sex as a proxy is so ill fit to the purported ends as it is here. And to the extent Congress might seek simply to ensure an "opportunity" for a relationship, little administrative inconvenience would seem to accompany a sex-neutral requirement of presence at birth, knowledge of birth, or contact between parent and child prior to a certain age.

The claim that § 309(a)(4) substantially relates to the achievement of the goal of a "real, practical relationship" thus finds support not in biological differences but instead in a stereotype—*i.e.,* "the generalization that mothers are significantly more likely than fathers . . . to develop caring relationships with their children." *Miller, supra,* at 482-483 (Breyer, J., dissenting). Such a claim relies on "the very stereotype the law condemns," *J. E. B.* [*v. Alabama ex rel. T. B.,* 511 U.S. 127, 138 (1994)] (internal quotation marks omitted), "lends credibility" to the generalization, *Mississippi Univ. for Women* [*v. Hogan,* 458 U.S. 718, 730 (1982)], and helps to convert that "assumption" into "a self-fulfilling prophecy," *ibid.* Indeed, contrary to this stereotype, Boulais has reared Nguyen, while Nguyen apparently has lacked a relationship with his mother.

The majority apparently tries to avoid reliance on this stereotype by characterizing the governmental interest as a "demonstrated opportunity" for a relationship and attempting to close the gap between opportunity and reality with a dubious claim about what is "almost axiomatic." But the fact that one route is wisely forgone does not mean that the other is plausibly taken. The inescapable conclusion instead is that § 309(a)(4) lacks an exceedingly persuasive justification.

In denying petitioner's claim that § 309(a)(4) rests on stereotypes, the majority articulates a misshapen notion of "stereotype" and its significance in our equal protection jurisprudence. The majority asserts that a "stereotype" is "defined as a frame of mind resulting from irrational or uncritical analysis." This Court has long recognized, however, that an impermissible stereotype may enjoy empirical support and thus be in a sense "rational." Indeed, the stereotypes that underlie a sex-based classification "may hold true for many, even most, individuals." *Miller,* 523 U.S., at 460 (Ginsburg, J., dissenting). But in numerous cases where a measure of truth has inhered in the generalization, "the Court has rejected official actions that classify unnecessarily and overbroadly by gender when more accurate and impartial functional lines can be drawn." *Ibid.*

Nor do stereotypes consist only of those overbroad generalizations that the reviewing court considers to "show disrespect" for a class. The hallmark of a stereotypical sex-based classification under this Court's precedents is not whether the classification is insulting, but whether it "relie[s] upon the simplistic, outdated assumption that gender could be used as a 'proxy for other, more germane bases of classification.'" *Mississippi Univ. for Women, supra,* at 726 (quoting *Craig, supra,* at 198).

* * *

C

The Court has also failed even to acknowledge the "volumes of history" to which "[t]oday's skeptical scrutiny of official action denying rights or opportunities based on sex responds." [*Virginia,* 518 U.S.] at 531. The history of sex discrimination in laws governing the transmission of citizenship and with respect to parental responsibilities for children born out of wedlock counsels at least some circumspection in discerning legislative purposes in this context.

Section 309 was first enacted as § 205 of the Nationality Act of 1940, 54 Stat. 1139-1140. The 1940 Act had been proposed by the President, forwarding a report by a specially convened Committee of Advisors, including the Attorney General. The Committee explained to Congress the rationale for § 205, whose sex-based classification remains in effect today:

> [T]he Department of State has, at least since 1912, uniformly held that an illegitimate child born abroad of an American mother acquires at birth the nationality of the mother, in the absence of legitimation or adjudication establishing the paternity of the child. This ruling is based . . . on the ground that the mother in such case stands in the place of the father . . . . [U]nder American law the

mother has a right to custody and control of such child as against the putative father, and *is bound* to maintain it as its *natural guardian.* This rule seems to be in accord with the old Roman law and with the laws of Spain and France.

To Revise and Codify the Nationality Laws of the United States, Hearings on H. R. 6127 before the House Committee on Immigration and Naturalization, 76th Cong., 1st Sess., 431 (1945) (reprinting Message from the President, Nationality Laws of the United States (1938)) (emphasis added and internal quotation marks and citations omitted).

Section 309(a)(4) is thus paradigmatic of a historic regime that left women with responsibility, and freed men from responsibility, for nonmarital children. Under this law, as one advocate explained to Congress in a 1932 plea for a sex-neutral citizenship law, "when it comes to the illegitimate child, which is a great burden, then the mother is the only recognized parent, and the father is put safely in the background." Naturalization and Citizenship Status of Certain Children of Mothers Who Are Citizens of the United States, Hearing on H. R. 5489 before the House Committee on Immigration and Naturalization, 72nd Cong., 1st Sess., 3 (testimony of Burnita Shelton Matthews); *see also id.,* at 5 (citizenship law "permit[s] [the father] to escape the burdens incident to illegitimate parenthood"). Unlike § 309(a)(4), our States' child custody and support laws no longer assume that mothers alone are "bound" to serve as "natural guardians" of nonmarital children. The majority, however, rather than confronting the stereotypical notion that mothers must care for these children and fathers may ignore them, quietly condones the "very stereotype the law condemns," *J. E. B.,* 511 U.S., at 138 (internal quotation marks omitted).

* * *

III

* * *

As to the question of deference [afforded to Congress in the exercise of its immigration and naturalization power], the pivotal case is *Fiallo* v. *Bell,* 430 U.S. 787 (1977). *Fiallo,* however, is readily distinguished. *Fiallo* involved constitutional challenges to various statutory distinctions, including a classification based on the sex of a United States citizen or lawful permanent resident, that determined the availability of a special immigration preference to certain aliens by virtue of their relationship with the citizen or lawful permanent resident. *Id.,* at 788-792. The Court, emphasizing "the limited scope of judicial inquiry into immigration legislation," [*id.*] at 792, rejected the constitutional challenges. The Court noted its repeated prior emphasis that " 'over no conceivable subject is the legislative power of Congress more complete than it is over' the admission of aliens." *Ibid.* (quoting *Oceanic Steam Nav. Co.* v. *Stranahan,* 214 U.S. 320, 339 (1909)).

The instant case is not about the admission of aliens but instead concerns the logically prior question whether an individual is a citizen in the first place. A predicate for application of the deference commanded by *Fiallo* is that the individuals concerned be aliens. But whether that predicate obtains is the very matter at issue in this case. *Cf. Miller,* 523 U.S., at 433, n.10 (opinion of Stevens, J.) ("[T]he Government now argues . . . that an alien outside the territory of the United States has no substantive rights cognizable under the Fifth Amendment. Even if that is so, the question to be decided is whether petitioner is such an alien or whether, as [petitioner] claims, [petitioner] is a citizen. Thus, we must address the merits to determine whether the predicate for this argument is accurate" (internal quotation marks and citation omitted).) Because §§ 301 and 309 govern the conferral of citizenship at birth, and not the admission of aliens, the ordinary standards of equal protection review apply. *See id.,* at 480-481 (Breyer, J., dissenting).

* * *

No one should mistake the majority's analysis for a careful application of this Court's equal protection jurisprudence concerning sex-based classifications. Today's decision instead represents a deviation from a line of cases in which we have vigilantly applied heightened scrutiny to such classifications to determine whether a constitutional violation has occurred. I trust that the depth and vitality of these precedents will ensure that today's error remains an aberration. I respectfully dissent.

55: Naturalization Procedures (add after first full paragraph)

Special Provisions for Children

As noted in the preceding excerpt, children usually attain naturalization derivatively when their parents are naturalized. Children adopted overseas by U.S. citizen parents are not derivatively naturalized, as their parents are already U.S. citizens. In 2000, Congress enacted legislation that granted automatic naturalization to such children residing in the United States with citizen parents. Child Citizenship Act of 2000, Pub. L. 106-395, 144 Stat. 1631 (2000) (amending INA § 320). Under the Act, a foreign-born child under the age of 18 who has one citizen parent, resides in the custody of that citizen parent and is residing in the United States as a permanent resident, automatically becomes a citizen. The INS estimates that perhaps as many as 75,000 children currently living in the United States will benefit from the statute as well as the approximately 20,000 adopted children of U.S. citizens who are admitted as permanent resident aliens annually.

Note that the law applies to both natural and adopted children. Under what circumstances might a natural child need to take advantage of the legislation?

58: CitizenshipUSA (add to end of carryover paragraph)

The Department of Justice's Office of Inspector General conducted a detailed investigation of the CitizenshipUSA program. Its report, released July 31, 2000, concluded that the program had not been initiated for political purposes but that the INS had "failed to address known system weaknesses before implementing a program that they knew would tax that system as it never had been taxed before." An executive summary of the report and its conclusions are available on-line. *An Investigation of the Immigration and Naturalization Service's Citizenship USA Initiative,* http://www.usdoj.gov/oig/igspercr1.htm.

62: Knowledge of History and Civics (add as new paragraph at end of note 2)

The Hmong Veterans Naturalization Act, Pub. L. 106-207, 114 Stat. 316 (2000), provided an exemption from the English-language requirement and "special considerations" regarding the civics requirement for refugees admitted from Laos who "served with a special guerrilla unit, or irregular forces, operating from a base in Laos in support of the United States military at any time during the period beginning February 28, 1961, and ending September 18, 1978." Later, Pub. L. 106-415, 114 Stat. 1810 (2000), extended these benefits to widows of eligible veterans.

80: Waiver of the Naturalization Oath (add new note 4 after carryover paragraph)

4. Pub. L. 106-448, 114 Stat. 1939 (2000), waived the oath of allegiance for those applicants whose disability prevents them for understanding the oath. Section 337(a) of the INA was amended to authorize the Attorney General to waive the taking of the oath by a person "if in the opinion of the Attorney General the person is unable to understand, or to communicate an understanding of, its meaning because of a physical or developmental disability or mental impairment." A person for whom the oath is waived is considered "to have met the requirements of section 316(a)(3) with respect to attachment to the principles of the Constitution and well disposition to the good order and happiness of the United States."

93: Dual Nationality (add at end of note 1)

See generally Martin, *New Rules on Dual Nationality for a Democratizing Globe: Between Rejection and Embrace*, 14. Geo. Immig. L.J. 1 (1999) .

118: Administrative Denaturalization (add new paragraph to note 6)

In *Gorbach v. Reno*, 219 F.3d 1087 (9th Cir.2000) (en banc), the Ninth Circuit held that the Attorney General lacked statutory authority to administratively revoke naturalization. The court rejected the government's argument that the power to denaturalize is inherent in the power to naturalize, concluding that the 1990 amendments to the INA "shifted the power to naturalize citizens from federal and state courts to the Attorney General, but left intact the district court denaturalization proceeding." The court stressed the importance of U.S. citizenship in the following terms:

> Citizenship in the United States of America is among our most valuable rights. For many of us, it is all that protects our life, liberty, and property from arbitrary deprivation. The world is full of miserable governments that protect none of these rights. Many of us would be dead or never conceived in wretched places in other countries, had we or our ancestors not obtained American citizenship. ... An executive department cannot simply decide, without express statutory authorization, to create an internal executive procedure to deprive people of those rights without even going to court.

Id. at 1098. In January 2001, a permanent injunction was entered prohibiting the government from invoking the administrative denaturalization procedures. *See* 78 Interp.Rel. 442 (2001).

Chapter Two: Foundations of the Immigration Power

174: Later Developments (add at end of carryover paragraph)

For more on the 1996 changes, see Morawetz, *Understanding the Impact of the 1996 Deportation Laws and the Limited Scope of Proposed Reforms*, 113 Harv. L. Rev. 1938 (2000)

172-75: Later Developments

Issues relating to immigration and immigrants have remained prominent in Congress since the casebook went to press in early 1998. While nothing became law that approached the basic restructuring of the Immigration and Nationality Act in 1996, numerous significant measures addressed discrete topics, and certain trends are discernible. Other chapters discuss these developments in greater detail.

Some amendments to the INA changed the rules for some nonimmigrant categories and introduced new ones. Congress responded to vigorous lobbying from businesses adversely affected by a cap on temporary work visas (in a category known as H-1B) by increasing the cap several times, while subjecting employers to additional requirements meant to satisfy critics of the program. Congress added several new nonimmigrant categories in 1998-2000. The Legal Immigrant Family Equity Act (LIFE Act) created V visas to allow the admission of spouses and minor children of permanent residents who have been waiting more than three years for their own permanent resident status. Congress also expanded the K visa category for fiancés and fiancées of U.S. citizens to expedite the admission of new spouses of citizens. There are other new nonimmigrant categories for victims of sex trafficking and slave labor in the United States, and for victims of abuse resulting from a specified list of crimes. Congress is also actively considering several proposals to expand admission of workers, especially agricultural workers. A guestworker program with Mexico has figured prominently in talks between Presidents George W. Bush and Vicente Fox.

Other new provisions concerned relief from removal and adjustment of status to permanent residency. For example, the LIFE Act temporarily revived §245(i), a provision that allows aliens who have been present in the country illegally to become permanent residents without leaving the United States, if they fit one of the immigrant categories—primarily through family ties to U.S. citizens or permanent residents or through U.S. employment. Section 245(i) matters a great deal because it allows those who qualify to avoid bars to permanent residency that would be triggered if they had to leave the country to pick up a visa. The Battered Women Immigrant Protection Act of 2000 made it generally easier for battered spouses and children of U.S. citizens or permanent residents to remain in the United States in lawful status on their own, without requiring the cooperation of the batterer. Some relief from removal provisions addressed only specific nationality groups. For example, the Haitian Refugee Immigration Fairness Act of 1998 opened up permanent residency to Haitians on terms similar to those for Nicaraguans and Cubans under the *de facto* amnesty in the 1997 Nicaraguan Adjustment and Central American Relief Act (NACARA).

Taken together, these developments concerning nonimmigrant categories and relief from removal may signal a trend toward changing lawful immigration indirectly—not by changing basic immigrant categories, but rather by easing the transition from nonimmigrant to permanent resident, and by allowing those here unlawfully to become lawful permanent residents through relief from removal. The new T, U, and V nonimmigrant visas foresee adjustment to permanent resident status, as does one of the two principal proposals for a Mexican guestworker program.

Other amendments to the INA do not fit into either of these two trends but merit mention nonetheless. An important set of enactments addressed citizenship requirements, for example by easing English-language and civics requirements for Hmong veterans, eliminating the naturalization oath for certain disabled applicants, and providing for the automatic naturalization of children born overseas to U.S. citizen parents or adopted by U.S. citizen parents.

217: Deportation and Punishment (add at end)

For further reading, see Pauw, *A New Look at Deportation As Punishment: Why At Least Some of the Constitution's Criminal Procedure Protections Must Apply*, 52 Admin. L. Rev. 305 (2000); Bleichmar, *Deportation as Punishment: A Historical Analysis of the British Practice of Banishment and Its Impact on Modern Constitutional Law*, 14 Geo. Immig. L.J. 115 (1999) .

218: Modern Attacks on "Plenary Power" (add at end)

A growing body of scholarship has explored the role of race—a theme obviously central to the *Chinese Exclusion Case*—in the development of immigration law and policy. *See, e.g.,* Saito, *Alien and Non-Alien Alike: Citizenship, "Foreignness," and Racial Hierarchy in American Law*, 76 Or. L. Rev. 261 (1997); Romero, *The Congruence Principle Applied: Rethinking Equal Protection Review in Federal Alienage Classifications After* Adarand Constructors, Inc. v. Pena, 76 Or. L. Rev. 425 (1997) ; Chin, *Segregation's Last Stronghold: Race, Discrimination and the Constitutional Law of Immigration*, 46 UCLA L. Rev. 1 (1998); Johnson, *Race Matters: Immigration Law and Policy Scholarship, Law in the Ivory Tower, and the Legal Indifference of the Race Critique*, U. Ill. L. Rev. 525 (2000) (criticizing this casebook among other works for paying inadequate attention to race and/or to critical race theory).

Chapter Three: Federal Agencies and Courts

247-51: The Immigration and Naturalization Service (add at end of page 248)

By FY 2001, INS's budget grew to over $5 billion and its staffing level exceeded 33,000. President Bush's first budget proposal contemplates continued significant growth, looking to a $5.5 billion budget for FY 2002 and staffing growth to over 36,000 employees. 78 Interp.Rel. 296, 810 (2001).

INS is making increasing use of its website (http://www.ins.usdoj.gov) to provide information to the public, covering, for example, regulatory developments, policy changes, and breaking news. Also available there are the governing laws and regulations, as well as printable versions of most of the INS forms that applicants and practitioners commonly need. In addition, INS launched a new telephone hot-line (1-800-375-5283) in early 2000, meant to provide better access to information on immigration benefits and services. The telephone service is available in both English and Spanish, and early feedback suggests that it affords notably easier access to useful answers, including through live assistance, than earlier phone systems.

249: The Border Patrol (add at end of final full paragraph)

Congress continues to fund steady increases in the ranks of the Border Patrol. In 2001, there were over 9,000 Border Patrol agents, and a major hiring push continues. The Bush administration projects the deployment of over 11,000 agents by the end of FY 2003, which would represent, according to its figures, a 175 percent increase since 1993. 78 Interp.Rel. 810 (2001).

250: Adjudications (add at end of first full paragraph)

Applications for benefits have risen steeply in recent years, partly because Congress has added several new programs, with their own intricately detailed requirements. According to INS's FY 2000 year-end statistical report, the agency received nearly 5.5 million applications and petitions for immigration benefits that year, plus another 460,000 applications for naturalization.

256: Immigration Judges (add at end of third paragraph)

The immigration court caseload did not grow as EOIR projected in the mid-1990s, owing largely to the new authorities given to INS under the 1996 IIRIRA to issue removal orders (expedited removal and administrative removal, discussed in Chapter Eight) or to enforce previously issued removal orders (reinstatement, also discussed in Chapter Eight) without the involvement of an immigration judge. IJ receipts peaked in FY 1997 at 297,000, declined to 232,000 by FY 1999, and resumed their climb in FY 2000, reaching 254,000 that year. The total number of judges remains at just over 200.

257-59: Appeals

The caseload of the BIA grew even more steeply than projected, with receipts hovering around 30,000 each year from FY 1997 through 2000. In response, EOIR expanded the Board to 21 members and continues to make provision for temporary members drawn from the ranks of current immigration judges and administrative law judges, as well as retired Board members and IJs. The Board also began implementing new streamlining regulations in November 1999. They allow a single member to issue an affirmance, without opinion, of the appealed decision if he or she finds "that the result reached in the decision under review was correct; that any errors in the decision under review were harmless or nonmaterial." 8 C.F.R. § 3.1(a)(7). The immigration judge's opinion then becomes the final agency determination for purposes of any further appeals.

The EOIR website (http://www.usdoj.gov/eoir) provides useful information, including statistical reports and practice manuals, as well as easy access to local immigration court rules and BIA precedent decisions.

262: The Department of State

Immigration-related information is available from the Department of State's Visa Services website (http://travel.state.gov/visa_services.html). The latest information on immigrant visa processing (showing visa allocation priority dates now being processed—an indication of how far down the waiting list the Department is currently reaching) may be found at the Visa Bulletin site (http://travel.state.gov/visa_bulletin.html).

262-63: The United States Information Agency

On October 1, 1999, the USIA was integrated into the Department of State, pursuant to the Foreign Affairs Reform and Restructuring Act of 1998, Pub. L. No. 105-277, Div. G, 112 Stat. 2681-761, in order to assure better coordination of its activities with overall U.S. foreign policy goals. Authority over waivers of the two-year foreign residence requirement that applies to many exchange visitors (before they can obtain permanent status in the United States), INA § 212(e), now rests with the visa office in the Department's Bureau of Consular Affairs.

263-68: Restructuring (add at end, after note 4)

5. In 1999, a set of restructuring proposals put forward by a Washington think-tank, the Carnegie Endowment for International Peace, drew considerable attention. D. Papademetriou, T.A. Aleinikoff, & D. Meyers, *Reorganizing the U.S. Immigration Function: Toward a New Framework for Accountability* (1998). Determined to rise above the "reactive" proposals that had so far received the main attention, the authors suggested that migration operations should all be consolidated in a new cabinet-level agency, perhaps known as the Department of Migration and Citizenship, based loosely on the model of the Environmental Protection Agency. It would combine all of the migration-related functions currently performed by the Departments of Justice, State, and Labor, and would be internally organized so as to separate enforcement and adjudication functions. As a second alternative, the report suggested elevating the immigration function within the Department of Justice. A central change would be the creation of separate Divisions of Immigration Enforcement and Immigration Services, both of which would report to a newly created position of

Associate Attorney General for Immigration, who would be one of the five or six top officers of the Department.

By late 1999 both the executive branch and Congress had developed restructuring proposals that followed the general lines of Carnegie's Option 2. Both plans would have separated INS's enforcement and service functions, placing them in two new bureaus within the Department of Justice. Moreover, the DOJ plan and most congressional versions had these units reporting to a new Associate Attorney General who would specialize in immigration matters. But agreement could not be reached on details as the 1999 congressional term came to an end, and the executive branch could not proceed with such a reorganization without congressional approval. Although there was some hope for a revival of restructuring plans in 2000, the issue was shelved as the campaign year heated up. George W. Bush pledged on the campaign trail to pursue the separation of immigration enforcement and services, and Administration statements have reiterated the general theme since the inauguration. President Bush's choice for the post of INS Commissioner also seemed to signal continued interest in significant restructuring. He announced in April 2001 that he would nominate James Ziglar, a lawyer with considerable business and management experience, who had been serving since 1998 as Senate Sergeant-at-Arms. As of the time of this writing, however, Ziglar has not been confirmed and the Administration has issued no detailed restructuring plan. 76 Interp.Rel. 1161, 1249, 1606 (1999); 77 *id.* 377, 1480 (2000); 78 *id.* 738, 921 (2001).

Chapter Four: Admissions: Categories and Procedures

284: Characteristics of Immigrants (add at end of section A.1.a.)

The Census Bureau reported that the foreign-born population of the United States reached an all-time high of 28.4 million in 2000, up from 9.6 million in 1970. On a percentage basis, however, the 2000 figure amounted to 10.4 percent of total population, which remains well below the 14.7 percent foreign-born recorded in 1910. One-third of the current foreign-born population comes from Mexico or Central America. Foreign-born residents age 25 and older were as likely as natives to be college graduates (26 percent), but a lower percentage of the foreign born finished secondary school. Only 67 percent have at least a high school education, compared with 87 percent of the native-born, although these patterns vary widely by region of birth (from 37.3 percent for Central America to 83.8 percent from Asia). As a group, the foreign-born earn less than natives and are more likely to live in poverty. Thirty-seven percent of the foreign-born are naturalized citizens. U.S. Census Bureau, *The Foreign-Born Population in the United States,* Current Population Reports, Mar. 2000 (issued Jan. 2001) . This report is based on the Current Population Survey, not the comprehensive 2000 census, for which results will be issued over the following three years.

The Bureau reported that immigrants are learning English at an accelerated pace and catching up educationally more quickly than earlier generations. *Census Finds Immigrants Blending in Faster, Easier,* U.S.A. Today, Dec. 27, 2000, at 11A. For a more pessimistic interpretation of the latest statistics, see Camarota, *The Slowing Progress of Immigrants: An Examination of Income, Home Ownership, and Citizenship, 1970-2000,* Center for Immigration Studies Backgrounder, Mar. 2001.

On the related but separate question of ethnic origin, the Census Bureau reported that by 1999 the Hispanic population (not necessarily foreign born) made up 12.5 percent of the U.S. population (35.3 million people), a growth of 39 percent in one decade. The population who identified themselves as of Asian and Pacific Island origin grew by 43 percent, to 10.8 million people. For a comparison, the African-American population grew by 14 percent, to 35 million, and the non-Hispanic white population by seven percent, to 224.6 million. *Population, States Briefs,* Migration News, Sept. 2000; 78 Interp.Rel. 670 (2001).

287: Add to Table 4.4

Table 4A

Immediate Relatives Admitted, FY 1997-98

Fiscal Year	Number Admitted
1997	322,440
1998	284,270

Source: INS Office of Policy and Planning, Annual Report, Legal Immigration, Fiscal Year 1998, July 1999.

292: Diversity Immigration

The interest in diversity immigration has increased, even as the number of admissions available has dropped to 50,000 (as a result of an offset to cover admissions authorized by NACARA, see Casebook pp. 285 n.4, 775-78, 1167-71). Over 13 million applications were filed for each of the FY 2001 and 2002 lotteries, of which 2 million for 2001 and 3 million for 2002 were disqualified for failing to follow the instructions. *See* 77 Interp.Rel. 912-13 (2000), 78 *id.* 848 (2001). The largest shares of admissions for 2002 were awarded to applicants from Ghana, Nigeria, and Sierra Leone.

294: Add to Table 4.7

Table 4.7A

Immigrants Admitted by Major Category of Admission, FY 1997-98

Category	1998	1997
All immigrants	**660,477**	**798,378**
Immediate relatives of U.S. citizens	**284,270**	**322,440**
Family-sponsored preferences	**191,480**	**213,331**
1st preference	17,717	22,536
2nd preference	88,488	113,681
3rd preference	22,257	21,943
4th preference	63,018	55,171
Employment-based preferences	**77,517**	**90,607**
1st preference	21,408	21,810
2nd preference	14,384	17,059
3rd preference	34,317	42,596
4th preference	6,584	7,781
5th preference	824	1,361
Diversity Programs	**45,499**	**49,374**
Refugees and Asylees	**54,709**	**112,158**
Other (including parolees, cancellation of removal, Amerasians)	**6,981**	**10,404**

Source: INS Office of Policy and Planning, Annual Report, Legal Immigration, Fiscal Year 1998, July 1999.

It should be noted that the decline in overall admissions largely reflects processing bottlenecks, particularly in INS's completion of adjustments of status, rather than any significant decline in immigration demand. During these years, INS examination resources were partially diverted to cope with record demand for naturalization and also to fix naturalization processing problems as a priority matter. INS was also still coping with a major increase in adjustment demand stemming from the enactment of INA § 245(i). *See* Casebook pp. 504-06 and material for p. 507 *infra*. INS has estimated that legal immigration for the four-year period encompassing FY 1995-98 would have been 450,000-550,000 higher if not for the backlogs in adjustment of status. INS News Release, Aug. 11, 1999, http://www.ins.usdoj.gov/graphics/publicaffairs/newsrels/Legal.htm. As of 2001, INS has embarked on a new priority effort to improve adjustment processing and to reduce delays, which had reached two years or more, to the target processing time of six months from filing to approval.

296: Ceilings and Floors (add at end of carryover paragraph)

Section 104 of the American Competitiveness in the Twenty-first Century Act (AC21), Pub. L. 106-313, 114 Stat. 1251 (2000), added a new INA § 202(a)(5), which essentially eliminates per-country ceilings for the employment-based categories, as long as fewer than the full annual limit for employment-based visas available are being used. The law has no effect on the per-country ceilings as applied to family-based categories. *See* Klasko, *American Competitiveness in the 21st Century: H-1Bs and Much More,* 77 Interp.Rel. 1689, 1692 (2000) .

297: Table 4.8 (add after existing table)

Table 4.8A

Visa Preference Admissions for July 2001

	Worldwide	China	India	Mexico	Philippines
FAMILY CATEGORIES					
1st	1-01-97	1-01-97	1-01-97	1-01-90	5-22-88
2A	9-22-96	9-22-96	9-22-96	10-22-94	9-22-96
2B	1-01-93	1-01-93	1-01-93	10-22-91	1-01-93
3rd	1-01-96	1-01-96	1-01-96	1-01-74	12-8-87
4th	10-8-89	10-8-89	5-8-88	10-8-89	9-01-79
EMPLOYMENT CATEGORIES					
1st	Current	Current	Current	Current	Current
2nd	Current	Current	Current	Current	Current
3rd	Current	Current	Current	Current	Current
Unskilled	Current	Current	Current	Current	Current
4th	Current	Current	Current	Current	Current
Religious	Current	Current	Current	Current	Current
5th	Current	Current	Current	Current	Current

Source: U.S. Department of State, Bureau of Consular Affairs, Visa Bulletin.

July 2001 represents the first time in many years that all employment-based categories are current. This somewhat surprising situation largely derives from the changes made by AC21, enacted in October 2000. (*See* material for p. 296 *supra*.) The "current" status of the subcategory for unskilled workers, in particular, may prove to be a short-term anomaly, because only 5,000 admissions per year will be available to the unskilled in succeeding fiscal years, owing to offsets for NACARA admissions. (*See* Casebook, p. 284 n.4.) For June 2001, visas were available for unskilled workers only if their priority date was before May 1, 1999—still a major improvement over the seven-year wait reflected in Table 4.8 of the Casebook.

The most recent visa admission chart may always be found at the State Department's Visa Bulletin website (http://travel.state.gov/visa_bulletin.html).

319: Notes to *Fiallo v. Bell* (add at end of notes)

5. In *Nguyen v. INS*, 121 S.Ct. 2053 (2001), a 5-4 majority upheld against a gender discrimination challenge a somewhat comparable statutory distinction between the mothers and fathers of out-of-wedlock children for purposes of transmitting U.S. citizenship at birth. U. S. citizen mothers would transmit citizenship almost automatically, but citizen fathers had to pursue additional specified administrative steps before the child reached 18 in order for the child to be considered a citizen. The Court stated that the statute was constitutional even under the heightened scrutiny normally applied to gender distinctions; therefore it did not have to reach the issue whether a less demanding standard would apply in the immigration and naturalization field. *Nguyen* is treated more comprehensively in the material for pp. 29-43 *supra*.

338: IMFA and the Problem of Spouse Abuse (add at end of last paragraph of the section)

Other critics found further shortcomings in the 1994 amendments meant to protect battered spouses and children, which had been enacted as part of the Violence Against Women Act of 1994 (VAWA), Pub.L. 103-322, 108 Stat. 1902-1955. *See, e.g.,* Espenoza, *No Relief for the Weary: VAWA Relief Denied for Battered Immigrants Lost in the Intersections*, 83 Marquette L. Rev. 163 (1999) (proposing the elimination of the good moral character requirement for VAWA self-petitioners and the addition of a new judicial recommendation against deportation for battered immigrants). Congress acted to address many of the criticisms in the Battered Immigrant Women Protection Act of 2000 (often called VAWA 2000), which was enacted as §§ 1501-1513 of the Victims of Trafficking and Violence Protection Act of 2000, Pub.L.106-386, 114 Stat.1464, 1518. For a highly useful summary of the provisions, see Gilbert, *Family Violence and U.S. Immigration Law: New Developments*, Immigration Briefings, Mar. 2001.

VAWA 2000 expands the class of battered spouses and children who can self-petition, particularly through elimination of the requirement that extreme hardship be shown. INA § 204(a)(1)(A)(iii), (A)(iv), (A)(v), (B)(ii), (B)(iii), (B)(iv). It also provides discretion to examiners to find that the petitioner possesses good moral character despite certain criminal convictions, if the criminal act was "connected to the alien's having been battered or subjected to extreme cruelty." INA § 204(a)(1)(C). Certain other grounds of inadmissibility and deportability can be waived or overcome if the petitioner shows that the violation had "a connection" to the battery or cruelty. *See, e.g.,* INA §§ 212(a)(9)(C)(ii), 237(a)(7). Other existing inadmissibility and deportability waivers are expanded to make self-petitioners eligible. VAWA 2000, § 1505(c)-(f). The special avenue of relief from removal known as cancellation was also expanded as it applies to the victims of battery by U.S. citizen or LPR family members. INA § 240A(b)(2). And access to the benefits of special legislation legalizing certain Central Americans, Cubans, Haitians, and others is extended to the principal beneficiaries' battered spouses and children. VAWA 2000, §§ 1509-1511.

Finally, in order to encourage victims to come forward and assist law enforcement, VAWA 2000 and its parent statute, the Victims of Trafficking Act, create two new nonimmigrant visa categories for certain victims of abuse- or trafficking-related crimes if they are being helpful in prosecution or investigation of the perpetrators. The T visa category (victims of human trafficking offenses) is limited to 5,000 per year and usually requires a showing of extreme hardship were the person to be removed. The U category (based on abuse resulting from a list of specified crimes) is capped at 10,000 annually. Such nonimmigrants are eligible to adjust to permanent resident status after three years, if they continue their cooperation and meet certain other requirements. INA §§ 101(a)(15)(T), (U); 214(n), (o); 245(*l*) (both subsections so designated).

346: Notes to *Young v. Reno* (add at end of carryover paragraph)

In *Nguyen v. INS* (material for pp. 29-43 *supra*), the Supreme Court dealt with an argument that Congress should have pursued its objectives through a statute that confers citizenship on an out-of-wedlock child of a U.S. citizen father whenever "an actual father-child relationship is proved," rather than specifying concrete acts that the father would have to perform in order to transmit citizenship. The Court observed with approval that Congress rejected this approach, "perhaps because of the subjectivity, intrusiveness, and difficulties of proof that might attend an inquiry into any particular bond or tie," opting instead for "an easily administered scheme." 121 S.Ct. at 2053.

347: Notes to *Young v. Reno* (add at end of note 3)

The *Chevron* doctrine was limited in *United States v. Mead Corp.*, 121 S.Ct. 2164 (2001). The Court ruled that "administrative implementation of a particular statutory provision qualifies for *Chevron* deference when it appears that Congress delegated authority to the agency generally to make rules carrying the force of law, and that the agency interpretation claiming deference was promulgated in the exercise of that authority." *Id.* at 2171. The opinion suggests that interpretations embodied in notice-and-comment rulemaking and adjudications in a "relatively formal administrative procedure" would ordinarily meet this test. Less formal statements of the agency's interpretation, like the Customs Service "ruling letter" at issue in that case, are entitled only to a lower level of deference under *Skidmore v. Swift & Co.*, 323 U.S. 134, 139-40, 65 S.Ct. 161, 89 L.Ed. 124 (1944) . Under *Skidmore*, the "fair measure of deference" varies with the circumstances, and courts should look "to the degree of the agency's care, its consistency, formality, and relative expertness, and to the persuasiveness of the agency's position." 121 S.Ct. at 2171. Justice Scalia filed a vigorous lone dissent, calling the decision "one of the most significant opinions ever rendered by the Court in dealing with judicial review of administrative action. Its consequences will be enormous, and almost uniformly bad." *Id.* at 2189.

356: Labor Certification: Background and Basic Procedures (add after carryover paragraph)

Demand for labor certification increased considerably as the economy improved over the last few years. At the same time, federal funding cuts for DOL and for the State Employment Security Agencies (SESAs, which play a key role in normal individual labor certification) decreased the administrative capacity to handle the caseload. Delays have run as high as three years or more in certain states and regions. Moreover, even after approval of the labor certification, employers thereafter faced worsening processing delays at INS for adjudication of the I-140 visa petition and, in most cases, of an adjustment of status application. In late 1996, DOL therefore issued General Administration Letter (GAL) 1-97, with the intent of encouraging more SESAs to use streamlined procedures. 73 Interp.Rel. 1458 (1996). The primary alternative procedure, known as Reduction in Recruitment (RIR), has assumed increasing importance in succeeding years. (GAL 1-97 was amended as a result of litigation, in ways not pertinent to the discussion here. The currently operative version appears at 64 Fed.Reg. 23983 (1999).)

To qualify for RIR, the employer must demonstrate that the application is for an occupation "for which there is little or no availability," that it contains no restrictive requirements, that the job is being offered at the prevailing wage, and that the employer has conducted "adequate recruitment" over the six months before filing the application, using "sources normal to the occupation and industry." GAL 1-97, at B.2. Employers who normally conduct on-going recruitment for multiple openings are best positioned to take advantage of RIR, but on-going recruitment for a single opening can also qualify. RIR frees the employer from participating in the ordinarily mandatory 30-day recruitment under SESA supervision, which can only take place after the application is filed. If the SESA forwards the application to the certifying officer as an RIR application, it will receive priority adjudication, which can mean a final decision in a matter of weeks—an enormous advantage given the significant backlogs in standard processing. A similar fast-track processing opportunity, known as "limited processing review," is available for other situations where the SESA regards approval as a clear case. *Id.* at C.3. *See* Maclean, *The Labor Certification Process*, in 1 Immigration and Nationality Law Handbook, 2000-01 Edition, 377, 390-91 (AILA 2000) ; Stanton, *Changing Paradigms for Labor Certification: New Strategies, Opportunities, and Risks*, Immigration Briefings, Sept. 1997.

358: Labor Certification: Background and Basic Procedures (add after Trillin article)

The Dictionary of Occupational Titles (D.O.T.) can be found online at http://www.oalj.dol.gov/libdot.htm. The Department of Labor is also in the process of replacing the D.O.T. by a new computerized database system called O*NET (Occupational Information Center). See 75 Interp.Rel. 1622 (1998). It can be found online at http://online.onetcenter.org.

365: Notes to *Information Industries* (add after note 3):

4. The American Competitiveness in the Twenty-first Century Act (AC21), Pub.L. 106-313, 114 Stat. 1251 (2000), added a modest-looking subsection (j) to INA § 204 that may have enormous long-term implications for the traditional labor certification system. It provides:

> **Job flexibility for long delayed applicants for adjustment of status to permanent residence.**—A petition under subsection (a)(1)(D) for an individual whose application for adjustment of status pursuant to section 245 has been filed and remained unadjudicated for 180 days or more shall remain valid with respect to a new job if the individual changes jobs or employers if the new job is in the same or a similar occupational classification as the job for which the petition was filed.

The labor certification likewise remains valid under these circumstances. INA § 212(a)(5)(A)(iv).

This measure is in part a response to long backlogs in INS processing of adjustments of status, which reached as long as two years or more in several districts in recent years—delays that were often added to lengthy delays in securing labor certification. And it was enacted as part of legislation that focused mainly on correcting problems related to H-1B nonimmigrant visas. *See* material for pp. 395-98 *infra*. (A high percentage of current employment-based immigration consists of workers who began work with the employer in the H-1B category, a status that can last up to six years, and who then adjust status without leaving the country. INS and DOL processing delays were often taking valued employees who appeared to qualify for a current category well past the six-year mark.) But 180 days is not usually considered a long delay in this context; this period is in fact INS's target processing time for adjustments once the system is reformed and more adequately funded and staffed. More importantly, § 204(j) subtly but fundamentally challenges the underlying protection premises of labor certification altogether—to the point that one commentator suggests that this section "may sound the death knell for labor certification." Weiss, *Employment-based (EB) Immigration at the Millennium: An Examination of the Immigration Act of 1990, Its Aftermath, and The American Competitiveness in the Twenty First Century Act*, Immigration Briefings, Dec. 2000, at 15.

Consider what follows once the 180-day processing time is exceeded. The alien can switch to another job or employer in the same or similar occupational classification (a crucial concept whose exact meaning remains to be defined). The employee's taking of a new job in a different region will render irrelevant any protection to U.S. workers ostensibly provided by the labor certification, which was premised on a finding that there were no U.S. workers available *at the place* mentioned in the original application. See INA § 212(a)(5)(A)(i)(I). Prevailing wages—a key determination meant to implement the statutory command that there be no adverse effect on wages and working conditions of U.S. workers from the hiring of the alien—are also determined, in most instances, according to a specific geographic market. Will the new employer in a high-wage region now be allowed to pay the lower wage?

Further, in adjudicating the related I-140 petitions, INS has traditionally paid close attention to whether the petitioning employer is capable of paying the wage or salary stated in the labor certification process. Will this requirement apply to the new employer? As of what time period—the time the adjustment is approved, or the time when the original labor certification or I-140 was filed or decided? The statute does not appear to require a revised application for adjustment of status, or even notice to INS that a change of jobs has occurred. Moreover, after the employee has switched jobs (following the passage of 180 days), suppose the original employer withdraws the I-140 visa petition—an unsurprising reaction in such circumstances. One commentator argues that it would be illogical to give the original employer power to affect the alien's status in this fashion, because the whole point of this provision appears to be to make sure the alien is no longer tied to a particular employer after 180 days. Klasko, *supra*, material for p. 296, at 1695. The implementing regulations for § 204(j) will have to deal with these challenging technical and conceptual issues.

365-67: The "Prevailing Wage" Requirement

By rulemaking the Department of Labor overruled the BALCA's *Hathaway* decision as it applies to certain employees, essentially reinstating the *Tuskegee* approach for the following: researchers employed by colleges and universities, federally funded research and development centers operated by colleges and universities, and federal research agencies. The prevailing wage for such employees is therefore to be determined by reference to nonprofit institutions, and not by comparison to researchers employed by private, for-profit employers. 63 Fed.Reg. 13756-67 (1998). *See* 75 Interp.Rel. 429 (1998). The American Competitiveness and Workforce Improvement Act of 1998 (ACWIA), Pub. L. 105-277, Title IV, § 415, 112 Stat. 2681, added a new INA § 212(p) that incorporates this approach to prevailing wages into the statute, but for a wider class of workers. ACWIA applies this methodology to employees of institutions of higher education and of affiliated nonprofit entities, and to employees of all nonprofit and governmental research organizations. DOL has provided additional guidance on prevailing wage determinations in General Administration Letter (GAL) 2-98 and GAL 1-00. *See* 77 Interp.Rel. 694 (2000), 74 id. 1712 (1997).

372-73: National Interest Waivers for EB-2

INS has significantly tightened the standards for national interest waivers of the job offer and labor certification requirements, potentially available under INA § 203(b)(2)(B) for workers who fit the second employment-based preference. It did so by designating as a precedent the Administrative Appeals

Office (AAO) decision in *Matter of New York State Dept. of Transportation (NYSDOT)*, Int.Dec. 3363 (Assoc. Comm'r 1998) , discussed in 75 Interp.Rel. 1289-99 (1998). The AAO now requires the employer to show that the alien will be employed "in an area of substantial intrinsic merit" and that "the proposed benefit will be national in scope." The AAO continued:

The final threshold is * * * specific to the alien. The petitioner seeking the waiver must persuasively demonstrate that the national interest would be adversely affected if a labor certification were required for the alien. The petitioner must demonstrate that it would be contrary to the national interest to potentially deprive the prospective employer of the services of the alien by making available to U.S. workers the position sought by the alien. The labor certification process exists because protecting the jobs and job opportunities of U.S. workers having the same objective minimum qualifications as an alien seeking employment is in the national interest. An alien seeking an exemption from this process must present a national benefit so great as to outweigh the national interest inherent in the labor certification process.

Stated another way, the petitioner, whether the U.S. employer or the alien, must establish that the alien will serve the national interest to a substantially greater degree than would an available U.S. worker having the same minimum qualifications.

In 1999, Congress enacted additional specifications stating when a national interest waiver should be granted for physicians who agree to serve for a specified number of years in a medically underserved area. INA § 203(b)(2)(B)(ii). For an assessment of the early implementation of the *NYSDOT* standards, see Waxman, *New York State Department of Transportation: National Interest Waivers One Year Down the Road*, 76 Interp.Rel. 1641 (1999) . *See also* Rosser, Note, *The National Interest Waiver of IMMACT 90*, 14 Geo. Immig. L.J. 165 (1999) .

377: The Future of Labor Certification (add at end of section, before Exercise)

In addition to the implications of the new § 204(j), *see* material for p. 365 *supra,* the Department of Labor is considering major changes to the labor certification process. The tentative reengineering proposals, outlined in a notice in the Federal Register, 65 Fed.Reg. 51777 (2000), would make most labor certification processing similar to the current RIR (reduction in recruitment) process described *supra*, material for p. 356. Noting that labor certification is "complicated, costly, and time consuming," and that cuts in DOL funding have driven its processing times above two years in many states, DOL recognizes that changes are needed. The proposal would also centralize much more of the processing and decisionmaking in DOL regional offices, reducing the role of the state employment security agencies (SESAs). In particular, it would cut out from most cases the 30-day mandatory recruitment process conducted in part through the SESA.

Under the preliminary proposal, the employer would need to secure a prevailing wage determination from the SESA before filing for labor certification, but DOL hopes to standardize and streamline the process using machine-readable forms and new technology. The employer would have to conduct "an adequate test of the labor market * * * through sources normal to the occupation and industry during the 6-month period preceding the filing" of the labor certification application. Recruitment efforts would contain both mandatory steps and alternative steps chosen by the employer, but DOL envisions this as being similar to current RIR procedures. Hence an employer with a continuous hiring process could rely on normal recruitment processes undertaken before it contemplated seeking labor certification, assuming that the prevailing wages and working conditions were offered. Once able to document such a labor-market test, the employer would file the actual application for labor certification, in machine-readable form. DOL expects to have technology that will search for certain selection criteria or flags, so as to target questionable applications for a closer audit. It will also pull some applications at random for audit. Applications not audited, DOL says, should receive an approval within 7-21 working days. An audit could result in certification after the closer review, denial, or an order for additional recruiting supervised by the SESA.

377-79: Investors as Immigrants

Usage of the investor visa provisions increased in 1996 and 1997, a change INS attributed to two factors: statutory amendments in 1992 creating a new pilot program that eased the requirements of showing direct job creation for covered "regional centers," Pub.L. 102-395, Title VI, § 610, 106 Stat. 1874 (1992), and the growing involvement of private-sector promoters who began to market the program overseas. *INS Reports to Congress on the EB–5 Investor Visa Program*, 76 Interp.Rel. 595 (1998) . Competing promoters developed complex financing schemes that minimized the real exposure and up-front cash requirements of the participating investors. INS initially approved many such plans, but in December 1997 put a hold on questionable petitions, on the basis of a lengthy new legal analysis from the General Counsel's office. *General Counsel Criticizes Immigrant Investor Arrangements, Sparking Controversy*, 75 Interp.Rel. 323 (1998) ; Schmitt, *Abuses are Cited in Trade of Money for U.S. Residence*, N.Y.Times, Apr. 13, 1998, at A1. In 1998, the AAO issued four precedent decisions that clarified INS's interpretation of the governing regulations, largely along the lines marked out by the General Counsel's office, with the effect that many of the previous investment arrangements were judged not to qualify. *See Matter of Soffici*, Int.Dec. 3359 (Assoc. Comm'r 1998) ; *Matter of Izumii*, Int.Dec. 3360 (Assoc. Comm'r 1998) ; *Matter of Hsiung*, Int.Dec. 3361 (Assoc. Comm'r 1998) ; and *Matter of Ho*, Int.Dec. 3362 (Assoc. Comm'r 1998) .

The changes have been challenged in court. One court upheld INS's current approach, holding, *inter alia,* that it did not need to be implemented through notice-and-comment rulemaking. *R.L. Investment Partners v. INS*, 86 F.Supp.2d 1014 (D.Haw.2000) Another court sustained INS's position against most of the litigants' challenges, but it remanded for consideration of whether there was an invalid retroactive application in a subset of cases. The latter cases involved investors who had already immigrated to the United States based on initial INS approval, but whose investments were judged noncompliant under the new precedent decisions when the aliens applied two years later for removal of their conditional status (thus leaving them deportable). *See* 78 Interp.Rel. 875 (2001) (discussing the unreported case of *Chang v. United States*).

386: Nonimmigrants

[Delete footnote 30 as obsolete.]

394: H-2A Nonimmigrants (add at end of section)

INS and the Department of Labor have published regulations meant to streamline H-2A processing, primarily by assigning to DOL the responsibility, formerly held by INS, to adjudicate the employer's petition for temporary agricultural workers. Formerly such a petition was filed separately with INS after the employer received labor certification from DOL. Under the new regulations, the employer will therefore file a single packet of materials, with fee, with DOL. The new procedures are now slated to go into effect in October 2001. 77 Interp.Rel. 1001, 1624 (2000). An estimated 25,000 to 35,000 H-2A visas are now issued each year. 78 *id.* 414 (2001).

In 2000 and 2001, interest grew in new measures for agricultural workers, further fueled by the endorsement of an agricultural guestworker program by Mexico's new President Vicente Fox. Two principal alternatives have garnered the main attention, although several variations have been discussed. One alternative, exemplified in a proposal championed by Senator Phil Gramm (R-Tex.), would provide for a new program admitting agricultural workers for up to a year, but with added incentives and enforcement measures to assure that the stay is only temporary. The workers would be fully covered by U.S. labor laws during this period. Workers could apply for a new permit after returning home, but would be ineligible for permanent residence. The second framework also contemplates expanded temporary admissions, but workers who remain in agriculture for a stated period, usually five years, could then gain legal permanent residence. The latter proposals generally make special provision for those who have already worked illegally in U.S. agriculture for specified periods. Some critics resist either such measure, from a variety of different perspectives: because the programs would reward illegal action, because they would not succeed, despite their proponents' claims, in reducing illegal migration, or because they would foster exploitation by employers. No reform proposal was enacted in 2000, but a summit between Presidents Bush and Fox in March 2001 endorsed priority study by a bilateral working group, headed by their foreign ministers, of migration issues. The group will look both at temporary worker programs "with an emphasis on circularity" and at "regularization of undocumented Mexicans in the United States." Joint Statement of the US-Mexico High Level Working Group on Migration, April 4, 2001. It remains to be seen exactly what the group will propose and what Congress will come to accept. For more information on the various proposals and the ongoing debate, see 78 Interp.Rel. 236, 414, 642 (2001); Carnegie

Endowment for Int'l Peace, Mexico-U.S. Migration: A Shared Responsibility (2001) (prepared by a binational U.S.-Mexico Migration Panel); D. Papademetriou & M. Heppel, Balancing Acts: Toward a Fair Bargain on Seasonal Agricultural Workers (Int'l Migration Series: Carnegie Endowment for Int'l Peace, 1999) ; Holley, *Bad Hosts*, Legal Times, Apr. 9, 2001, at 58; Kirschten, *Labor: Immigrants Without Immigration,* National Journal, Feb. 10, 2001, at 430; P. Martin, *Guest Worker Programs for the 21st Century,* Center for Immigration Studies Backgrounder, Apr. 2000; Aleinikoff, *The Green Card Solution,* The American Prospect, Dec. 20, 1999.

395-96: Nonimmigrants (add at end of footnote 31)

The H-1A category lapsed in 1997. In 1999, Congress enacted the Nursing Relief for Disadvantaged Areas Act of 1999 (NRDAA), Pub. L.106-95, 113 Stat. 1312, which created a new H-1C category for nurses and uses an attestation process similar to that for the former H-1A provisions. The new statute, however, which sunsets after four years, allows the temporary admission of no more than 500 nurses per year, for a maximum stay of three years, and only when they will be employed in a Health Professional Shortage Area.

398: H-1B Nonimmigrants (add at end of section)

When the 65,000 cap on H-1B admissions was reached again in May 1998, with nearly five months left in the fiscal year, businesses that were adversely affected lobbied for a congressional remedy. In response, Congress incorporated into the omnibus appropriations bill passed in October a temporary increase in the ceiling for three years. But Congress coupled that relief with reform measures meant to address the concerns of long-time critics of the H-1B program. American Competitiveness and Workforce Improvement Act of 1998 (ACWIA), Pub. L. 105-277, Title IV, 112 Stat. 2681. The principal amendments were codified in INA §§ 212(n), 214(c)(9), and 286(s). *See* 75 Interp.Rel. 1472 (1998), 76 *id.* 37, 105 (1999). Final INS regulations were published in February 2000. 65 Fed.Reg. 10678 (2000). DOL published voluminous interim final regulations implementing ACWIA, as well as subsequent legislation described below, in December 2000. 65 Fed.Reg. 80110 (2000). They include a newly drafted form ETA 9035, which must be used for the employer's labor condition application, and they also incorporate certain provisions that had been declared invalid in the 1996 *National Association of Manufacturers* litigation (mentioned in the Casebook) because of insufficient compliance with the notice-and-comment requirements of the APA.

Under the 1998 ACWIA, the caps on H-1B admissions rose to 115,000 for FY 1999 and 2000, then were to recede to 107,500 for 2001, before reverting to 65,000 thereafter. In order to discourage overuse of the provision, however, and also to create a pool of funds meant to help reduce the future need for H-1B workers, ACWIA imposed a $500 fee on an employer's initial petition for an H-1B worker or for a first extension of a worker's H-1B status. The funds are to be used primarily for job training programs for U.S. workers, college scholarships for low-income students in engineering, math, and computer science, and certain other science enrichment courses. Colleges, universities, and nonprofit research institutions are exempt from the fee. ACWIA also created new obligations for employers who are "H-1B dependent"—meaning firms of more than 50 employees for which H-1B workers constitute at least 15 percent of the workforce, or specified higher percentages for smaller firms. Such firms must generally provide more elaborate assurances in their labor condition applications (LCAs) that the H-1Bs do not displace U.S. workers and that they have taken good-faith steps to recruit U.S. workers. The Act increased enforcement and penalties against violating employers.

INS reached the initial 115,000 ceiling in June 1999, three months before the end of the fiscal year, partly owing to the carryover caseload resulting from the early stop to H-1B admissions in 1998. (Later studies revealed that INS apparently overshot the cap for FY 1999.) *See* 76 Interp.Rel. 858 (1999); *id.* 1552 (1999). But a booming economy and high demand in high-tech industries, which were major users of H-1B admissions, meant that the cap was reached even earlier in FY 2000. INS published a notice in mid-March suspending further H-1B applications unless they indicated a start date after October 1, 2000, which was the start of the next fiscal year. 65 Fed.Reg. 15178 (2000). As a result, members of Congress proposed several new bills to raise the cap, temporarily or permanently, and to adjust the various qualifications and fees. See 77 Interp.Rel. 261, 297, 334, 369 (2000). Critics argued that the bill was not needed, that the high-tech industry would be adequately supplied with U.S. workers if it offered competitive salaries, that H-1B workers are paid considerably less than American workers with the same skills, or that they can be exploited because of their dependence on the employer for maintaining H-1B status and eventually acquiring LPR status. *See, e.g,* Matloff, *This Program Exploits Programers,* Newsday, Dec. 22, 2000, at A49; Matloff, *High-Tech Cheap Labor,* Wash. Post, Sept. 12, 2000, at A35; Donnelly, *Indefinitely Temporary: Senate Boost to High-Tech Guest Workers Will Block Green Cards,* Center for Immigration Studies Backgrounder, Mar. 2000; Cohn & Roche, *Indentured Servants for High-Tech Trade,* Baltimore Sun, Feb. 21, 2000.

These voices did not prevail against the effective lobbying of industry. In October 2000, Congress enacted the American Competitiveness in the Twenty-first Century Act, Pub. L. 106-313, 114 Stat. 1251 (2000), sometimes known as AC21. It increased the H-1B limit to 195,000 for each of fiscal years 2001, 2002, and 2003. The limit reverts to 65,000 in fiscal 2004. AC21 exempts important classes of H-1B employees from the cap, however, principally those who work for colleges, universities or nonprofit research organizations and related entities. This provision in effect allows tens of thousands of additional H-1B admissions above the cap each year. A companion bill increased the employer's fee from $500 to $1000, with slightly revised exemptions. Pub.L. 106-311, 114 Stat. 1247 (2000). A section of AC21 known as the "H-1B portability" provision allows someone previously granted H-1B status to begin working for a new employer upon that employer's filing of a new "non-frivolous" H-1B petition, rather than having to wait for INS approval of the new petition. AC21 also provides for the extension of the H-1B status beyond the former limit of six years in certain circumstances, primarily when the request for labor certification and adjustment of status (to obtain permanent resident status in one of the EB categories) has been pending for more than 365 days. AC21 § 106. *See* Klasko, *American Competitiveness in the 21st Century: H-1Bs and Much More,* 77 Interp.Rel. 1689 (2000) ; INS Fact Sheet, *Changes to the H-1B Program, 77 id.* 1732 (2000).

Ironically, the declining fortunes of the high-tech industry in 2001 may have reduced demand for H-1B visas about the time that the increased caps were taking effect. The decline has also led to lay-offs of many H-1B workers. Under the law, once they lose their employment, such workers are immediately out of status and are supposed to leave the country—a rude shock, because a high percentage of H-1B workers traditionally expect eventually to gain permanent immigration through the employment. There are an estimated 425,000 H-1B workers currently employed in the United States. 78 Interp.Rel. 608 (2001); *Labor, H-1B,* Migration News, July 2001.

Are the 1998 and 2000 changes to the H-1B provision good policy? What are their implications for the protections to U.S. workers that provide the theoretical basis of the labor certification requirements in the employment-based preference categories?

429: Crimes

In 1999, Congress broadened the inadmissibility ground for drug convictions in INA § 212(a)(2)(C) to include those who "endeavor" to engage in the illicit activity, and to include any spouse, son, or daughter of an inadmissible alien who benefited from the illicit activity within the past five years, and "knew or reasonably should have known that the financial or other benefit was the product of such illicit activity."

In July 1999, the INS issued a memo on inadmissibility under INA § 212(a)(3)(E)(ii) of aliens who have engaged in genocide. The memo's purpose is "to increase awareness among Service Officers of this ground of inadmissibility, and provide education that there are currently aliens who are inadmissible" under this ground. The memo focuses on events in Rwanda during 1994 and provides guidance to INS officers who suspect that an alien was involved in genocide there. *See* 76 Interp.Rel. 1165 (1999).

429-30: Immigration Control

For useful overviews of the unlawful presence and overstay inadmissibility grounds, see Burkemper, *The Impact of The IIRIRA's Unlawful Presence and Overstay Provisions on Temporary Workers,* 76 Interp.Rel. 1749 (1999); Yale-Loehr, *Beating the Bar: Avoiding, Delaying or Remedying Unlawful Presence,* 3 Bender's Imm. Bulletin 779 (1998). In June 1999, the State Department issued a consolidated summary of guidance on INA § 222(g), *see* 76 Interp.Rel. 977 (1999).

454: Notes on National Security and Constitutional Constraints on Inadmissibility Grounds (add at end of note 5)

Several recent federal appeals court decisions have addressed important issues arising out of § 219 designations:

a. In *People's Mojahedin Organization of Iran v. United States Department of State*, 182 F.3d 17 (D.C.Cir.1999), *cert. denied*, 529 U.S. 1104, 120 S.Ct. 1846, 146 L.Ed. 788 (2000), the People's Mojahedin Organization of Iran and the Liberation Tigers of Tamil Eelam (of Sri Lanka) sought judicial review of the Secretary of State's decision to designate them as foreign terrorist organizations under INA § 219. These organizations argued that the § 219 designation procedure deprived them of due process of law. The Court of Appeals for the D.C. Circuit rejected their challenges, noting first that as entirely foreign entities they have no constitutional rights, so that any rights they enjoy are statutory only. The court then declined to review the determination that the organizations' activities threaten the security of U.S. nationals or the national security of the United States, finding that these are nonjusticiable determinations pertaining to foreign policy. The court did find it within its review power—but then sustained on the merits—the determinations that these organizations are "foreign" and "engage in terrorist activities."

b. In *Humanitarian Law Project v. Reno*, 205 F.3d 1130 (9th Cir.2000), *cert. denied*, 121 S.Ct. 1226, 149 L.Ed.2d 136 (2001), the Ninth Circuit considered whether Congress may, consistent with the First Amendment, enact criminal penalties for contributing material support to organizations designated as foreign terrorist organizations under § 219. The plaintiffs were organizations and individuals who wished to donate to two organizations designated under § 219: the Kurdistan Workers Party ("PKK")and the Liberation Tigers of Tamil Eelam. The plaintiffs argued that their support would aid only nonviolent humanitarian and political activities, and that the ban on support would infringe their associational rights under the First Amendment. The plaintiffs also argued that the grant of § 219 designation authority to the Secretary of State violates the First and Fifth Amendments, and that the criminal penalty statute is unconstitutionally vague. In rejecting the first of these arguments, the Ninth Circuit panel first distinguished between advocacy and membership on the one hand, and providing material support on the other. Regulation of the latter warrants only intermediate scrutiny. The court continued:

> When we review under the intermediate scrutiny standard, we must ask four questions: Is the regulation with [sic] the power of the government? Does it promote an important or substantial government interest? Is that interest unrelated to suppressing free expression? And, finally, is the incidental restriction on First Amendment freedoms no greater than necessary?
>
> Here all four questions are answered in the affirmative. First, the federal government clearly has the power to enact laws restricting the dealings of United States citizens with foreign entities; such regulations have been upheld in the past over a variety of constitutional challenges. Second, the government has a legitimate interest in preventing the spread of international terrorism, and there is no doubt that that interest is substantial. Third, this interest is unrelated to suppressing free expression because it restricts the actions of those who wish to give material support to the groups, not the expression of those who advocate or

believe the ideas that the groups supports.

So the heart of the matter is whether AEDPA is well enough tailored to its end of preventing the United States from being used as a base for terrorist fundraising. Because the judgment of how best to achieve that end is strongly bound up with foreign policy considerations, we must allow the political branches wide latitude in selecting the means to bring about the desired goal. Plaintiffs argue that the prior statutory scheme, which allowed the donation of humanitarian assistance to those who were not directly involved in terrorist activity, *see* 18 U.S.C. § 2339A(b) (1994) (amended 1996), was properly tailored and the current statutory scheme is therefore overbroad. But the fact that the prior statutory scheme was narrower tells us nothing about whether the current scheme is overbroad, because we don't know how well the prior scheme worked. Presumably Congress thought that it did not work well enough and so decided to broaden it. Moreover, the Supreme Court has held that the government need not select the least restrictive or least intrusive means of accomplishing its purpose.

Congress explicitly incorporated a finding into the statute that "foreign organizations that engage in terrorist activity are so tainted by their criminal conduct that any contribution to such an organization facilitates that conduct." AEDPA § 301(a)(7), 110 Stat. at 1247. It follows that all material support given to such organizations aids their unlawful goals. Indeed, as the government points out, terrorist organizations do not maintain open books. Therefore, when someone makes a donation to them, there is no way to tell how the donation is used. Further, as amicus Anti-Defamation League notes, even contributions earmarked for peaceful purposes can be used to give aid to the families of those killed while carrying out terrorist acts, thus making the decision to engage in terrorism more attractive. More fundamentally, money is fungible; giving support intended to aid an organization's peaceful activities frees up resources that can be used for terrorist acts. We will not indulge in speculation about whether Congress was right to come to the conclusion that it did. We simply note that Congress has the fact-finding resources to properly come to such a conclusion. Thus, we cannot say that AEDPA is not sufficiently tailored.

205 F.3d 1135-36.

The court also upheld the Secretary of State's designation authority, finding it not "unfettered," and that any limits on judicial review were "a necessary concomitant of the foreign affairs power." *Id.* at 1137. However, the court upheld a preliminary injunction against enforcement of the prohibition to the extent that it applied to providing "personnel" and "training," on the ground that those terms were unconstitutionally vague. "Someone who advocates the cause of the PKK could be seen as supplying them with personnel . . . [b]ut advocacy is pure speech protected by the First Amendment." And "a plaintiff who wishes to instruct members of a designated group on how to petition the United Nations to give aid to their group could plausibly decide that such protected expression falls within the scope of the term 'training.'" *Id.* at 1152.

　　c. In *National Council of Resistance of Iran v. Department of State*, 251 F.3d 192 (D.C.Cir.2001) , the Court of Appeals for the D.C. Circuit dealt with several issues that it had not reached in *People's Mojahedin Organization of Iran*. The National Council of Resistance of Iran and the People's Mojahedin of Iran—which the Secretary of State had found to be alter egos of each other—sued to challenge their designations in 1999 as foreign terrorist organizations. This was the same People's Mojahedin that had failed to show sufficient presence in the United States to mount a constitutional challenge to its designation as a foreign terrorist organization in 1997. *See People's Mojahedin Organization of Iran v. United States Department of State*, discussed earlier this note.

　　This time, however, the court found that both organizations had sufficient presence in 1999 to invoke the Fifth Amendment to the U.S. Constitution. The court then found that the designation process deprived them of previously held rights to "hold bank accounts, and to receive material support or resources from anyone within the jurisdiction of the United States." *Id.* According to the court, these were deprivations of life, liberty, or property to which the Due Process Clause applies:

> The most obvious rights to be impaired by the Secretary's designation are the petitioners' property rights. Specifically, there is before us at least a colorable allegation that at least one of the petitioners has an interest in a bank account in the United States. As they are one, if one does, they both do. We have no idea of the truth of the allegation, there never having been notice and hearing, but for the present purposes, the colorable allegation would seem enough to support their due process claims. *Russian Volunteer Fleet v. United States,* 282 U.S. 481, 491-92, 51 S.Ct. 229, 75 L.Ed. 473 (1931), makes clear that a foreign organization that acquires or holds property in this country may invoke the protections of the Constitution when that property is placed in jeopardy by government intervention. This is not to say that the government cannot interfere with that and many other rights of foreign organizations present in the United States; it is only to say that when it does so it is subject to the Due Process Clause.

251 F.3d at —. The court went on to hold that due process requires prior notice: "the Secretary must afford the limited due process available to the putative foreign terrorist organization prior to the deprivation worked by designating that entity as such with its attendant consequences, unless he can make a showing of particularized need." *Id.* Finally, the court spelled out what kind of process it had in mind:

> * * * To make plain what we have assumed above, those procedures which have been held to satisfy the Due Process Clause have "included notice of the action sought," along with the opportunity to effectively be heard. [*Mathews v. Eldridge*, 424 U.S.

319,] 334, 96 S.Ct. 893 [, 47 L.Ed.2d 18 (1976)]. This, we hold, is what the Constitution requires of the Secretary in designating organizations as foreign terrorist organizations under the statute. The Secretary must afford to the entities under consideration notice that the designation is impending. Upon an adequate showing to the court, the Secretary may provide this notice after the designation where earlier notification would impinge upon the security and other foreign policy goals of the United States.

The notice must include the action sought, but need not disclose the classified information to be presented *in camera* and *ex parte* to the court under the statute. This is within the privilege and prerogative of the executive, and we do not intend to compel a breach in the security which that branch is charged to protect. However, the Secretary has shown no reason not to offer the designated entities notice of the administrative record which will in any event be filed publicly, at the very latest at the time of the court's review. We therefore require that as soon as the Secretary has reached a tentative determination that the designation is impending, the Secretary must provide notice of those unclassified items upon which he proposes to rely to the entity to be designated. There must then be some compliance with the hearing requirement of due process jurisprudence—that is, the opportunity to be heard at a meaningful time and in a meaningful manner recognized in *Mathews, Armstrong [v. Manzo*, 380 U.S. 545, 552, 85 S.Ct. 1187, 14 L.Ed.2d 62 (1965)], and a plethora of other cases. We do not suggest "that a hearing closely approximating a judicial trial is necessary." *Mathews*, 424 U.S. at 333, 96 S.Ct. 893. We do, however, require that the Secretary afford to entities considered for imminent designation the opportunity to present, at least in written form, such evidence as those entities may be able to produce to rebut the administrative record or otherwise negate the proposition that they are foreign terrorist organizations.

It is for this reason that even in those instances when post-deprivation due process is sufficient, our review under § 219(b) is not sufficient to supply the otherwise absent due process protection. The statutory judicial review is limited to the adequacy of the record before the court to support the Secretary's executive decision. That record is currently compiled by the Secretary without notice or opportunity for any meaningful hearing. We have no reason to presume that the petitioners in this particular case could have offered evidence which might have either changed the Secretary's mind or affected the adequacy of the record. However, without the due process protections which we have outlined, we cannot presume the contrary either.

Id. The court did not order the designations vacated, but rather instructed "that the petitioners be afforded the opportunity to file responses to the nonclassified evidence against them, to file evidence in support of their allegations that they are not terrorist organizations, and that they be afforded an opportunity to be meaningfully heard by the Secretary upon the relevant findings." *Id.* The court added: "While not within our current order, we expect that the Secretary will afford due process rights to these and other similarly situated entities in the course of future designations." *Id.*

464-71: The Public Charge Provision

In May 1999, the INS published proposed regulations "to establish clear standards governing a determination that an alien is inadmissible . . . , or has become deportable, on public charge grounds." 64 Fed.Reg. 28676 (1999). For commentary, see Wheeler, *Affidavit of Support: The Ten Most Common Mistakes*, 5 Bender's Imm. Bulletin 125 (2000); Wheeler, *Affidavit of Support: The Year in Review*, 4 Bender's Imm. Bulletin 97 (1999); *INS Provides Important Clarification on Public Charge Standards for Immigrants Receiving Public Benefits*, 76 Interp.Rel. 843 (1999); Joaquin & Cancilla, *Protecting Immigrants and the Community: A New Approach to Public Charge Determinations*, 76 Interp.Rel. 885 (1999). In 2001, the required income at the 125 percent level for four persons is $22,063, or one wage-earner working full-time at $11.03 per hour. Higher minimums apply to Hawaii and Alaska. *See* 66 Fed.Reg. 10695 (2001).

490: Nonimmigrant Admissions (add at end of last full paragraph)

Congress finally made the visa waiver program permanent in 2000, with some modest changes in the criteria, including new provisions to include persons coming on business aircraft and not only on commercial carriers. Visa Waiver Permanent Program Act, Pub.L. 106-396, 114 Stat. 1637 (2000). The program currently covers 29 countries, 22 of which are in Europe. 77 Interp.Rel. 1755 (2000).

491: Immigrant Visas and Visa Petitions (add at end of last full paragraph on the page)

VAWA 2000 eased the requirements for self-petitioning by battered spouses and children. *See* material for p. 338 *supra.*

502: Notes on Adjustment of Status (add at end of note 3)

Because of the limit on judicial review set forth in INA § 242(a)(1)(B), enacted in 1996, a court would not have jurisdiction to review a decision of the immigration judge and BIA like that in *Jain.* Courts are divided, however, as to whether they still have jurisdiction to review an INS examiner's denial of adjustment when no removal proceeding is underway. *Compare Mart v. Beebe*, 94 F.Supp.2d 1120 (D.Or.2000) (jurisdiction exists) *with Amoakowaa v. Reno*, 94 F.Supp.2d 903 (N.D.Ill.2000) (no jurisdiction).

506: The Special Adjustment Provisions of INA § 245(i) (add at end of section)

The LIFE Act and the V visa. Congress voted in late 2000 for a limited reopening of the § 245(i) window, with a grandfathering provision similar to the one enacted in late 1997. It covers persons who were in the United States on the date of enactment, December 21, 2000, and whose sponsors filed a visa petition or labor certification application no later than April 30, 2001. The changes came in a pair of related bills, the Legal Immigrant Family Equity Act (LIFE Act), Pub.L. 106-533, Tit. XI, 114 Stat. 2762 (2000), and the LIFE Act Amendments, Pub.L. 106-554, Tit. XV, Div. B, 114 Stat. 2763 (2000). Allowing this new group to adjust status means that they can potentially escape the impact of the three- and ten-year bars imposed by INA § 212(a)(9)(B). Lengthy lines materialized at INS offices as the deadline drew near, and tens of thousands of applicants filed the initial papers needed to take advantage of this measure. Shortly thereafter, President Bush called for an extension of the time to file, and the House passed a measure that would add four months to the application window. The Senate has not yet acted as of the time of this writing, but some extension, possibly of a full year, appears likely to pass. *See* 78 Interp.Rel. 873 (2001).

Also recognizing that many beneficiaries of the earlier grandfather provision may have to wait years before obtaining full legal status, and that some families might be separated in the meantime, Congress created a new nonimmigrant category, the V visa, to alleviate some of this hardship. A spouse or minor child who is the beneficiary of a second-preference petition filed on or before December 21, 2000, may obtain a V visa once more than three years have elapsed since the petition was filed. This measure will permit entry if the person is outside the United States or the acquisition of a lawful status via adjustment, if already present here. Work authorization is also provided. Certain inadmissibility grounds are also waived, most notably the three- and ten-year bars of § 212(a)(9)(B). INA §§ 101(a)(15)(V), 214(o).

The main purpose of the limited revival of § 245(i) is clearly not to generate revenue, but to permit a large cohort of currently undocumented migrants, who have the family or employment relationship necessary for eventual LPR status, to escape the effects of § 212(a)(9)(B). What impact, then, does this new legislation have on the self-enforcement policy that underlay initial adoption of the three- and ten-year bars (*see* Casebook, p. 431)? Should Congress take a different approach? *See* Martin, *Waiting for Solutions*, Legal Times, May 28, 2001, at 66 (arguing that the bars have failed to serve the objectives originally envisioned, that "spasmodic" extensions of 245(i) further undercut any enforcement impact and serve neither the policies of the restrictionists nor those of immigration advocates, and that instead the bars should be repealed).

507: Modern Admission Procedures (add before the section on Parole)

Note on Delays in Processing and Special Procedures to Expedite

A major reality of today's admission and adjustment procedures is delay. It can take two years or more to obtain individual labor certification from the Department of Labor. (DOL initiatives to reduce these delays and eventually to reengineer labor certification are described, *supra,* material for pp. 356, 377.) Visa petition approvals from INS can occupy six months to a year. If the applicable preference category is backlogged, this delay may be of no practical consequence, because the visa priority date is established by the date of the *application*, and the INS approval can be expected well before the time when the person could immigrate in any case. But for preference categories that are current (in 2001 this means exclusively the employment-based visa categories) and for immediate relatives (particularly newlyweds), such delays are a real imposition. Further, when INS concentrated examination resources on naturalizations in the late 1990s, adjustment of status petitions suffered as a consequence, languishing in some parts of the country for two or three years between filing and decision. Naturalization processing has now largely returned to the target time of approximately six months from application to approval, and INS has redirected resources toward catching up on adjustments. President Bush has announced a five-year $500 million initiative to achieve a universal six-month processing standard for all immigration applications and petitions. *See* 78 Interp.Rel. 810 (2001).

Congress has not waited for these improvements to materialize, however. In 2000, Congress mandated various studies and plans to achieve greater currency in adjudication. It also adopted several special measures meant to work around some of the delays. For example, Congress adopted a new nonimmigrant visa category, to be known as K-3, for the spouses of U.S. citizens. The longstanding K-1 visa, for fiancés and fiancées of U.S. citizens, permitted entry in order to marry in this country within 90 days of admission. Historically, no special provision had been made for U.S. citizens who marry overseas, on the assumption that their spouses could enter promptly as immediate relatives, for which there is no quota. Delayed visa petition processing, however, often meant that a marriage abroad would be followed by lengthy separation before the foreign spouse could immigrate. With a K-3 visa, the spouse may enter and obtain work authorization while awaiting approval of the visa petition and eventual adjustment of status. Only the consular officer in the country where the marriage occurred may issue the K-3 visa, and the U.S. citizen must have filed the I-130 visa petition and a special K-3 petition. INA §§ 101(a)(15)(K)(ii), 214(p). (The V visa, described *supra,* material for pp. 504-06, also provides interim legal status and work authorization for persons undergoing lengthy waits for adjustment of status, although its main benefit will apply to persons who are affected by backlogs in the FS-2A preference category, rather than by processing delays as such.)

For business-related visas and applications, Congress went even further in dealing with the consequences of processing delays. For example, it adopted a new INA § 286(u) to permit INS to charge a $1000 fee (in addition to the normal fee) for premium processing of employment-based petitions and applications, assuring an INS decision within 15 days of receipt. The first regulations to implement this program were adopted in June 2001, focusing on certain business-related nonimmigrant categories. Later expansions are expected. 66 Fed.Reg. 29862 (2001). The H-1B portability provision, and the extension of the H-1B status beyond the previous limit of six years for certain nonimmigrants who have completed labor certification and are awaiting adjustment, also respond to INS and DOL delays, in a manner that is especially generous to the businesses involved. *See* material for pp. 395-98 *supra.* The same is true of the rather striking provision, INA § 204(j), allowing an applicant for an employment-based preference to change jobs or employers in the same or similar field after an adjustment application has been pending for 180 days. *See* material for p. 365 *supra*.

Are these changes good policy? Will they prove counterproductive, as INS diverts resources to adjudicate the additional applications, such as the extra K-3 petition? Should they be ended if the Bush initiative succeeds in bringing most processing within the six-month target time? Is premium processing for those who can afford an extra fee an appropriate part of American immigration policy? In any case, should it be limited to business-related applications?

510: Parole (add at end of section)

Under pre-1996 practice, parole was limited to excludable aliens and could not be granted to entrants without inspection (EWIs) or to persons who had been inspected and admitted, because those persons had already effected an entry. (A variety of other administrative practices, including "extended voluntary departure" and "deferred enforced departure" grew up to accommodate roughly equivalent exercises of discretion for those categories.) After the 1996 Act, parole is now available as well to EWIs, because that Act reclassifies EWIs as applicants for admission. An opinion issued by the INS General Counsel discusses this legal interpretation. 76 Interp.Rel. 1050, 1067 (1999). It also notes that the authority now possessed by immigration judges to consider bond redeterminations for EWIs (but not for other applicants for admission—*i.e.*, not for arriving aliens, whose release is to be decided solely by INS district directors) amounts to an exercise of the parole power. 8 C.F.R. § 236.1(d)(1) (added by the regulations implementing the 1996 Act). Old BIA rulings stating that parole could be granted only by INS have been superseded, to this specific extent, by the regulations.

Chapter Five: Constitutional Protection of Aliens After Admission

538-50: Welfare Legislation in 1996 and 1997 (substitute for *Abreu*)

CITY OF CHICAGO v. SHALALA
United States Court of Appeals, Seventh Circuit, 1999.
189 F.3d 598, cert. denied, 529 U.S. 1036, 120 S.Ct. 1530, 146 L.Ed.2d 345 (2000).

RIPPLE, CIRCUIT JUDGE.

The City of Chicago, along with several city officials and an intervenor class of legal permanent residents, brought suit against the Secretary of Health and Human Services and other federal officers to challenge certain provisions of the Personal Responsibility and Work Opportunity Reconciliation Act of 1996, Pub.L. No. 104-193, 110 Stat. 2105 (1996) ("the Welfare Reform Act" or "the Act"), that restrict certain noncitizens' eligibility for welfare benefits. The plaintiffs alleged that the provisions of the Act that disqualify most legal aliens from receiving Food Stamps, Supplemental Security Income ("SSI"), and other welfare benefits violate the Fifth Amendment's Due Process Clause. The district court granted the defendants' motion to dismiss, and the plaintiffs appeal. For the reasons set forth in the following opinion, we affirm the judgment of the district court.

BACKGROUND

A. The Welfare Reform Act

The Welfare Reform Act significantly restricted the eligibility of noncitizens lawfully in the United States to receive welfare benefits. *See* Pub.L. No. 104-193, 110 Stat. 2105, 2262-64 (1996).[1] Section 402(a) of the Act provides that, subject to certain exceptions, "qualified alien[s]" are not eligible to receive SSI or Food Stamp benefits. 8 U.S.C. § 1612(a) (1998).[2] As defined in § 431 of the Act, qualified aliens include permanent resident aliens, asylees, refugees, aliens who are paroled into the United States, aliens whose deportation is being withheld, aliens who have been granted conditional entry, certain Cuban and Haitian entrants, and certain "battered" aliens. *See id.* § 1641.[3]

---

[1] Congress has amended the Act twice since its original enactment in 1996. *See* Balanced Budget Act of 1997, Pub.L. No. 105-33, §§ 5301-5304, 5306, 5562-5563, 111 Stat. 251 (1997); Agricultural Research, Extension, and Education Reform Act of 1998, Pub.L. No. 105-185, §§ 503-508, 112 Stat. 523 (1998). The amendments restored eligibility for welfare benefits to some noncitizens by expanding the exceptions to the provisions excluding aliens from eligibility. This opinion will refer to the provisions of the Welfare Reform Act that are currently codified, as amended, in Title 8 of the United States Code.

[2] The SSI program provides supplemental security income to low-income individuals who are blind, disabled, or 65 or older. *See* 42 U.S.C. § 1381 et seq. The Food Stamp program provides food purchasing assistance to households with low income and few resources. *See* 7 U.S.C. § 2011 et seq.

[3] The Act also provides that, subject to certain exceptions, "illegal" or "undocumented" aliens--aliens who do not meet the definition of "qualified alien"--are

Section 402(a)(2) enumerates several exceptions that allow various subgroups within the qualified alien population to remain eligible for SSI, Food Stamps, or both. Refugees, asylees, aliens whose deportation is being withheld, certain Cuban and Haitian entrants, and certain Amerasian immigrants remain eligible for 7 years after the date they are admitted to the United States or are granted the relevant status. *See id.* § 1612(a)(2)(A). Permanent resident aliens who have worked for 40 qualifying quarters, as well as aliens who are veterans or on active duty (and their spouses and dependent children), retain their eligibility for the benefits. *See id.* § 1612(a)(2)(B), (C). Aliens lawfully residing in the United States who were receiving SSI benefits as of the date of enactment (August 22, 1996) retain their eligibility for SSI. *See id.* § 1612(a)(2)(E). Aliens who were receiving Food Stamps on the date of enactment remained eligible thereafter for a limited grace period, which is now over. *See id.* § 1612(a)(2)(D)(ii). Aliens who were lawfully residing in the United States on the date of enactment retain eligibility for SSI if they are blind or disabled and for Food Stamps if they are "receiving benefits or assistance for blindness or disability" within the meaning of the Food Stamp Act of 1977. *Id.* § 1612(a)(2)(F). Members of Indian tribes, as defined in 25 U.S.C. § 450b(e), and certain American Indians born in Canada remain eligible for the benefits. *See* 8 U.S.C. § 1612(a)(2)(G). Aliens who received SSI benefits after July 1996 on the basis of an application filed before January 1, 1979, also retain eligibility for SSI. *See id.* § 1612(a)(2)(H). Aliens who were either 65 or older or under 18, and were lawfully residing in the United States on the date of enactment, remain eligible for Food Stamps. *See id.* § 1612(a)(2)(I), (J). Finally, certain Hmong and Highland Laotians who are lawfully residing in the United States, and their spouses and dependent children, remain eligible for Food Stamps. *See id.* § 1612(a)(2)(K).

In § 402(b) of the Act, Congress authorized the states, subject to certain exceptions, to determine the eligibility of qualified aliens for three other federal benefit programs: Temporary Assistance for Needy Families ("TANF"), Social Services Block Grants ("SSBG"), and Medicaid. *See id.* § 1612(b). The exceptions to this provision, enumerated in § 402(b)(2), are similar to the exceptions in § 402(a)(2) and provide that certain subgroups are eligible for the designated federal programs.

* * *

DISCUSSION
* * *

A. Standard of Review

In order to assess the constitutionality of § 402 of the Welfare Reform Act, we must first determine the appropriate level of scrutiny for judicial review of the legislative enactment at issue. In *Graham v. Richardson*, 403 U.S. 365, 91 S.Ct. 1848, 29 L.Ed.2d 534 (1971), the Supreme Court held that a state statute that denies welfare benefits to resident aliens (or denies benefits to resident

---

ineligible for any federal public benefit, including SSI and Food Stamps. *See* 8 U.S.C. § 1611. However, the provisions governing illegal aliens are not at issue in this lawsuit.

aliens who have not resided in the United States for a specified number of years) violates equal protection. *See id.* at 376, 91 S.Ct. 1848. Noting that aliens are a "'discrete and insular' minority," *id.* at 372, 91 S.Ct. 1848 (quoting *United States v. Carolene Prods. Co.*, 304 U.S. 144, 152-53 n.4, 58 S.Ct. 778, 82 L.Ed. 1234 (1938)), the Court applied "heightened" or "close judicial scrutiny" to the statutes at issue. *Id.* The Court, however, limited its holding to state legislation. Indeed, the Court devoted several paragraphs of its opinion to distinguishing between state authority to make alienage-based classifications and federal authority to do so. *See id.* at 376-78, 91 S.Ct. 1848. The Court acknowledged that the federal government's plenary authority over issues of immigration and naturalization provided an additional justification to invalidate state statutes that conflicted with overriding national policies in this area. *See id.*

Indeed, in *Mathews v. Diaz*, 426 U.S. 67, 96 S.Ct. 1883, 48 L.Ed.2d 478 (1976), the Court made clear that the standard of scrutiny applied to state legislation in *Richardson* does not govern judicial review of federal legislation involving alienage. In *Diaz*, the Supreme Court upheld federal legislation that restricted certain aliens' eligibility for a medical insurance program based on the duration of their residence in the United States and on their admission for permanent residence.[10] The Court emphasized that "responsibility for regulating the relationship between the United States and our alien visitors has been committed to the political branches of the Federal Government," and therefore judicial review of decisions made by Congress or the President in the area of immigration and naturalization must be narrow. *Id.* at 81-82, 96 S.Ct. 1883. Although the Court did not adopt explicitly the "rational basis" standard of scrutiny, it in effect applied rational basis review, upholding the legislation because it was not "wholly irrational." *Id.* at 83, 96 S.Ct. 1883. The Court explicitly distinguished the *Richardson* case and explained that state and federal alienage classifications must be treated differently because of Congress' plenary authority to regulate the conditions of entry and residence of aliens. *See id.* at 84-85, 96 S.Ct. 1883. In short, we believe that the *Diaz* case is directly on point on the issue of what level of scrutiny should be applied to Congressional regulation of aliens' welfare benefits. *See Rodriguez v. United States*, 169 F.3d 1342, 1350 (11th Cir.1999).[11]

---

[10] Notably, the Court characterized the issue in *Diaz* as not whether discrimination between citizens and aliens is permissible but whether discrimination within the class of aliens is permissible, because the statute excluded only those aliens who had not been in the United States for a minimum of 5 years and those who had not received permanent residence. *See Diaz*, 426 U.S. at 80, 96 S.Ct. 1883. Similarly in this case, the classifications at issue can be characterized as discrimination *among* aliens, as Congress has excluded some but not all aliens from eligibility for certain welfare benefits. As discussed above, Congress carved out numerous categories of aliens who remain eligible for such benefits. *See* 8 U.S.C. §§ 1612(a)(2), 1613(b).

[11] *See also Kiev v. Glickman*, 991 F.Supp. 1090, 1095-97 (D.Minn.1998); *Abreu v. Callahan*, 971 F.Supp. 799, 807-11 (S.D.N.Y.1997); *cf. Campos v. FCC*, 650 F.2d 890, 894 (7th Cir.1981) (holding broadly that federal alienage-based classifications are subject only to narrow judicial review, and sustaining legislation conditioning the grant of commercial radio operator licenses on citizenship).

The plaintiffs submit that *Diaz* is not the controlling authority in this case. We shall set forth briefly why we cannot accept this argument. First, the plaintiffs submit that the Court's more recent holding in *Adarand Constructors, Inc. v. Pena*, 515 U.S. 200, 115 S.Ct. 2097, 132 L.Ed.2d 158 (1995), makes clear that the strict scrutiny applied in *Richardson* should apply to federal alienage classifications as well. In *Adarand*, the Supreme Court articulated a general rule that equal protection analysis under the Fifth Amendment is the same as it is under the Fourteenth Amendment. *See id.* at 217, 115 S.Ct. 2097. However, *Adarand* itself acknowledged an exception to this general rule for cases in which special deference to the political branches of the federal government is appropriate. *See id.* at 217-18, 115 S.Ct. 2097 (citing *Hampton v. Mow Sun Wong*, 426 U.S. 88, 96 S.Ct. 1895, 48 L.Ed.2d 495 (1976), a case involving federal exercise of the immigration power).

The plaintiffs also submit that the holding of *Diaz* should be limited to cases in which a durational residency requirement is necessary to maintain the fiscal integrity of an insurance program. We cannot read any such limitation into the Court's holding in *Diaz*. The Court relied on the rational link between duration of residency and the fiscal soundness of an insurance program only when evaluating whether the statute at issue satisfied the rational basis test, not when determining what level of scrutiny should apply. We therefore see no reason to limit the Court's articulation of the rational basis standard to the particular factual situation of that case.

The plaintiffs further argue that, even if federal laws enacted under Congress' plenary immigration power are subject to rational basis review, the Welfare Reform Act is not such a law because it does not regulate the terms or conditions of immigration or naturalization. A statute that makes indigent aliens deportable, they submit, would constitute an exercise of the immigration power, but the Welfare Reform Act's withdrawal of welfare benefits from resident aliens, by contrast, is not within the scope of the immigration power. We cannot accept this argument. We believe that the Court's analysis in *Diaz* makes clear that, for purposes of equal protection analysis, Congress' interest in regulating the relationship between our alien visitors and the national government ought not to be defined in such narrow terms as to preclude application of the rational basis test in a case such as the present one involving eligibility for government benefits. *See Diaz*, 426 U.S. at 81-83, 96 S.Ct. 1883 (characterizing Congress' decision to restrict certain aliens' eligibility for welfare benefits as a decision "in the area of immigration and naturalization" and noting that "the responsibility for regulating the relationship between the United States and our alien visitors has been committed to the political branches of the Federal Government"); *see also Rodriguez*, 169 F.3d at 1349.[12] In sum, we conclude that, under the holding

---

[12] The amicus suggests that deferential review is warranted only when federal legislation actually regulates "core immigration functions," not whenever the legislation merely affects immigrants. In support of this contention, the amicus cites cases that invalidated statutes that "affected" noncitizens. However, none of the cited cases addresses this issue as directly as does the *Diaz* case.

in *Diaz*, the provisions of the Welfare Reform Act at issue in this case must be reviewed under rational basis scrutiny.

The intervenors additionally submit that, even if strict scrutiny does not apply, at least some intermediate level of scrutiny should be employed. Relying on *Plyler v. Doe*, 457 U.S. 202, 102 S.Ct. 2382, 72 L.Ed.2d 786 (1982), they argue that, because the Act imposes a severe and permanent deprivation upon a discrete and disadvantaged class, the alienage-based classification must be subjected to intermediate scrutiny. In *Plyler*, the Supreme Court applied intermediate scrutiny to a state law excluding illegal immigrant children from public education. *See id.* at 223-24, 102 S.Ct. 2382. As the Eleventh Circuit pointed out in *Rodriguez*, however, the *Plyler* case involved a state law, and nothing in the Court's opinion suggests that *Diaz* would not apply (or that heightened scrutiny would apply) if the law were federal. *See Rodriguez*, 169 F.3d at 1349-50. In fact, *Plyler* cited *Diaz* to point out that the deference owed to Congress in matters of aliens' status within our borders does not apply to state classifications of aliens. *See Plyler*, 457 U.S. at 225, 102 S.Ct. 2382. The Court stated:

> The States enjoy no power with respect to the classification of aliens. *See Hines v. Davidowitz*, 312 U.S. 52, 61 S.Ct. 399, 85 L.Ed. 581 (1941). This power is "committed to the political branches of the Federal Government." [*Mathews v. Diaz*, 426 U.S. at 81, 96 S.Ct. 1883]. Although it is "a routine and normally legitimate part" of the business of the Federal Government to classify on the basis of alien status, *id.* at 85, 96 S.Ct. 1883, and to "take into account the character of the relationship between the alien and this country," *id.* at 80, 96 S.Ct. 1883, only rarely are such matters relevant to legislation by a State.

Id. (parallel citations omitted). Because the law at issue in the case before us is a federal enactment, *Plyler* does not alter our reliance on *Diaz* for the application of rational basis review to the provisions of the Welfare Reform Act.

B. Application of the Rational Basis Test

We turn now to the application of the rational basis test. The Supreme Court has admonished that "rational-basis review in equal protection analysis 'is not a license for courts to judge the wisdom, fairness, or logic of legislative choices.'" *Heller v. Doe*, 509 U.S. 312, 319, 113 S.Ct. 2637, 125 L.Ed.2d 257 (1993) (quoting *FCC v. Beach Communications, Inc.*, 508 U.S. 307, 313, 113 S.Ct. 2096, 124 L.Ed.2d 211 (1993)). Rather, a statute survives rational basis scrutiny "if there is a rational relationship between the disparity of treatment and some legitimate governmental purpose." *Id.* at 320, 113 S.Ct. 2637. Moreover, under rational basis review, Congress need not actually articulate the legitimate purpose or rationale that supports the classification at issue. Instead, a statute "must be upheld against equal protection challenge if there is any reasonably conceivable state of facts that could provide a rational basis for the classification." *Id.* (quoting *Beach Communications*, 508 U.S. at 313, 113 S.Ct. 2096) (internal quotation marks omitted). We are required, under the rational basis standard, "to accept a legislature's generalizations even when there is an imperfect fit between means and ends. A classification does not fail rational-basis review because it 'is not made with mathematical nicety or because in practice it results in some inequality.'" *Id.* at 321, 113 S.Ct. 2637 (quoting *Dandridge v. Williams*, 397 U.S. 471, 485, 90 S.Ct. 1153, 25 L.Ed.2d 491 (1970) (quoting *Lindsley v. Natural Carbonic Gas Co.*, 220 U.S. 61, 78, 31 S.Ct. 337, 55 L.Ed. 369 (1911))) (internal quotation marks omitted).

The policy objectives that Congress hoped to achieve through the enactment of the Welfare Reform Act are set forth in 8 U.S.C. § 1601. First, Congress stated that the Act's provisions are intended to foster the legitimate governmental purpose of encouraging aliens' self-sufficiency. It is Congress' stated policy that "aliens within the Nation's borders not depend on public resources to meet their needs, but rather rely on their own capabilities and the resources of their families, their sponsors, and private organizations." 8 U.S.C. § 1601(2)(A). The plaintiffs submit that, because federal immigration policy already prohibits the immigration of those who are likely to become public charges, the benefits at issue in this case serve only as a safety net. Therefore, they contend, it is irrational to remove this safety net in an effort to encourage aliens to be more reliant on their families, sponsors, and private organizations because it is precisely those aliens who are unable to rely on such alternate sources of support who need the benefits in the first place. Moreover, they argue, removing welfare benefits from aliens who are elderly, disabled, or children will not help them become self-reliant because they are simply unable to work.

Whatever the merits of this criticism of the Welfare Reform Act, as a matter of public policy, we cannot say that the statute is rendered irrational simply because *some* aliens who are unable to work will not be induced to provide for themselves. In Congress' view, such aliens ought to rely on their families, sponsors, or private organizations for support, rather than on the public welfare rolls. The statute is reasonably related to that goal. Indeed, even if some aliens have no access to support from these alternate sources, the citizenship requirement is still rationally related to the goal of encouraging aliens to rely on private, not public, resources to meet their needs. *See Heller*, 509 U.S. at 321, 113 S.Ct. 2637 (noting that rational basis review requires courts to "accept a legislature's generalizations even when there is an imperfect fit between means and ends"); *Zehner v. Trigg*, 133 F.3d 459, 463 (7th Cir.1997) ("[T]he classification need not be the most narrowly tailored means available to achieve the desired end."); *see also Kiev*, 991 F.Supp. at 1099-1100; *Abreu v. Callahan*, 971 F.Supp. 799, 818 (S.D.N.Y.1997).

Congress has stated its policy that "the availability of public benefits not constitute an incentive for immigration to the United States." 8 U.S.C. § 1601(2)(B). Although reasonable individuals certainly can disagree on the wisdom of controlling immigration through such a policy, we must conclude that the provisions of the Welfare Reform Act are rationally related to the legitimate governmental goal of discouraging immigration that is motivated by the availability of welfare benefits. In reference to state welfare benefits, the Supreme Court has acknowledged that "[a]lien residency requirements for welfare benefits necessarily operate . . . to discourage entry into or continued residency in the State." *Richardson*, 403 U.S. at 379, 91 S.Ct. 1848. We cannot say, therefore, that it was irrational for Congress to conclude that removal of federal welfare benefits would have a similar deterrent effect on immigration into the United States. The plaintiffs submit that there is no rational connection between withdrawing benefits from legal resident aliens who were already in the United States when the Act was enacted and the goal of deterring future immigrants from coming here to reap welfare benefits. Although the Act may be overinclusive in this respect, again, rational basis scrutiny does not require a perfect fit. We therefore are constrained to hold that there is a rational relationship between the Welfare Reform Act's restriction of aliens' eligibility for welfare benefits and the legitimate governmental goal of deterring immigration that is motivated by the availability of those benefits.

Section 1612 also declares that Congress wanted to preserve the public fisc by reducing the rising costs of operating federal benefits programs. The plaintiffs suggest, however, that the distinction between citizens and noncitizens is no more rationally related to the general goal of saving money than would be a distinction between brown-eyed people and all other people; disqualifying any subset of eligible people will save money. But again, we cannot say that it was irrational for Congress to decide to achieve its budget objectives by eliminating aliens from these programs.[14] In effectuating the governmental goal of cost savings, Congress had to start somewhere and "must be allowed leeway to approach a perceived problem incrementally." *Beach Communications*, 508 U.S. at 316, 113 S.Ct. 2096. Moreover, Congress was entitled to conclude that achieving savings by eliminating these benefits to aliens was sufficiently compatible with the other policy objectives that it sought to foster through this legislation.

The Executive Branch, defending the constitutionality of the statute before this court, offers a further justification not found in Congress' statement of policy. It submits that the Act's provisions are rationally related to the legitimate governmental purpose of encouraging naturalization. The Act gives resident aliens in need of welfare benefits a strong economic incentive to become naturalized citizens. The plaintiffs again argue overinclusiveness,

---

[14] Congress had before it evidence that aliens were receiving welfare benefits in increasing numbers. *See, e.g., Supplemental Security Income: Problem Areas and Possible Reforms, Hearing on Supplemental Security Income Before the Senate Comm. on Finance*, 1995 WL 128208 (F.D.C.H. Mar. 27, 1995) ("Another factor underlying the growth of SSI . . . is the rapid growth of aliens on the rolls. According to the General Accounting Office, in 1993 the number of aliens on SSI was 683,000, or about 12% of the SSI caseload, up from 3% in 1982, at an annual cost of $3.3 billion . . . . The rising share of alien recipients is not unique to SSI; it has been observed in each of the major federal public assistance programs—Medicaid, SSI, AFDC, and Food Stamps . . . ." (footnote omitted)); *Proposals to Reduce Illegal Immigration, Hearing Before the Senate Comm. on the Judiciary*, 1995 WL 110439 (F.D.C.H. Mar. 14, 1995) ("The number of SSI recipients who are aliens has been increasing steadily. In December 1994, there were a little more than 738,000 aliens receiving SSI benefits. This is double the number of aliens receiving benefits 5 years ago. Alien recipients now constitute nearly 12 percent of the total number of SSI recipients.").

contending that the statute removes from eligibility certain aliens who cannot seek naturalization, such as elderly or disabled aliens who cannot demonstrate language proficiency or an understanding of United States history and government. The plaintiffs further submit that it is irrational to use the threat of starvation and homelessness to goad people into naturalization. Again, whatever the merits of these arguments in the public policy arena, we cannot accept them as a basis for rendering the statute unconstitutional. This court and other courts of appeals have recognized the legitimacy of this governmental interest in encouraging naturalization. *See, e.g., Campos v. FCC*, 650 F.2d 890, 894 (7th Cir.1981); *Mow Sun Wong v. Campbell*, 626 F.2d 739, 745 (9th Cir.1980), *cert. denied*, 450 U.S. 959, 101 S.Ct. 1419, 67 L.Ed.2d 384 (1981). The Supreme Court assumed in *Hampton v. Mow Sun Wong*, 426 U.S. 88, 96 S.Ct. 1895, 48 L.Ed.2d 495 (1976), that the "national interest in providing an incentive for aliens to become naturalized" would justify a citizenship requirement for federal civil service employment. *Id.* at 105, 96 S.Ct. 1895. We cannot say, therefore, that it would be irrational for Congress to conclude that restricting the availability of welfare benefits to aliens would provide incentive for aliens to seek naturalization. *See Kiev*, 991 F.Supp. at 1100; *Abreu*, 971 F.Supp. at 817-18. As we have already mentioned, rational basis scrutiny does not require a perfect fit between this legitimate governmental purpose and the means chosen to achieve it.

The plaintiffs submit finally that the Act fails rational basis review because it was motivated by impermissible animus toward noncitizens. We disagree. As the Supreme Court made clear in *Diaz*, "it is obvious that Congress has no constitutional duty to provide all aliens with the welfare benefits provided to citizens." *Diaz*, 426 U.S. at 82, 96 S.Ct. 1883. "In the exercise of its broad power over naturalization and immigration, Congress regularly makes rules that would be unacceptable if applied to citizens .... The fact that an Act of Congress treats aliens differently from citizens does not in itself imply that such disparate treatment is 'invidious.'" *Id.* at 79-80, 96 S.Ct. 1883. In light of the various rationales discussed above, we cannot say that the Welfare Reform Act is "inexplicable by anything but animus toward the class that it affects." *Romer v. Evans*, 517 U.S. 620, 632, 116 S.Ct. 1620, 134 L.Ed.2d 855 (1996).

Finally, we note that the Welfare Reform Act also contains a number of exceptions to its general exclusion of aliens from the welfare programs. Like the situation that confronted the Supreme Court in *Diaz*, therefore, we have a statutory scheme that, strictly speaking, distinguishes not between citizens and aliens but rather among subclasses within the alien population. *See Diaz*, 426 U.S. at 80, 96 S.Ct. 1883. Nevertheless, we do not believe that the exceptions carved out by Congress from its general prohibition against benefits to aliens, detracts from the rationality of the overall statutory scheme. Although Congress did not articulate a reason for each of these exceptions, we must accept Congress' determination because we can discern "a rational relationship between the disparity of treatment and some legitimate governmental purpose." *Heller*, 509 U.S. at 320, 113 S.Ct. 2637. As the Court of Appeals for the Eleventh Circuit explained in *Rodriguez v. United States*, 169 F.3d 1342 (11th Cir.1999), several of the exceptions extend benefits to aliens who have made special contributions to this Country.[15]   It certainly is not irrational for Congress to reward such service or to encourage other aliens to make similar contributions in the future. Five of the other exceptions ensure benefits to individuals who have sought refuge in this Country because of especially difficult conditions in their own countries.[16] Certainly, humanitarian concerns can constitute a rational basis for distinguishing among aliens. Although some might disagree with the distinctions Congress has made in this regard, such line-drawing is its prerogative, not the judiciary's. *See Heller*, 509 U.S. at 319, 113 S.Ct. 2637. Nor was it irrational for Congress to have excluded from the general ban those already residing in the United States who have an affliction or a condition that makes them particularly vulnerable to poverty.[17] No doubt, there is some question whether Congress included within the excepted class all those who should have been included. Drawing such lines, however, is a legislative task for Congress.   "[D]ifferences between the eligible and the ineligible are differences in degree rather than differences in the character of their respective clams." *Diaz*, 426 U.S. at 83-84, 96 S.Ct. 1883. The provision permitting the continuation of SSI benefits for those who are already receiving them and who appear to continue to meet the eligibility criteria is similarly not irrational; Congress was entitled to weigh the cost of terminating such a program against the cost of continuation.   Finally, members of Indian tribes have a unique historical relationship with the Federal Government, and therefore it certainly was not irrational for Congress to determine that it ought to continue to provide them benefits.[19]

CONCLUSION

We conclude that the citizenship requirements in § 402 of the Welfare Reform Act do not offend equal protection. We hold that *Mathews v. Diaz* requires the application of rational basis review and that the Act survives that level of scrutiny because it is rationally related to legitimate governmental purposes. Accordingly, the judgment of the district court is affirmed.

Affirmed.

550-51: Notes on the 1996 and 1997 Welfare Legislation

[Change the references to *Abreu* to *City of Chicago*.]

As noted in footnote one in *City of Chicago*, Congress restored food stamps in June 1998 for about 225,000 legal immigrant children, noncitizen

---

[15] In this category are aliens who have assisted the Nation's economy by working at least 40 quarters (10 years), aliens who are veterans or active military personnel, and members of the Hmong and Highland Laotian tribes who provided assistance to the United States during the Vietnam War. *See* 8 U.S.C. § 1612(a)(2)(B), (C), (K).

[16] In this category are refugees, asylees, aliens whose deportation has been withheld because of fear of persecution, and certain Cuban, Haitian and Amerasian immigrants. *See* 8 U.S.C. § 1612(a)(2)(A).

[17] Included in this category are those who resided in the United States at the time of the passage of the statute and who are blind, disabled, or in their old age or youth. *See* 8 U.S.C. § 1612(a)(2)(E), (F), (I), (J).

[19] *See* 8 U.S.C. § 1612(a)(2)(G).

seniors, disabled noncitizens, and refugees who had been in the United States as of August 22, 1996. *See* Agricultural Research, Extension, and Education Reform Act, Pub. L. No. 105-185, 112 Stat 523 (1998). And in October 1998, Congress restored benefits for about 20,000 additional elderly and disabled immigrants. *See* Noncitizen Benefit Clarification and Other Technical Amendments Act, Pub. L. No. 105-306, 112 Stat. 2926 (1998). Combined with other partial restorations in 1997, these enactments have restored SSI eligibility for virtually all noncitizens receiving benefits on August 22, 1996, as well as food stamp eligibility for some noncitizens receiving benefits on that date. The bars for future arrivals remain intact.

551-52: Note on State Welfare Legislation

For an overview of state measures pursuant to the 1996 Welfare Act and a detailed argument that the constitutional immigration power is an exclusively federal power that may not be devolved by statute to the states, see Wishnie, *Laboratories of Bigotry?: Devolution of the Immigration Power, Equal Protection, and Federalism*, 76 N.Y.U. L. Rev. 493 (2001).

552-55: Notes on Constitutional Limits on Federal Alienage Classifications

[Change the references to *Abreu* to *City of Chicago*, and change the references to Judge Kaplan to Judge Ripple.]

Chapter Six: Unauthorized Migrants in the United States

601: Estimating the Unauthorized Population (add at bottom of page)

Early analysis of 2000 Census data suggests that the number of undocumented migrants residing in the United States may be far higher than earlier estimates—perhaps totaling 11 million. *See* Zitner, *Immigrant Tally Doubles in Census Count: U.S. has twice as many undocumented workers as estimated*, L.A. Times, Mar. 10, 2001, at A1 (2001 WL 2468491) .

624: Border Enforcement (add at end of note 1)

See generally P. Andreas, Border Games: Policing the U.S.-Mexico Divide (2000).

625: Apprehension Data (add at end of note 2)

According to the INS, apprehensions at the southwest border reached 1.64 million in fiscal year 2000 (up 7 percent from the previous fiscal year). Immigration and Naturalization Service, Monthly Statistical Report, September 2000 FY Year End Report (Oct. 31, 2000) . For the first quarter of fiscal year 2001, however, apprehensions declined by 14 percent in comparison to the first quarter of fiscal year 2000. Immigration and Naturalization Service, Monthly Statistical Report First Quarter Ending December 2000 (Jan. 31, 2001) . It is not yet clear what has caused the decline—economic conditions in the two countries, deterrence through enforcement, fewer migrants traveling home and seeking (unlawful) re-entry, or a combination of these and other factors.

640: Employer Sanctions (add at end of note 2)

In recent years, INS interior enforcement activities have dropped dramatically. In fiscal year 2000, INS completed 1189 cases against employers—a 34 percent decrease from the previous fiscal year and barely one quarter of the cases completed in fiscal year 1998. *See* Immigration and Naturalization Service, Monthly Statistical Report, September 2000 FY Year End Report (Oct. 31, 2000); Immigration and Naturalization Service, Monthly Statistical Report, September 1999 FY Year End Report (Oct. 29, 1999).

651: IRCA Legalization (add after first full paragraph)

To paraphrase Mark Twain, the death of the so-called "late amnesty" cases was greatly exaggerated. The Legal Immigration Family Equity Act (LIFE Act), Pub. L. 106-533, Tit. XI, 114 Stat 2762 (2000), and the LIFE Act Amendments, Pub. L. 106-554, Tit. XV, Div. B, 114 Stat. 2763 (2000), provide class members in the *Catholic Social Services* case and two other long-running cases challenging 1986 legalization regulations an opportunity to file applications for adjustment to permanent resident status. Applicants must still demonstrate eligibility under the criteria set forth in IRCA to gain status. The Act also grants work authorization to family members of class members and provides them protection against removal. Section 1104 of LIFE Act, *as amended by* §§ 1502-1504 of the LIFE Act Amendments.

677: Proposition 187 (add after first full paragraph)

The Proposition 187 litigation was ultimately settled after Gray Davis was elected governor of California. The state agreed to drop its appeal of Judge Pfaelzer's decision, thereby leaving in place the lower court's invalidation of provisions that barred undocumented children from public school and required state employees to check status and report suspected undocumented aliens to the INS. In exchange, plaintiffs agreed to accept the sections of the initiative that made it a crime to produce and use false documents. *See* McDonnell, *Prop. 187 Talks Offered Davis Few Choices*, L.A. Times, July 30, 1999, at A3 (1999 WL 2181861). Settlement of the case, of course, meant that the Supreme Court would not be presented with an opportunity to revisit its decision in *Plyler v. Doe.*

Chapter Seven: Deportability and Relief From Removal

717: *AADC v. Reno* **(add at end of note 1)**

The Supreme Court vacated and remanded the decision of the Ninth Circuit. *Reno v. American-Arab Anti-Discrimination Committee*, 525 U.S. 471, 119 S.Ct. 936, 142 L.Ed.2d 940 (1999). The decision dealt principally with judicial review—the Court found that INA § 242(g) deprived the district court of jurisdiction to hear the plaintiffs' claims (*see* Chapter Eight in this Supplement); but Justice Scalia, writing for the Court, had the following to say about the First Amendment as it related to the aliens' "selective prosecution" claim:

> Finally, we must address respondents' contention that, since the lack of prior factual development for their claim will render the § 242(a)(1) exception to § 242(g) unavailing; since habeas relief will also be unavailable; and since even if one or both were available they would come too late to prevent the "chilling effect" upon their First Amendment rights; the doctrine of constitutional doubt requires us to interpret § 242(g) in such fashion as to permit immediate review of their selective-enforcement claims. We do not believe that the doctrine of constitutional doubt has any application here. As a general matter—and assuredly in the context of claims such as those put forward in the present case—an alien unlawfully in this country has no constitutional right to assert selective enforcement as a defense against his deportation.
>
> Even in the criminal-law field, a selective prosecution claim is a *rara avis*. Because such claims invade a special province of the Executive—its prosecutorial discretion—we have emphasized that the standard for proving them is particularly demanding, requiring a criminal defendant to introduce "clear evidence" displacing the presumption that a prosecutor has acted lawfully. * * *
>
> These concerns are greatly magnified in the deportation context. Regarding, for example, the potential for delay: Whereas in criminal proceedings the consequence of delay is merely to postpone the criminal's receipt of his just deserts, in deportation proceedings the consequence is to permit and prolong a continuing violation of United States law. Postponing justifiable deportation (in the hope that the alien's status will change—by, for example, marriage to an American citizen—or simply with the object of extending the alien's unlawful stay) is often the principal object of resistance to a deportation proceeding, and the additional obstacle of selective-enforcement suits could leave the INS hard pressed to enforce routine status requirements. And as for "chill[ing] law enforcement by subjecting the prosecutor's motives and decisionmaking to outside inquiry": What will be involved in deportation cases is not merely the disclosure of normal domestic law-enforcement priorities and techniques, but often the disclosure of foreign-policy objectives and (as in this case) foreign-intelligence products and techniques. The Executive should not

have to disclose its "real" reasons for deeming nationals of a particular country a special threat—or indeed for simply wishing to antagonize a particular foreign country by focusing on that country's nationals—and even if it did disclose them a court would be ill equipped to determine their authenticity and utterly unable to assess their adequacy. Moreover, the consideration on the other side of the ledger in deportation cases—the interest of the target in avoiding "selective" treatment—is less compelling than in criminal prosecutions. While the consequences of deportation may assuredly be grave, they are not imposed as a punishment, see *Carlson v. Landon,* 342 U.S. 524, 537, 72 S.Ct. 525, 96 L.Ed. 547 (1952). In many cases (for six of the eight aliens here) deportation is sought simply because the time of permitted residence in this country has expired, or the activity for which residence was permitted has been completed. Even when deportation is sought because of some act the alien has committed, in principle the alien is not being punished for that act (criminal charges may be available for that separate purpose) but is merely being held to the terms under which he was admitted. And in all cases, deportation is necessary in order to bring to an end *an ongoing violation* of United States law. The contention that a violation must be allowed to continue because it has been improperly selected is not powerfully appealing.

To resolve the present controversy, we need not rule out the possibility of a rare case in which the alleged basis of discrimination is so outrageous that the foregoing considerations can be overcome. Whether or not there be such exceptions, the general rule certainly applies here. When an alien's continuing presence in this country is in violation of the immigration laws, the Government does not offend the Constitution by deporting him for the additional reason that it believes him to be a member of an organization that supports terrorist activity.

In her concurrence, Justice Ginsburg agreed that § 242(g) deprived the federal courts of jurisdiction over respondents' pre-final-order suit, because the First Amendment does not require immediate judicial consideration of plaintiffs' selective enforcement plea. On the substance of the First Amendment issue, Ginsburg wrote:

> The petition for certiorari asked this Court to review the merits of respondents' selective enforcement objection, but we declined to do so, granting certiorari on the jurisdictional question only. We thus lack full briefing on respondents' selective enforcement plea and on the viability of such objections generally. I would therefore leave the question an open one. I note, however, that there is more to "the other side of the ledger" than the Court allows.
>
> It is well settled that "[f]reedom of speech and of press is accorded aliens residing in this country." *Bridges v. Wixon,* 326

U.S. 135, 148, 65 S.Ct. 1443, 89 L.Ed. 2103 (1945). Under our selective prosecution doctrine, "the decision to prosecute may not be deliberately based upon an unjustifiable standard such as race, religion, or other arbitrary classification, including the exercise of protected statutory and constitutional rights." *Wayte v. United States*, 470 U.S. 598, 608, 105 S.Ct. 1524, 84 L.Ed.2d 547 (1985) (internal citations and quotation marks omitted). I am not persuaded that selective enforcement of deportation laws should be exempt from that prescription. If the Government decides to deport an alien "for reasons forbidden by the Constitution," *United States v. Armstrong*, 517 U.S. 456, 463, 116 S.Ct. 1480, 134 L.Ed.2d 687 (1996), it does not seem to me that redress for the constitutional violation should turn on the gravity of the governmental sanction. Deportation, in any event, is a grave sanction. As this Court has long recognized, "[t]hat deportation is a penalty—at times a most serious one—cannot be doubted." *Bridges*, 326 U.S., at 154, 65 S.Ct. 1443; see also *ibid.* (Deportation places "the liberty of an individual . . . at stake . . . . Though deportation is not technically a criminal proceeding, it visits a great hardship on the individual and deprives him of the right to stay and live and work in this land of freedom."); G. Neuman, Strangers to the Constitution: Immigrants, Borders, and Fundamental Law 162 (1996) ("Deportation has a far harsher impact on most resident aliens than many conceded 'punishment[s]'. . . . Uprooting the alien from home, friends, family, and work would be severe regardless of the country to which the alien was being returned; breaking these attachments inflicts more pain than preventing them from being made.").

In sum, were respondents to demonstrate strong likelihood of ultimate success on the merits and a chilling effect on current speech, and were we to find the agency's action flagrantly improper, precedent and sense would counsel immediate judicial intervention. But respondents have made no such demonstration. Further, were respondents to assert a colorable First Amendment claim as a now or never matter—were that claim not cognizable upon judicial review of a final order—again precedent and sense would counsel immediate resort to a judicial forum. In common with the Attorney General, however, I conclude that in the final judicial episode, factfinding, to the extent necessary to fairly address respondents' claims, is not beyond the federal judiciary's ken.

Justice Souter dissented on the ground that the district court had jurisdiction. This part of his opinion addresses the First Amendment argument:

The approach I would take in this case avoids a troubling problem that the Court chooses to address despite the fact that it was not briefed before the Court: whether selective prosecution claims have vitality in the immigration context. Of course, in principle, the Court's approach itself obviates the need to address that issue: if respondents' suit is barred by § 242(g), the Court need not address the merits of their claims. Yet the Court goes on, in what I take as dictum, to argue that the alien's interest in avoiding selective treatment in the deportation context "is less compelling than in criminal prosecutions," either because the alien is not being punished for an act he has committed, or because the presence of an alien in the United States is, unlike a past crime, "an ongoing violation of United States law" (emphasis deleted). While the distinctions are clear, the difference is not. The interest in avoiding selective enforcement of the criminal law, shared by the government and the accused, is that prosecutorial discretion not be exercised to violate constitutionally prescribed guaranties of equality or liberty. See *United States v. Armstrong*, 517 U.S. 456, 464-465, 116 S.Ct. 1480, 134 L.Ed.2d 687 (1996); *Wayte v. United States*, 470 U.S. 598, 608, 105 S.Ct. 1524, 84 L.Ed.2d 547 (1985). This interest applies to the like degree in immigration litigation, and is not attenuated because the deportation is not a penalty for a criminal act or because the violation is ongoing. If authorities prosecute only those tax evaders against whom they bear some prejudice or whose protected liberties they wish to curtail, the ongoing nature of the nonpayers' violation does not obviate the interest against selective prosecution.

No doubt more could be said with regard to the theory of selective prosecution in the immigration context, and I do not assume that the Government would lose the argument. That this is so underscores the danger of addressing an unbriefed issue that does not call for resolution even on the Court's own logic. Because I am unconvinced by the Court's statutory interpretation, and because I do not think the Court should reach the selective prosecution issue, I respectfully dissent.

Note that the Court's comments on the selective prosecution claim do not necessarily apply to a direct First Amendment challenge to the underlying deportability ground.

For a detailed discussion of the Court's opinions, *see* Neuman, *Terrorism, Selective Deportation and the First Amendment after* Reno v. AADC, 14 Geo. Immig. L.J. 313 (2000); Cole, *Damage Control? A Comment on Professor Neuman's Reading of* Reno v. AADC, 14 Geo. Immig. L.J. 347 (2000); Martin, *On Counterintuitive Consequences and Choosing the Right Control Group: A Defense of* Reno v. AADC, 14 Geo. Immig. L.J. 363 (2000).

718-21: Retroactivity (add at end of carryover paragraph on page 721)

The Second Circuit affirmed Judge Weinstein's opinion on retroactivity in *Henderson v. INS*, 157 F.3d 106 (2d Cir.1998), *cert. denied*, 526 U.S. 1004, 119 S.Ct. 1141, 143 L.Ed.2d 209 (1999) .

In *INS v. St. Cyr*, 121 S.Ct. 2271 (2001), the Supreme Court concluded that Congress' repeal of relief from deportation under INA § 212(c) should not be applied retroactively, and that therefore "§ 212(c) relief remains available for aliens * * * whose convictions were obtained through plea agreements and who, notwithstanding those convictions, would have been eligible for § 212(c) relief at the time of their plea under the law then in effect." *Id.* slip op. at 36. Applying norms of statutory interpretation that disfavor the retrospective application of statutes, the Court stated that legislation "may not be applied retroactively * * * absent a clear indication from Congress that it intended such a result." It found "nothing in IIRIRA unmistakably indicating that Congress considered the question whether to apply its repeal of § 212(c) retroactively" to aliens such as St. Cyr. (The Court also relied upon the additional canon of construction that ambiguities in deportation statutes should be resolved in favor of the alien.) Importantly, however, the Court appeared to cast no doubt on Congress' power to adopt retroactive immigration legislation—provided the intent to do so was unambiguously expressed.

725: Document Fraud (add after cite to Walters v. Reno in second full paragraph)

The district court's opinion was affirmed by the Ninth Circuit, 145 F.3d 1032 (9th Cir.1998) (upholding, with one minor alteration, permanent injunction issued by lower court).

725: Crime-related Grounds (add at end of first paragraph under subheading b)

See Kanstroom, *Deportation, Social Control, and Punishment: Some Thoughts About Why Hard Laws Make Bad Cases*, 113 Harv. L. Rev. 1889 (2000); Morawetz, *Understanding the Impact of the 1996 Deportation Laws and the Limited Scope of Proposed Reforms*, 113 Harv. L. Rev. 1938 (2000).

730: Crimes Involving Moral Turpitude (add as new concluding paragraph to note 1)

Take, for instance, the problem of drunk driving. Should driving-under-the-influence be deemed a "crime involving moral turpitude"? What role should current social attitudes play in deciding this question? In *Matter of Lopez-Meza*, Int.Dec. 3423 (BIA 1999), the Board held that an Arizona conviction for aggravated driving under the influence constituted a crime involving moral turpitude. The majority concluded that simple DUI does not "reflect conduct that is necessarily morally reprehensible or that indicates such a level of depravity or baseness that it involves moral turpitude." However, a person guilty of aggravated DUI—which requires a showing that the driver knowingly drove with a suspended, canceled, revoked or refused license—"commits a crime so base and so contrary to the currently accepted duties that persons owe to one another and to society in general that it involves moral turpitude." The Board distinguished *Lopez-Meza* in *Matter of Torres-Varela*, 23 I&N Dec. 78 (BIA 2001), which involved another Arizona conviction for aggravated DUI; in *Torres-Varela*, the aggravating factor was prior convictions for DUI, not DUI with knowledge of a prohibition against driving at any time (as in *Lopez-Meza*). The majority held that "multiple convictions for the same DUI offense, which individually is not a crime involving moral turpitude, do not, by themselves, aggregate into a conviction for a crime involving moral turpitude." A dissenting opinion asserted that "the 'aggregating' factor in *Matter of Lopez-Meza*, driving with a knowledge that one is forbidden to drive, is no greater 'a deviance from the accepted rules of contemporary morality' . . . than the 'aggregating' factor here: choosing to drink and drive, knowing that one has already been convicted twice of this inherently dangerous offense." Assume that you are a member of the Board. How would you identify "accepted rules of contemporary morality" and whether certain conduct deviated so far from such rules as to constitute moral turpitude?

739: Aggravated Felonies (delete second full paragraph and *In re Batista-Hernandez* and insert)

MATTER OF CRAMMOND
Board of Immigration Appeals (*en banc*), 2001.
23 I & N Dec. 9.

GUENDELSBERGER, BOARD MEMBER:
* * *
I. FACTS AND PROCEDURAL HISTORY

The respondent is a native and citizen of Belize who entered the United States as a lawful permanent resident on March 7, 1988. The record reflects that the respondent was convicted on March 23, 1998, in the Superior Court of California, Ventura County, of two separate crimes: (1) residential burglary, in violation of section 459 of the California Penal Code, for which he was sentenced to 210 days in jail and 3 years of probation; and (2) unlawful sexual intercourse, in violation of section 261.5(c) of the California Penal Code, for which he was sentenced to 90 days in jail, to run consecutive to his sentence for the burglary conviction, and 3 years of probation.

The respondent's motion to reopen relates solely to our November 4, 1999, determination that his conviction for unlawful sexual intercourse was for an "aggravated felony" within the meaning of section 101(a)(43)(A) of the Immigration and Nationality Act, and that he was consequently removable under section 237(a)(2)(A)(iii) of the Act, and ineligible for certain forms of relief as a result of that aggravated felony conviction. *See generally* 8 C.F.R. § 3-2(c)(l).

Specifically, the respondent argues that his March 23, 1998, conviction for "unlawful sexual intercourse" can no longer be considered a conviction for an "'aggravated felony" under section 101(a)(43)(A) of the Act, because the state court reduced the offense from a felony to a misdemeanor. Consequently, he argues that he should be allowed to pursue relief from removal because he is not an "aggravated felon." In support of his motion, he has submitted a copy of a computer printout reflecting docket entries for October 21, 1999, in the Ventura County Superior Court, which indicate that the respondent's offense was reduced to a misdemeanor.[1]

---

[1] The Service has not challenged the respondent's contention that his crime was reduced from a felony to a misdemeanor under state law.

II. ISSUE

The issue in this case is whether the respondent has been convicted of an "aggravated felony" under section 101(a)(43)(A) of the Act. This determination turns on whether that section includes a conviction for a misdemeanor, as opposed to a felony, and whether the misdemeanor/felony distinction is governed by state or federal law.

The issue we decide here concerns only the interpretation of section 101(a)(43)(A). Our examination of other sections is for the purpose of determining whether their language or structure may shed light on the intended scope of section 101(a)(43)(A).

III. ANALYSIS

A. Section 101(a)(43)(A) of the Act

Section 101(a)(43) of the Act defines the categories of offenses that Congress has determined merit treatment as "aggravated felonies" under the immigration laws. Section 101(a)(43)(A) includes the crime of "sexual abuse of a minor" within the definition of an aggravated felony. Specifically, the statute provides, in pertinent part as follows:

> The term "aggravated felony" means--
> (A) murder, rape, or sexual abuse of a minor;
> . . . .

The term applies to an offense described in this paragraph whether in violation of Federal or State law .. . . .

Section 101(a)(43)(A) of the Act. The issue before us is whether the language of the statute mandates that an offense described in section 101(a)(43)(A) be a "felony" offense.

Interpretation of statutory language begins with the terms of the statute itself, and if those terms, on their face, constitute a plain expression of congressional intent, they must be given effect. *Chevron, U.S.A., Inc. v. Natural Resources Defense Council, Inc.*, 467 U.S. 837, 842-43 (1984). The legislative purpose is presumed to be expressed by the ordinary meaning of the words used. *INS v. Phinpathya*, 464 U.S.183, 189 (1984). In discerning congressional intent, the words of a statute must be read in their context and with a view to their place in the overall statutory scheme, as the meaning (or the ambiguity) of certain words or phrases may only become evident when placed in context.

We do not find a clear expression of congressional intent in the plain language of section 101(a)(43) of the Act. The choice of the term "aggravated felony," as opposed to more generic terms such as "aggravated offense" or "aggravated crime," does suggest that Congress intended to restrict the listed offenses to felonies. On the other hand, there is no explicit reference in section 101(a)(43)(A) requiring that the crimes included there be felonies.

Looking beyond section 101(a)(43)(A), some of the other aggravated felony provisions refer to other federal statutes, or they require minimum sentences or minimum monetary loss amounts for an offense to qualify as an aggravated felony. Specifically, section 101(a)(43)(B) requires, by reference to federal statutes regarding illicit trafficking in a controlled substance at 21 U.S.C.

§ 802 and drug trafficking at 18 U.S.C. § 924(c), that an offense be punishable as a felony.

Section 101(a)(43)(F) of the Act refers specifically to the federal definition of a "crime of violence" in 18 U.S.C. § 16, which requires that any crime falling within § 16(b) be a felony but contains no such requirement for offenses falling within § 16(a). It further provides a specific minimum sentence of "at least 1 year" for the offense. Thus, this section has been found to include crimes that are not "felonies" within the federal definition of that term.[3] *See United States v. Pacheco*, 225 F.3d 148 (2d Cir.2000) (finding, for sentence enhancement purposes, that a misdemeanor offense for which the alien had been sentenced to a 1-year suspended sentence was an aggravated felony within the meaning of the Act); *Wireko v. Reno*, 211 F.3d 833 (4th Cir.2000) (finding that the plain language of section 101(a)(43)(F) contains no requirement that the offense have been a felony, and concluding that the alien's misdemeanor conviction for sexual battery was for an aggravated felony). Section 101(a)(43)(G) also defines as aggravated felonies theft or burglary offenses for which the sentence is "at least 1 year," without further qualification. *See* United States v. Graham, 169 F.3d 787 (3d Cir.) (finding, for sentence enhancement purposes, that a misdemeanor theft conviction for which the term of imprisonment is 1 year is an aggravated felony conviction under section 101(a)(43)(G)), *cert. denied*, 528 U.S. 845 (1999).

* * *

Where the language of the statute is ambiguous, we turn to traditional tools of statutory construction, such as the legislative history or other statutes where Congress may have spoken subsequently and more specifically regarding the issue at hand. Although legislative statements have less force than the plain language of the statute, such statements are helpful to corroborate and underscore a reasonable interpretation of the statute. There is little indication in other sections of the Act or in the overall statutory scheme of Congress' intentions concerning the offenses listed in section 101(a)(43)(A). However, the addition of section 237(a)(2)(E) of the Act as a ground of removability,[4] which includes such crimes against children as child abuse, child neglect, and child abandonment, suggests that Congress intended "sexual abuse of a minor" offenses under section 101(a)(43)(A) to be limited to felony offenses. This is indicated by the fact that lesser sexual abuse offenses would be covered under section 237(a)(2)(E).

The language in former section 212(c) of the Act also supports the position that aggravated felony crimes are necessarily felony offenses. That section barred relief to an alien who was "convicted of one or more aggravated felonies and has served for such felony or felonies a term of imprisonment of at

---

[3] The federal definition of a "felony" requires that the minimum term of imprisonment be "more than 1 year." 18 U.S.C. § 3559(a)(5) (1994).

[4] Section 237(a)(2)(E) of the Act was added by section 350 of the IIRIRA, 110 Stat. at 3009-640.

least 5 years."[5] The reference to "such felony" suggests that, at least at the time this amendment was enacted, aggravated felonies were considered felony offenses. Similarly, as discussed in Board Member Filppu's concurring opinion, the IIRIRA left intact at least one provision in the Act in which the term "such felon" is used in reference to a person convicted of an aggravated felony.

The legislative history of section 101(a)(43) of the Act indicates that Congress intended to include only the most serious offenses within the aggravated felony definition. The term "aggravated felony" was first introduced to the Act by section 7342 of the Anti-Drug Abuse Act of 1988, Pub. L. No. 100-690, 102 Stat. 4181, 4469 ("ADAA"). As stated in the House Conference Report accompanying S. 358, which resulted in amendments to the aggravated felony definition by section 501 of the Immigration Act of 1990, Pub. L. No. 101-649, 104 Stat. 4978, 5048, the intent of the 1990 amendments was to "broaden[] the list of serious crimes, conviction of which results in various disabilities and preclusion of benefits under the Immigration and Nationality Act." H.R. Conf. Rep. No. 101-955 (1990), *reprinted in* 1990 U.S.C.C.A.N. 6784, 6797.

Since the ADAA first used and defined the term aggravated felony in 1988, Congress has expanded the definition on several occasions, signaling its growing concern over criminal aliens. One of the bills containing amendments to the aggravated felony definition proposed limiting aggravated felonies to those crimes that would have a base offense level of 12 or more under the United States Sentencing Guidelines ("U.S.S.G."). *See* H.R. 22, 104th Cong. (1995). According to chapter 5, Part A, Zone D of the U.S.S.G. Sentencing Table, a base offense level of 12 provides, with one exception, for a minimum term of imprisonment of 12 to 18 months. *See* 18 U.S.C.A. ch.5, pt. A (West 1996).

In the legislative history accompanying the bill that set forth the proposed amendments to section 101(a)(43)(A) of the Act that were eventually enacted in the IIRIRA, the Committee on the Judiciary referred to the offenses under that section as felonies. Specifically, in discussing the amendments precluding an alien convicted of an aggravated felony from applying for adjustment of status, the Committee noted that "[b]ecause of the expanded definition of 'aggravated felony' provided by sec. 161 of the bill, aliens who have been convicted of most felonies, if sentenced to at least 1 year in prison, will be ineligible for this relief." S. Rep. No. 104-249, at 40 (1996) (emphasis added).

Overall, the legislative history and other interpretive aids provide less than clear guidance as to whether Congress intended that offenses falling within the aggravated felony definition at section 101(a)(43)(A) should be limited to felony offenses.

It is not evident from the language of the statute or from the legislative history whether Congress intended that an offense listed in section 101(a)(43)(A) must be a felony in order to be considered an aggravated felony. We therefore turn to the "longstanding principle of construing any lingering

---

[5] This language was added to former section 212(c) by section 511 of the Immigration Act of 1990, Pub. L. No. 101-649,104 Stat. 4978, 5052. Section 2I2(c) was repealed by section 304(b) of the IIRIRA, 110 Stat. at 3009- 597.

ambiguities in deportation statutes in favor of the alien." *See INS v. Cardoza-Fonseca*, 480 U.S. 421, 449 (1987) (citing *INS v. Errico*, 385 U.S. 214, 225 (1966); *Costello v. INS*, 376 U.S. 120, 128 (1964); *Fong Haw Tan v. Phelan*, 333 U.S. 6, 10 (1948)). The consequences of a finding that a crime is an "aggravated felony" are severe. Congress has specifically noted its intention that aliens convicted of such crimes should be subjected to various disabilities under the immigration laws and precluded from nearly all forms of relief. In light of these harsh consequences, we resolve the ambiguity presented by this case in favor of the respondent. Thus, we find that if an alien has been convicted of an offense of "murder, rape, or sexual abuse of a minor," that conviction must be for a "felony" in order for the crime to be considered an "aggravated felony" under section 101(a)(43)(A) of the Act.

We recognize that the United States Court of Appeals for the Seventh Circuit has recently determined that section 101(a)(43)(A) of the Act encompasses state misdemeanor convictions for sexual abuse of a minor. *See Guerrero-Perez v. INS*, [242 F.3d 727] (7th Cir.2001). The court in *Guerrero-Perez* noted that, although it would ordinarily defer to the Board's interpretation of Immigration law, the Board's decision in the case before it was "silent with regard to the issue of whether Guerrero's misdemeanor conviction can be deemed an aggravated felony." *Id.* at [731]. Therefore, the court addressed the issue as a matter of first impression. After examining the structure and evolution of section 101(a)(43), the court concluded that "Congress, since it did not specifically articulate that aggravated felonies cannot be misdemeanors, intended to have the term aggravated felony apply to the broad range of crimes listed in the statute, even if these include misdemeanors." *Id.* at [737].

In *Guerrero-Perez*, the Seventh Circuit focused primarily upon two factors in reaching its conclusion. First, it found that the grouping of sexual abuse of a minor with murder and rape in section 101(a)(43)(A) was "a fairly strong indication, albeit a limited one" that Congress intended both misdemeanor and felony convictions for sexual abuse of a minor to be considered aggravated felonies. *Id.* at [736]. Second, it emphasized the word "means" in the definition of aggravated felony. We find it difficult to accept these factors as dispositive. As to the first factor, the grouping of sexual abuse of a minor with murder and rape, crimes almost universally classified as felonies, appears to cut both ways, if not to provide greater support for the argument that Congress intended to cover only felony sexual abuse of a minor offenses. The second factor, the focus upon the term "means," does not necessarily resolve the issue of the significance of Congress' choice of the term "aggravated felony" to describe the overall category of offenses.

The Seventh Circuit confines its examination of the statute to section 101(a)(43) and does not address the use of the term "aggravated felony" in other sections of the Act. As discussed above, the term is used in other sections of the Act in contexts that suggest a focus on felony offenses. The Seventh Circuit does not address our decision and analysis in *Matter of Davis*, 20 I&N Dec. 536, 542-43 (BIA 1992), which emphasizes the importance, for purposes of uniformity, of a felony offense in order to have an aggravated felony under section 101(a)(43)(B) of the Act. Finally, the Seventh Circuit does not fully address the interpretive principle that we resolve doubts in favor of the more narrow construction of deportation statutes. For these reasons, after taking into account the analysis set forth in *Guerrero-Perez v. INS, supra*, we nevertheless conclude that an aggravated felony under section 101(a)(43)(A) of the Act must be a felony offense.

B. Respondent's Conviction

We have determined that an offense under section 101(a)(43)(A) of the Act must be a felony offense. The question remains whether the respondent's offense is a felony. Where a state criminal conviction is at issue, this determination turns on whether the state or the federal definition of a "felony" controls.

Important policy considerations favor applying a uniform federal standard in adjudicating removability and determining the immigration consequences of a conviction under the Act. The states use a variety of approaches in defining the term "felony."[6] To assure uniform treatment under the immigration laws, unless otherwise directed, we turn to the federal definition of a felony in applying the terms of the aggravated felony provision. We have followed this approach in many recent decisions that interpret the Act. This system of classification provides a uniform benchmark against which to assess the immigration consequences of individual state convictions, and it frees us from the necessity of relying on "'the vagaries of state law.'" *Matter of K-V-D-*, [Int.Dec. 3422 (BIA 1999)] at 7 (quoting *Matter of A-F-*, 8 I&N Dec. 429, 446 (BIA, A.G. 1959)). Thus, we find it appropriate to apply the federal definition of a felony in determining whether a state offense is a felony for immigration purposes.

Under federal law, an offense is defined as a felony if it is one for which the maximum term of imprisonment authorized is, at a minimum, "more than 1 year." 18 U.S.C. § 3559(a)(5) (1994). An offense is classified as a misdemeanor if the maximum authorized term of imprisonment is "one year or less," and the minimum authorized term of imprisonment is 5 days. 18 U.S.C. §§ 3559(a)(6)-(8).

At the time of our November 4, 1999, decision, the conviction documents in the record indicated that the respondent had been convicted of a "felony charge" under section 261.5(c) of the California Penal Code and that he had entered a plea with the understanding that he could be sentenced to a maximum penalty of 3 years in prison for the offense.

---

[6] For example, California does not differentiate between felony and misdemeanor offenses with respect to the maximum authorized term of imprisonment. Rather, a felony is defined as "a crime which is punishable with death or by imprisonment in the state prison," and all other offenses are considered misdemeanors or infractions. Cal. Penal Code § 17(a) (West 2000). California law provides that an offense is a misdemeanor under various circumstances when discretion is left to the state court to determine whether the offense shall be punished by imprisonment in the state prison, by a fine, or by imprisonment in the county jail. *See* Cal. Penal Code § 17(b). Other states have similarly vague categorizations of crimes that are not necessarily tied to the maximum authorized term of imprisonment. *See, e.g.,* Mass. Gen. Laws Ann. ch. 274. § 1 (West 2000).

In conjunction with his motion, however, the respondent has presented new evidence indicating that his offense has been reduced to a "misdemeanor." The pertinent language of the state statute at issue in this case provides as follows:

> Any person who engages in an act of unlawful sexual intercourse with a minor who is more than three years younger than the perpetrator is guilty of either a misdemeanor or a felony, and shall be punished by imprisonment in a county jail not exceeding one year, or by imprisonment in the state prison.

Cal. Penal Code § 261.5(c) (West 1998). As this language indicates, the statute is divisible, in that persons may be charged and convicted either for a crime punishable as a misdemeanor (with a maximum term of imprisonment in a county jail not exceeding 1 year) or for a crime punishable as a felony (by imprisonment in the state prison, if the term of imprisonment exceeds 1 year). Given the reduction of the respondent's crime to a "misdemeanor," we find that his conviction falls within that portion of the statute punishing misdemeanor offenses. The maximum term of imprisonment for the misdemeanor portion of section 261.5(c) of the California Penal Code is "imprisonment in a county jail not exceeding one year." Because the federal definition of a felony requires that the term of imprisonment be for "more than one year," 18 U.S.C. § 3559(a)(5), the respondent's conviction—if modified as indicated in the motion to reopen— would not be for an offense falling within the federal definition of a felony.

IV. CONCLUSION

In light of our determination that the new evidence presented by the respondent in conjunction with his motion constitutes prima facie evidence that the offense of which he was convicted, unlawful sexual intercourse, does not fall within the federal definition of a felony, we conclude that it is not an aggravated felony under section 101(a)(43)(A) of the Act. The new evidence is therefore material to the respondent's case, as the conviction would no longer appear to support a finding of removability under section 237(a)(2)(A)(iii) of the Act. Nor would it preclude him from seeking certain forms of relief from removal, for which he was previously found statutorily ineligible as a result of his conviction for an aggravated felony.

Accordingly, we find it appropriate to grant the respondent's motion to reopen and to remand this matter to the Immigration Judge for further proceedings. * * *

FILPPU, BOARD MEMBER, concurring.

I respectfully concur.

I agree with the majority that current subparagraph (A) of the "aggravated felony" definition is limited to felony convictions and that we should apply the federal "felony" definition for convictions falling within this subparagraph. *See* section 101(a)(43)(A) of the Immigration and Nationality Act. Unlike the majority, however, I do not find this to be a case in which we must invoke the rule of lenity. The ordinary approach to questions of statutory construction provides an answer.

* * *

The statutory context in which the term "aggravated felony" was introduced confirms for me that it then applied only to felonies. This term had its origin in section 7342 of the Anti-Drug Abuse Act of 1988, Pub. L. No. 100-690, 100 Stat. 4181, 4469 ("ADAA"), and was restricted to murder, drug trafficking crimes, illicit trafficking in firearms or destructive devices, and any attempts or conspiracies to commit such acts. These are obviously serious offenses. They are likely to be felonies, but perhaps not necessarily so.

Importantly, the ADAA also made other changes showing that the legislation was aimed at "felons." The ADAA revised the custody provisions of former section 242(a) of the Act, to require the Attorney General to take custody of "any alien convicted of an aggravated felony" and then directed that "the Attorney General shall not release *such felon* from custody." ADAA § 7343(a)(4), 102 Stat. at 4470 (emphasis added). The ADAA further added a new section 242A to the Act, which was designed to expedite the deportation of aliens convicted of aggravated felonies. *See* section 242A of the Act. New section 242A(b) provided in relevant part as follows:

> With respect to an alien convicted of an aggravated felony who is taken into custody by the Attorney General . . . the Attorney General shall, to the maximum extent practicable, detain any such felon at a facility at which other such aliens are detained.

ADAA § 7347(a), 102 Stat. at 4471, 4472 (emphasis added). This provision currently appears as section 238(a)(2) of the Act. The natural meaning of the term "aggravated felony" and these related statutory references to "such felon," which were part of the original enactment, seem to foreclose any reasonable argument that the term then was meant generally to include misdemeanors.

* * *

That does not end the matter, however. The "aggravated felony" definition has undergone a series of amendments. Rape and sexual abuse of a minor were added to section 101(a)(43)(A) of the Act by section 321(a)(l) of the Illegal Immigration Reform and Immigrant Responsibility Act of 1996, Division C of Pub. L. No. 104-208, 110 Stat. 3009-546, 3009-627 ("IIRIRA"). New legislation, of course, may alter the character or meaning of existing statutory language. Importantly, in this respect, the IIRIRA also amended other subparagraphs of the "aggravated felony" definition such that a literal reading of several subparagraphs would cover certain misdemeanor convictions in addition to felony convictions. *See, e.g.*, section 101(a)(43)(G) of the Act (providing that theft or burglary offenses are aggravated felonies if the term of imprisonment is at least 1 year).

The IIRIRA's inclusion of language covering certain misdemeanors within various subparagraphs of the "aggravated felony" definition creates uncertainty as to whether the IIRIRA fundamentally changed the original meaning of the term. Consequently, we must look beyond the use of the word "felony" in the original enactment to determine whether misdemeanor convictions fall within subparagraph (A), as amended by the IIRIRA.

The United States Supreme Court directs us to look at a statute as a whole when construing language that appears to be ambiguous. *See Food and Drug Admin. v. Brown & Williamson Tobacco Corp.*, 529 U.S. 120, 132 (2000); *John*

Hancock Mut. Life Ins. Co. v. Harris Trust & Sav. Bank, 510 U.S. 86, 94-95 (1993). The first place to look is in the IIRIRA itself, because the basic question to be resolved is whether the design of the IIRIRA effected a change in the prior meaning of the term "aggravated felony."

I find little guidance in section 321 or in section 322(a)(2) of the IIRIRA. *See* IIRIRA §§ 321, 322, 110 Stat. at 3009-627, 3009-629. These sections made the amendments to the aggravated felony definition. But no comprehensive design or pattern emerges to suggest that misdemeanor convictions were in general to be treated as "aggravated felon[ies]." Rather, sections 321 and 322(a)(2) of the IIRIRA extended the "aggravated felony" definition to some misdemeanors mainly by reducing the periods of imprisonment necessary for certain crimes to be treated as aggravated felonies. For example, prior to the IIRIRA, section 101(a)(43)(G) required the imposition of a 5-year sentence in order for a theft or burglary offense to be an aggravated felony. After enactment of the IIRIRA, the term of imprisonment was reduced to "at least one year," literally covering only those misdemeanors receiving the maximum sentence. *See* section 101(a)(43)(G) of the Act.

The phrase "aggravated felony" is a term of art. It does not mandate that the crimes actually be felonies when the literal language of a particular subparagraph includes offenses that are misdemeanors. Further, there is room to argue that the term "aggravated felony" must *generally* bear a different meaning after enactment of the IIRIRA in order to give effect to the literal language of those subparagraphs that now include misdemeanors. Indeed, one court has ruled that misdemeanor convictions are encompassed within section 101(a)(43)(A), but I agree with the majority that the court did so without the benefit of the analysis we provide today. *Guerrero-Perez v. INS*, [242 F.3d 737] (7th Cir.2001).

In the end, I find the inclusion of some "top-end" misdemeanors and a few others (*e.g.*, section 101(a)(43)(N) covers certain misdemeanor alien smuggling first offenses) to be scant evidence of a general design or objective to effect a significant departure from the meaning previously assigned to the term "aggravated felony." I would expect to find some mention of such a design in the legislative history of the IIRIRA.

Most importantly, the IIRIRA did not alter the term itself or make systematic changes to how the term is used elsewhere in the Act. The IIRIRA left it as an aggravated "felony." Had there been a broader intent to change the term's overall character, I would expect the term itself to have been amended in keeping with that intent, such that it might now be labeled an "aggravated crime" or an "aggravated offense."

* * *

Simply put, the overall design of the IIRIRA does not reflect any intent to change the original meaning of the term "aggravated felony" in general. The fact that the literal language of some subparagraphs would extend to a few misdemeanors is not a basis for concluding that all of the subparagraphs now cover misdemeanors too. The isolated inclusion by new legislation of a few misdemeanors within a lengthy catalogue of crimes does not, in my opinion, signal a legislative shift in the meaning of the principal term being defined, particularly when the new enactment, as a whole, fails to reflect any overall effort to change the natural meaning of the words used in that term.

It is a "fair assumption that Congress is unlikely to intend any radical departures from past practice without making a point of saying so." *Jones v. United States*, 526 U.S. 227, 234 (1999); *see Green v. Bock Laundry Machine Co.*, 490 U.S. 504, 521 (1989) (stating that a "party contending that legislative action changed settled law has the burden of showing that the legislature intended such a change"). The literal language of a few subparagraphs reflects a departure, but the structure and design of the IIRIRA as a whole do not. Consequently, I believe we must continue to give effect to the original design of section 101(a)(43) of the Act, except where the literal language of a particular subparagraph requires otherwise.

Current subparagraph (A) does not contain any explicit language overriding the original felony character of the definition. Thus, I conclude that an offense under subparagraph (A) must be a felony in order to qualify as an "aggravated felony."

> ROSENBERG, BOARD MEMBER, concurring [joined by one other member].
> I respectfully concur.

I agree with the majority that the respondent's 1998 misdemeanor conviction for unlawful sexual intercourse is not a conviction for an aggravated felony. Section 101(a)(43)(A) of the Immigration and Nationality Act. Specifically, I agree that the term "aggravated felony" in subparagraph (A) includes only a felony conviction for murder, rape, or sexual abuse of a minor, and that the accepted federal definition of a "felony" under 18 U.S.C. § 3559(a) (1994) applies in determining whether the respondent's state conviction constitutes a felony. Therefore, I concur in the result reached by the majority.

However, I find that the statutory language and legislative history pertaining to the term "aggravated felony" in general, and to subparagraph (A) in particular, provides a sound and reasoned basis for these conclusions. While I agree that "he term "aggravated felony" and the specific language of subparagraph (A) may not be altogether plain, the majority's own opinion belies its conclusion that "[t]here is little indication in other sections of the Act or in the overall statutory scheme of Congress' intentions concerning the offenses listed in section 101(a)(43)(A)." In particular, I cannot agree that "[o]verall, the legislative history and other interpretive aids provide less than clear guidance as to whether Congress intended [to limit the offenses covered by subparagraph (A)] to felony offenses." Similarly, I cannot agree that the language of the statute can be read to support "competing reasonable interpretations," as though the dissenting opinion provides but another equally tenable view we simply have chosen not to adopt.

* * *

II. REASONABLE BOARD INTERPRETATION OF AGGRAVATED FELONY

As I agree with the majority that we are only deciding the meaning of section 101(a)(43)(A) of the Act, I do not see the need to contrast subparagraph (A) with any of the other subparagraphs in section 101 (a)(43) in order to determine its meaning. Perhaps the majority only means to support its conclusion that the terminology in subparagraph (A) is ambiguous. Nevertheless, the majority's "[l]ooking beyond" subparagraph (A) to decisions addressing other subparagraphs of section 101(a)(43) of the Act in the sentence enhancement context suggests that it may view other paragraphs as encompassing misdemeanor convictions.

Even assuming that the majority draws no distinction between the language in subparagraph (A) and other subparagraphs of section 101(a)(43) of the Act, my concurring and dissenting colleagues exercise no such restraint. Both presume that certain subparagraphs of section 101(a)(43) of the Act, such as those referring to a sentence of "at least one year," necessarily encompass misdemeanor convictions. *See, e.g.*, sections 101(a)(43)(F), (G) of the Act.

I take issue with such conclusions, as there is no need to differentiate certain other subparagraphs of section 101(a)(43) as encompassing misdemeanor convictions in order to reach a reasonable interpretation of the scope of subparagraph (A). To do so improperly predetermines matters not at issue without giving the interested parties notice or an opportunity to be heard on those issues.

Although we are not deciding such issues today, the dissent raises some points regarding the construction of other subparagraphs of section 101(a)(43) of the Act that warrant a preliminary response. Principally, it is important to note that there are alternate readings of the 1996 amendments to certain subsections of the aggravated felony definition that are more than reasonable—and more reasonable than the construction posited by the dissent. Simply put, there is no reason to conclude that Congress meant for both misdemeanor and felony convictions to be included in the "aggravated felony" definition simply because Congress reduced the sentence requirement associated with felony convictions covered in certain subparagraphs from 5 years to 1 year.

For example, merely because the amendment to section 101(a)(43)(G) of the Act "[l]owers fine and imprisonment thresholds in the definition (from 5 years to 1 year . . .), thereby broadening the coverage of . . . theft . . . ,' S.Rep. No. 249, 104th Cong., 1996 WL 180026," does not mean that Congress intended to include misdemeanors in that category. *United States v. Graham, supra*, at 792 (alteration in original); *see also* section 101(a)(43)(F) of the Act (imposing an imprisonment threshold of 1 year). In particular, section 162 of Senate bill S. 1664 succinctly states: "Because of the expanded definition of 'aggravated felony' provided by sec. 161 of the bill, aliens who have been convicted of most *felonies, if sentenced to at least 1 year in prison*, will be ineligible" for relief barred by conviction for an aggravated felony. S. 1664, 104th Cong. § 162 (1996) (emphasis added); S. Rep. No. 104-249, at 17 (1996); *see also* H.R. Conf. Rep. No. 104-828, at 223 (1996) (House recedes to Senate amendment section 161). This language suggests that the Senate was concerned only with the range of sentences that would make a felony conviction an "aggravated felony." There is no suggestion that crimes classified as misdemeanors are to be transformed into "aggravated felonies" merely because of the sentence imposed. As the *Graham* court emphasized, "There is no evidence that Congress noticed that it was breaking the time-honored line between felonies and misdemeanors." *United States v. Graham, supra*, at 792.

My dissenting colleague completely misconstrues the import of our holding in *Matter of Davis*, 20 I&N Dec. 536 (BIA 1992). It is not that we "had no difficulty concluding that a misdemeanor offense was included within" the scope of section 101(a)(43) of the Act. It is that in *Davis*, we found that the statute required the conviction to be for a felony and adopted a federal standard as to whether an offense is a felony regardless of the label used by the state. In following this standard, some state misdemeanors have been treated as felonies and some state felonies have been treated as misdemeanors. In *Davis*, we found that a state misdemeanor was an aggravated felony because it qualified under the federal definition as a *felony*.

The question posited here is whether an offense that qualifies as a *misdemeanor* according to a federal standard can be an aggravated felony. *See United States v. Pacheco, supra*, at 158 (Straub, J.. dissenting) ("*If a felony is a crime punishable by more than one year, how, then, can an 'aggravated' felony include crimes punishable by just one year?*" (emphasis added)). I could not agree more with Judge Straub's view that "[t]o include misdemeanors within the definition of 'aggravated felony' turns the plain meaning of the word 'aggravated' entirely on its head, since in addition to not *being* felonies in the first place, misdemeanors are conventionally understood as being *less severe* than felonies, as well." *Id*.

It is entirely consistent with the meaning of the word "aggravated" and the meaning of the word "felony" to conclude that Congress meant only for persons who are convicted of a felony and sentenced for that felony to at least 1 year in prison to be affected by the definition. As Judge Straub emphasizes, one would never suggest that by adding the adjective "blue" to the noun "car," one could be attempting to define items that are not, in the first instance, cars. *See United States v. Pacheco, supra*, at 157 (Straub, J., dissenting). It makes far more sense to conclude that any *felony* conviction for murder, rape, or a crime involving sexual abuse of a minor qualifies as an "aggravated felony" conviction, even if the actual sentence imposed is less than 1 year. By contrast, it is reasonable that in decreasing the maximum sentences from 5 years to 1 year for offenses such as shoplifting or assault, Congress intended only for a felony conviction in these categories that is serious enough to result in at least a 1-year sentence to be classified as an aggravated felony conviction.

* * *

GRANT, BOARD MEMBER, dissenting [joined by eight other members].

I respectfully dissent. The decision of the majority too narrowly limits the scope of section 101(a)(43) of the Immigration and Nationality Act, by glossing over the contextual meaning of the statute's provisions, and is contrary to the holdings in several federal appellate decisions. These decisions properly conclude that the term "aggravated felony" is a term of art employed by Congress that encompasses *both* felonies *and* misdemeanors. Indeed, in the very recent case *Guerrero-Perez v. INS*, [242 F.3d 737] (7th Cir.2001), which is directly on point with the case before us, the United States Court of Appeals for the Seventh Circuit found that a misdemeanor conviction for criminal sexual abuse of a minor is an aggravated felony under subparagraph (A) of section 101 (a)(43). In light of these decisions, and in light of the history and construction of the statute at issue, I would find that the respondent's conviction for a crime of sexual abuse of a minor is an aggravated felony, regardless of whether it is classified by the state court as a misdemeanor or a felony offense.

The term "aggravated felony" was first used in a much shorter version of section 101(a)(43) of the Act in 1988. In 1996, Congress expanded the aggravated felony definition in three significant ways: first, it expanded the list of offenses that constitute aggravated felonies by specifically adding offenses that were misdemeanor offenses under federal statutes;[1] second, it trimmed from 5 years to 1 year the threshold sentence upon which crimes of violence and generic offenses such as theft and burglary may be considered aggravated felonies (thus allowing certain misdemeanor offenses to be included based on the sentence imposed);[2] and third, it added categories of offenses—for example, commercial bribery, counterfeiting, forgery, obstruction of justice, and perjury—for which a sentence of 1 year in prison brings the offense within the definition.[3] *See* Illegal Immigration Reform and Immigrant Responsibility Act of 1996, Division C of Pub. L. No. 104-208, §§ 321(a)(3), (4), 110 Stat. 3009-546, 3009-627 ("IIRIRA"); Antiterrorism and Effective Death Penalty Act of 1996, Pub. L. No. 104-132, §§ 440(e)(7), (8), 110 Stat. 1214, 1278 ("AEDPA").

The Seventh Circuit recently held that Congress' choice of the term to be defined—aggravated felony—cannot trump the definition that Congress has proceeded to assign to that term. *Guerrero-Perez v. INS, supra*, at [736-37]. In doing so, the court stated:

The structure of [section 101(a)(43)] reveals a desire on Congress' part not to limit aggravated felonies to only felony convictions. . . . The critical term in this section of the statute [deportability] is "aggravated felony" and Congress could have decided not to define this term, as it chose not to do so with regard to the term moral turpitude. However, rather than leave the question of what constitutes an aggravated felony open-ended, Congress said, "The term 'aggravated felony' means—. . ." and proceeded to list what crimes would be considered aggravated felonies. It is important to note that the term aggravated felony is placed within quotation marks and Congress then used the word "means" after this term. What is evident from the setting aside of aggravated felony with quotation marks and the use of the term "means" is that [section

---

[1] As amended, section 101(a)(43)(N) of the Act includes misdemeanor alien smuggling convictions under section 274(a)(2) of the Act, including first offenses under section 274(a)(2)(A), and only provides an exception for those persons convicted of a first offense if the smuggling involved the alien's spouse, child, or parent. Thus, a person convicted of an alien smuggling first offense that does not involve one of those specified family members has been convicted of an aggravated felony. *See Matter of Ruiz-Romero*, Interim Decision 3376 (BIA 1999). In addition, section 101(a)(43)(0), as amended, provides that convictions under section 275(a) of the Act, which includes misdemeanor convictions for the first offense of entry without inspection, are aggravated felony convictions if the alien was previously deported as an aggravated felon.

[2] *See* sections 101(a)(43)(F), (G) of the Act.

[3] *See* sections 101(a)(43)(R), (S) of the Act.

101(a)(43)] serves as a definition section. As a consequence, Congress had the option to use a variety of terms to reach the crimes listed within [section 101(a)(43)]. ... Congress had the discretion to use whatever term it pleased and define the term as it deemed appropriate. *See Stenberg v. Carhart*, 530 U.S. 914, 120 S.Ct. 2597, 2615 (2000) ("When a statute includes an explicit definition, we must follow that definition, even if it varies from that term's ordinary meaning."). The statute functions like a dictionary, in that it provides us with Congress' definition of the term "aggravated felony."

Id. (citation omitted). The Seventh Circuit thus rejected arguments identical to those presented in this case—that a misdemeanor conviction for sexual abuse of a minor cannot constitute a conviction for an "aggravated felony" because the crime is not a felony under state law. The majority's lean attempt to distinguish *Guerrero-Perez* begs the question that is asked and answered in the text quoted above: Congress' choice of a term to be defined has no meaning beyond that which is assigned by the subsequent definition, for "'[a] definition which declares what a term "means" . . . excludes any meaning that is not stated'." *Id.* (quoting *Colautti v. Franklin*, 439 U.S. 379, 393 n.10 (1979) (quoting 2A C. Sands, *Statutes and Statutory Construction* § 47.07 (4th ed. Supp. 1978))).

* * *

The majority is quick to move from the language of the aggravated felony definition itself to an attempt to discern the intent underlying the legislation. A careful examination of the language used by Congress in this section, however, allows us to interpret the meaning of the aggravated felony definition through general principles of statutory construction. Section 101(a)(43) has been, since its introduction into the Act, a single compound sentence listing a variety of offenses, not all of which constituted felonies. The definition was first enacted by section 7343 of the Anti-Drug Abuse Act of 1988, Pub. L. No. 100-690, 100 Stat. 4181, 4470 ("ADAA"), and included four categories of offenses: murder; drug trafficking; illicit trafficking in firearms or destructive devices; and any attempt or conspiracy "to commit any such act." Section 501(a) of the Immigration Act of 1990, Pub. L. No. 101-649, 104 Stat. 4798, among other changes, added two new categories of offenses: money laundering, and crimes of violence, as defined in 18 U.S.C. § 16, for which the term of imprisonment imposed was at least 5 years.

The aggravated felony definition was further amended by section 222(a) of the Immigration and Nationality Technical Corrections Act of 1994, Pub. L. No. 103-416, 108 Stat. 4320 ("INTCA"), which completely revised section 101(a)(43) from a single paragraph listing the 5 general categories of offenses, plus the "attempt and conspiracy" offenses, to a heterogenous compendium of offenses catalogued in 15 subparagraphs. Although restructured, the offenses nevertheless remained a single sentence modified by the following introductory phrase: "The term aggravated felony means—."

The Supreme Court has recently concluded that it is improper to adopt a construction of the text of a statute that attributes different meanings to the same phrase within the same sentence. *See Reno v. Bossier Parish Sch. Bd.*, 528 U.S.

320, 329-30 (2000). The definition contained in section 101(a)(43) is a single sentence that defines the term of art "aggravated felony." Through the various amendments over time, Congress has broadened the scope of the definition and has included various categories of crimes within this definition, both felonies and misdemeanors. Reading a felony limitation into the term "aggravated felony" for some parts of the definition but not for others is contrary to this principle of statutory construction. The term "aggravated felony," for our purposes, "means," without limitation, any of the offenses listed in the various subparagraphs of section 101(a)(43).

In 1992, prior to the more expansive amendments to the aggravated felony definition contained in the INTCA and the 1996 amendments, the Board examined a state misdemeanor "conspiracy" offense. *Matter of Davis*, 20 I&N Dec. 536 (BIA 1992). There, the Board held that a state misdemeanor conviction for conspiracy to distribute a controlled substance (cocaine) was an aggravated felony conviction because the underlying substantive offense constituted a "drug trafficking crime" under 18 U.S.C. § 924(c)(2). *Id.* at 545. The Board rejected an Immigration Judge's holding that the conspiracy offense would qualify as an aggravated felony only if the elements of that offense were analogous to the conspiracy provisions of the federal Controlled Substances Act. *Id.* at 539, 544-45. While it is true * * * that this holding was premised on precedents dealing with convictions for conspiracy to commit crimes involving moral turpitude, it is no less significant that the Board, in one of its first precedents construing section 101(a)(43), had no difficulty concluding that a misdemeanor offense was included within its scope.

The majority identifies no clear evidence that Congress has ever intended the term "felony" to impose a limiting construction. Rather, it posits that such a construction is possible due to the alleged "ambiguity" of a statute that uses the term "felony," but then lists myriad offenses, including ones which can be prosecuted as misdemeanors.[7] The reluctance to classify a particular offense as an aggravated felony—with all of the attendant consequences that the Act imposes on an alien who has committed such an offense—may be

---

[7] The concurrence of Board Member Filppu concludes, unlike the majority, that it was the clear intent of Congress in originally enacting section 101(a)(43) to limit its scope to felony offenses. Arguing from the "urtext" of the definition, which the concurrence asserts did not specifically include misdemeanor offenses, as well as from the Act's references to those covered by the definition as "felons," the concurrence concludes that this felony limitation remains in force—but only for those subparagraphs of the current definition that do not specifically list offenses that may be prosecuted as misdemeanors. As explained in the text, such assignment of different meaning with the same sentence of the Act is impermissible as a matter of statutory construction. The clear and unambiguous language of the current statute relieves us of the need to rely on the unexpressed intent of Congress in enacting the original version of section 101(a)(43), or to examine whether the subsequent amendments are consistent with that "original intent." *Cf. Seatrain Shipbuilding Corp. v. Shell Oil Co.*, 444 U.S. 572, 596 (1980) (providing that, while the views of subsequent Congresses cannot override the unmistakable intent of the enacting one, such views are entitled to significant weight when the precise intent of the enacting Congress is obscure).

understandable, but it is inherently subjective. Notably, from the entire history of judicial and administrative construction of this term, the majority cites no case which finds the ambiguity it has discovered here. The majority cites as evidence of "ambiguity" the fact that the Board has divided into four separate opinions in *this* case. I submit that it is the lack of clarity in the majority's opinion, and not any ambiguity in the statute, which has so fractured the Board on this occasion.

This lack of clarity is disturbing, and threatens great uncertainty in the administrative jurisprudence. The majority *appears* to propose that the term "aggravated felony" be given one meaning when applied to section 101(a)(43)(A) (*i.e.*, that it be construed as a felony requirement), but that it be attributed another meaning when applied to those subparagraphs that include misdemeanor offenses, either explicitly or by reference (*i.e.*, that it be construed as making no such additional requirement due to the conflict with the specific terms of the provision in question). Yet, on careful examination, the majority stops short of a firm conclusion on this point. The majority acknowledges a string of decisions by United States courts of appeals which find that misdemeanor convictions can constitute aggravated felonies (all involving offenses other than those listed in section 101(a)(43)(A) of the Act). It does not, however, state its own agreement with this finding. Thus, the majority decision not only improperly segregates subparagraph (A) from the rest of section 101 (a)(43), but clearly leaves open the possibility that it could construe die term "aggravated felony" to impose a felony prerequisite with respect to all crimes in the remaining subparagraphs of that section.

The majority thus leaves the Board on the horns of an untenable dilemma: either it presages an ultimate determination that Congress, in enacting and amending section 101(a)(43) of the Act, did not mean what it said when it included offenses that may be prosecuted as misdemeanors; or it leads to a future in which section 101(a)(43) will be interpreted by patchwork analysis, a felony prerequisite applying to some offenses and not to others. The first alternative is in derogation of the meaning of the Act. The second violates principles of statutory construction, improperly adopting a construction of the text that attributes different meanings to the same phrase within the same sentence. * * *

The second alternative also carries the seeds of its own collapse. If there is an overarching requirement, stemming from the phrase "aggravated felony," that certain listed offenses be felonies, that requirement should logically apply to all listed offenses. The outcome of this decision, as adumbrated by the concurring opinion of Board Member Rosenberg, could well lead to a conclusion that *no* offense may be classified as an "aggravated felony" unless that offense has been classified as a felony either by the convicting jurisdiction or by reference to a federal standard. However much I disagree with that outcome, it seems more logical than an approach that invests the phrase "aggravated *felony*" with the power to limit the reach of the definition in certain cases, *e.g.*, convictions for sexual abuse of a minor, but not in others, *e.g.*, a crime of violence under 18 U.S.C. § 16(a). *See* sections 101(a)(43)(A), (F) of the Act. Both sexual abuse of a minor and "§ 16(a)" crimes of violence can be prosecuted as misdemeanors. The rule, it seems, should be consistent for both.

I find the proper rule—that there is no overarching requirement that a crime listed or categorized under section 101 (a)(43) be a felony—inherent in the text of the statute. Without endorsing the majority's analysis-in-isolation of subparagraph (A), I note that this provision requires only that an offense be a crime of "murder, rape, or sexual abuse of a minor" in order to constitute an "aggravated felony." The offenses of "rape" and "sexual abuse of a minor" were added to subparagraph (A) by section 321 of the IIRIRA. *See* IIRIRA § 321, 110 Stat. at 3009-627. This provision contains no explicit requirement that the offenses listed therein be felony offenses, nor reference to a federal statute containing such a requirement. Although murder and rape were clearly felonies under the common law, the textual proximity of "sexual abuse of a minor" in section 101(a)(43) should not be used to infer that such is a requirement for any crime listed in that subparagraph. We have already determined that the phrase "sexual abuse of a minor" is to be given a broad reading, *Matter of Rodriguez-Rodriguez*, Interim Decision 3411 (BIA 1999), and in doing so have recognized the clear intent of Congress to impose severe immigration consequences on aliens who commit offenses of this type. That is consistent with finding that Congress intended to impose no "felony" limitation when it added this offense.

For these reasons, I would find that the new evidence the respondent seeks to submit for consideration, indicating that his felony offense has been reduced to a misdemeanor, is not material to our determination that his conviction was for an aggravated felony within the meaning of section 101(a)(43)(A) of the Act. I would find that his crime of sexual abuse of a minor is an aggravated felony under subparagraph (A), regardless of whether it is classified as a misdemeanor or a felony offense. Consequently, I would deny the motion to reopen.

Notes

1. The Seventh Circuit declined to reconsider its decision in *Guerrero-Perez v. INS*, 242 F.3d 737 (2001) , in light of *Matter of Crammond*. "We cannot adopt the approach that a splintered majority of the Board in *Crammond* supports. None of the positions articulated by the various Board Members who make up the majority present statutory interpretations that we have not considered previously." *Guerrero-Perez v. INS*, — F.3d — , 2001 WL 747384 (July 2, 2001). *See also United States v. Marin-Navarette*, 244 F.3d 1284 (11th Cir.2001) (conviction for misdemeanor of third-degree attempted child molestation constitutes "aggravated felony" under INA § 101(a)(43)(A) triggering 16-level increase in sentence for illegal reentry after deportation).

2. The definition of "aggravated felony" frequently poses difficult legal issues regarding the interpretation of other state and federal laws. For instance, INA § 101(a)(43)(F) classifies as an aggravated felony "a crime of violence as defined in section 16 of Title 18 [U.S. Code] ... for which the term of imprisonment [was] at least one year." The definition of "crime of violence" in 18 U.S.C. § 16 includes "any ... offense that is a felony and that, by its nature, involves a substantial risk that physical force against the person or property of another may be used in the course of committing the offense." Consider once again convictions for drunk driving. Whether or not DUI is a crime involving

moral turpitude, might it nonetheless constitute an aggravated felony because it involves a "a substantial risk" of physical force against another person or his or her property and is therefore a crime of violence under federal law? *Compare Tapia Garcia v. INS*, 237 F.3d 1216 (10th Cir.2001) and *Matter of Puente-Salazar*, Int.Dec. 3412 (BIA 1999) (en banc) (yes) with *United States v. Chapa-Garza*, 243 F.3d 921 (5th Cir.2001) (no, for sentence enhancement purposes).

See also (1) *Matter of K-V-D-*, Int.Dec. 3422 (BIA 1999) (en banc)— conviction under Texas state law for simple possession of a controlled substance is not an aggravated felony under INA § 101(a)(43)(B) where offense is not analogous to a drug trafficking crime under 18 U.S.C. § 924(c)(2) and is not a felony under federal law. The majority distinguished *United States v. Hinojosa-Lopez*, 130 F.2d 691 (5th Cir.1997), which reached a different conclusion regarding the statutory language for the purpose of criminal sentence enhancement under the U.S. Sentencing Guidelines.

(2) *Drakes v. Zimski*, 240 F.3d 246 (3d Cir.2000)—alien who gave false name after a traffic stop, was convicted of second-degree forgery under Delaware law, and was given a suspended sentence of one year committed an "aggravated felony" under INA § 101(a)(43)(R) (crime relating to forgery). *See generally* Bennett, *The Unconstitutionality of Nonuniform Immigration Consequences of "Aggravated Felony" Convictions*, 74 N.Y.U. L. Rev. 1696 (1999)).

747: Plea Bargains (add at end of first paragraph)

See *INS v. St. Cyr*, 121 S.Ct. 2271 (2001), n.48 (citing state statutes requiring trial judges to advise defendants in criminal cases that adverse immigration consequences may result from a plea agreement).

747: Plea Bargains (add in second full paragraph after cite to *United States v. Nagaro-Garbin*)

In re Resendiz, 25 Cal.4th 230, 19 P.3d 1171, 105 Cal.Rptr.2d 431 (2001) (an attorney's affirmative misrepresentation or erroneous advice regarding immigration consequences of a guilty plea can, in certain circumstances, constitute ineffective assistance of counsel; collateral nature of immigration consequences of a guilty plea is not a per se bar to an ineffective assistance claim).

759: Voluntary Departure (add at end of fourth full paragraph)

For a thorough discussion of the different requirements of the two voluntary departure provisions, see *Matter of Arguelles-Campos*, Int.Dec. 3399 (BIA 1999). Note that the Justice Department regulations have interpreted the statutory language "prior to the completion of [§ 240] proceedings" to mean "prior to or at the master calendar hearing at which the case initially calendared for a merits hearing." 8 C.F.R. § 240.26(b)(1)(i)(A). As Board Member Grant notes in a concurring opinion in *Arguelles-Campos*, "the initial master calendar hearing may take place months or even a year prior to the commencement of a hearing on the merits .... . Time and experience will tell whether this administrative interpretation, in practice, has limited the utility of the statutory scheme enacted by Congress." *See also Matter of Cordova*, Int.Dec. 3408 (BIA 1999) (immigration judge has duty to provide information about availability and requirements of § 240B(a) voluntary departure at the initial master calendar hearing or—if no master calendar hearing is held—prior to taking the *pleadings* in the matter).

766: Prosecutorial Discretion (add at end of first full paragraph)

In November 2000, INS Commissioner Doris Meissner issued a memorandum to INS field offices entitled "Exercising Prosecutorial Discretion," which stated that "[s]ervice officers are not only authorized by law but expected to exercise discretion in a judicious manner at all stages of the enforcement process—from planning investigations to enforcing final orders." The communication provides detailed guidance based on the fundamental principle that "INS officers may decline to prosecute a legally sufficient immigration case if the Federal immigration enforcement interest that would be served by prosecution is not substantial." The memo identifies a range of factors that should be considered in the exercise of prosecutorial discretion, including immigration history and status, length of stay in the U.S., criminal history, humanitarian concerns, likelihood of ultimately removing the alien, likelihood of achieving the enforcement goal by other means, the effect on future admissibility, cooperation with law enforcement officials, community attention, U.S. military service, and available INS resources. The memorandum is available on the INS website at: http://www.ins.usdoj.gov/graphics/lawregs/handbook/discretion.pdf

771-72: § 212(c)

As noted in the casebook, cancellation of removal replaced relief under an earlier provision of the INA, § 212(c), which IIRIRA repealed. Despite its repeal, § 212(c) will continue to be available for some aliens in years to come. First, IIRIRA included a "saving provision" that provided that IIRIRA's amendments would not apply to removal proceedings begun before the IIRIRA's effective date; thus aliens who were in proceedings before April 1, 1997 may still raise § 212(c) claims. Second, in the important decision of *INS v. St. Cyr*, 121 S.Ct. 2271 (2001) , the Supreme Court held that the restrictions on § 212(c) relief adopted by AEPDA and IIRIRA do not apply retroactively to aliens who pled guilty before the effective date of those statutes but whose proceedings began thereafter. For a summary of the complicated administrative and judicial proceedings on these issues, see 78 Interp.Rel. 278 (2001).

The Court had little trouble concluding that the repeal had retrospective, and potentially severe, effects in such cases:

> IIRIRA's elimination of any possibility of § 212(c) relief for people who entered into plea agreements with the expectation that they would be eligible for such relief clearly "attaches a new disability, in respect to transactions or considerations already past." *Landgraf* [*v. USI Film Products*, 511 U.S. 244, 269 (1994)]. * * * There can be little doubt that, as a general matter, alien defendants considering whether to enter into a plea agreement are acutely aware of the immigration consequences of their convictions. Given

the frequency with which § 212(c) relief was granted in the years leading up to AEDPA and IIRIRA, preserving the possibility of such relief would have been one of the principal benefits sought by defendants deciding whether to accept a plea offer or instead to proceed to trial.

* * * The potential for unfairness in the retroactive application of [AEDPA and IIRIRA restrictions on § 212(c)] * * * is significant and manifest. Relying upon settled practice, the advice of counsel, and perhaps even assurances in open court that the entry of the plea would not foreclose § 212(c) relief, a great number of defendants * * * agreed to plead guilty. Now that prosecutors have received the benefit of these plea agreements, agreements that were facilitated by the aliens' belief in their continued eligibility for § 212(c) relief, it would surely be contrary to "familiar considerations of fair notice, reasonable reliance, and settled expectations," *Landgraf*, 511 U.S., at 270, to hold that IIRIRA's subsequent restrictions deprive them of any possibility of such relief.

Id. at 31-34 (footnotes omitted). Would these same considerations apply to aliens who committed a crime before enactment but pled guilty thereafter? How about those convicted following a contested trial before enactment but whose removal proceedings began after enactment?

775: Haitians and NACARA

The casebook notes that NACARA did not provide relief to Haitian asylum seekers in the United States. A year after NACARA, Congress enacted the Haitian Refugee Immigration and Fairness Act of 1998, Pub. L. 105-277, Div. A, S 101(h) [Title IX], 112 Stat. 2681 (1998), which permits Haitians who had applied for asylum or been paroled into the United States before December 31, 1995 to adjust to permanent resident status. The Act gives covered Haitians relief comparable to that afforded Nicaraguans and Cubans under NACARA and better than that granted to Salvadorans and Guatemalans.

775: Continuous Residence or Physical Presence (add at end of note 1)

The "stop-time" rule of § 240A(d)(1) states that the period of continuous residence or continuous physical presence "shall be deemed to end . . . when the alien has committed an offense referred to in section 212(a)(2) that renders the alien inadmissible to the United States under section 212(a)(2) or removable from the United States under section 237(a)(2) or (4)." What stops the clock, the commission of the offense or a conviction that renders an alien removable? In *Matter of Perez*, Int.Dec. 3389 (BIA 1999) (en banc), a majority of the Board rejected the more generous reading, holding that the period of continuous residence came to an end with the commission of the offense.

777: Cancellation of Removal (add after note 2)

MATTER OF MONREAL-AGUINAGA
Board of Immigration Appeals (*en banc*), 2001.
23 I & N Dec. 56.

HOLMES, BOARD MEMBER:

* * *

I. BACKGROUND

In proceedings conducted in 1998, the respondent conceded that he was removable from the United States but applied for cancellation of removal under section 240A(b) of the Act, as well as for voluntary departure. * * *

The respondent is a 34-year-old native and citizen of Mexico who has been living in the United States since his entry in 1980. He has not returned to Mexico since coming to this country as a 14-year-old child. His wife, who was not statutorily eligible for cancellation of removal, voluntarily departed to Mexico shortly before the respondent's hearing on his application for cancellation of removal, and she took their infant United States citizen child with her. The couple's two older children have remained with the respondent in the United States. The oldest child is now 12 years old and the middle child is 8 years old. Both are United States citizens.

The respondent has been gainfully employed in this country since his entry as a teenager, and he provides the sole support for his two citizen children in this country, as well as sending money to his wife in Mexico. He has worked in an uncle's business continuously since 1991. The respondent's parents lawfully immigrated to this country in 1995, and his children sometimes spend time with these grandparents when their father is working. In addition, the respondent has seven siblings who reside lawfully in the United States, as well as a brother in Mexico who also works for the respondent's uncle. The respondent's oldest child testified at the hearing about his life in this country and his desire not to depart for Mexico, which he would do if his father was required to leave the United States.

There is no dispute that the respondent satisfies the good moral character and continuous physical presence requirements for cancellation of removal. Moreover, if he were found statutorily eligible for cancellation, we would grant relief in the exercise of discretion. In this latter regard, the Immigration Judge noted that this was a "sad" case, particularly in view of its effect on the United States citizen children, and the Immigration and Naturalization Service trial attorney characterized the respondent and his family as "really good people." Thus, the determinative issue before us is whether this respondent's United States citizen children or his lawful permanent resident parents will suffer "exceptional and extremely unusual hardship" if the respondent is ordered deported, as is required for him to establish statutory eligibility for cancellation of removal. The Immigration Judge concluded that this hardship requirement had not been met. We agree.

II. Meaning of the Term
"Exceptional and Extremely Unusual Hardship"

Under the prior law regarding suspension of deportation, an alien, such as this respondent, seeking that form of relief had to establish that he or his qualifying relative would suffer "extreme hardship" if deported. *See* section 244(a)(1) of the Act (repealed). In 1996, Congress replaced the suspension of deportation provisions of the Act with a form of relief entitled "Cancellation of Removal and Adjustment of Status for Certain Nonpermanent Residents." *See* section 240A(b) of the Act.

In enacting the cancellation statute, Congress narrowed the class of aliens who could qualify for relief. Under the present cancellation statute, an alien must have 10 years of continuous physical presence in this country, rather than the 7 years necessary under the previous requirements for suspension of deportation. Furthermore, under the new statute, hardship to the applicant for relief is not considered; only hardship to the alien's United States citizen or lawful permanent resident spouse, parent, or child may be considered. Finally, as indicated above, an alien must show that his or her qualifying relative would suffer exceptional and extremely unusual hardship if the alien is deported.

The cancellation statute does not further define the term "exceptional and extremely unusual hardship." It is axiomatic, however, that the interpretation of statutory language begins with the terms of the statute itself, and if those terms, on their face, constitute a plain expression of congressional intent, they must be given effect. Citing *INS v. Phinpathya*, 464 U.S. 183, 189 (1984), we have also recognized that the "legislative purpose is presumed to be expressed by the ordinary meaning of the words used." *Matter of Crammond*, 23 I&N Dec. 9, 11 (BIA 2001).

The terms "exceptional" and "extremely unusual" seemingly have ordinary meanings. "Exceptional" is defined as "[f]orming an exception; not ordinary; uncommon; rare." *Webster's New International Dictionary* 888 (2d ed. 1959). The added phrase "extremely unusual" plainly indicates circumstances in which the exception to the norm is very uncommon. The "plain meaning" of these terms becomes somewhat less clear, however, when appended to the term hardship, which can have multiple manifestations and inherently introduces an element of subjectivity into this statutory phrase. If the past 50 years have demonstrated nothing else with regard to the phrases "exceptional and extremely unusual hardship" and "extreme hardship," they have shown that reasonable people can agree that the meaning of these terms is "clear," but come to quite different conclusions as to their application in various factual situations. These are not terms of "fixed and inflexible content or meaning." *Matter of Hwang*, 10 I&N Dec. 448, 451 (BIA 1964) (addressing "extreme hardship").

It is obvious, however, under the plain meaning of the words used in the two statutes, that the hardship standard for cancellation of removal is a higher one than that under the suspension of deportation statute. The legislative history also plainly states that Congress intended to tighten the hardship standard, in part as a response to what it saw as a weakening of the extreme hardship requirement in certain precedent decisions of this Board. *See, e.g., Matter of 0-J-0-*, 21 I&N Dec. 381 (BIA 1996); *see also* H.R. Conf. Rep. No. 104-828 (1996).

Although the legislative history of section 240A(b)(1)(D) does not attempt to further define the term "exceptional and extremely unusual hardship," it does provide some guidance as to Congress' intent in adopting the term. The House Conference Report states that "[t]he managers have deliberately changed the required showing of hardship from 'extreme hardship' to 'exceptional and extremely unusual hardship' to emphasize that the alien must provide evidence of harm to his spouse, parent, or child *substantially beyond that which ordinarily would be expected to result from the alien's deportation.*" H.R. Conf. Rep. No. 104-828 (emphasis added). The legislative history also talks of this relief being available "in truly exceptional cases." *Id.* Thus, it appears that Congress intended that cancellation of removal should be available to nonpermanent residents only in compelling cases.

We are aware of the general rule that when "Congress adopts a new law incorporating sections of a prior law, Congress normally can be presumed to have had knowledge of the interpretation given to the incorporated law, at least insofar as it affects the new statute." *Lorillard v. Pons*, 434 U.S. 575, 581 (1978); *see also Matter of Acosta*, 19 I&N Dec. 211 (131A 1985). Here, only a phrase, not a whole section of law, was adopted from the prior law. The origins of the phrase "exceptional and extremely unusual hardship" are in the Immigration and Nationality Act of 1952, ch. 477, 66 Stat. 163 ("1952 Act"). There is both legislative history from the 1952 Act and subsequent case law involving this phrase that we can look to in an attempt to clarify its meaning.

Under the 1952 Act, as originally enacted, "exceptional and extremely unusual hardship" was the hardship standard applicable to all applicants for suspension of deportation.[1] The legislative history of the 1952 Act reflects that, at the time, Congress intended that the exceptional and extremely unusual hardship standard be a very high one indeed. The House Report states that suspension of deportation "should be available only in the very limited category of cases in which the deportation of the alien would be unconscionable." H.R. Rep. No. 82-1365 (1952), *reprinted in* 1952 U.S.C.C.A.N. 1653, 1718; S. Rep. No. 82-1137, at 25 (1952).

We are not persuaded, however, that the relevant cancellation standard should be that a respondent's deportation be "unconscionable" in its effect on a

---

[1] In 1962, Congress amended the suspension of deportation provisions, reconfiguring former section 244(a) from five subsections into two. The prior "exceptional and extremely unusual hardship" standard was retained for immigration offenders deportable under specified statutory grounds, principally relating to crime, fraud, and security, who also had to show 10 years of continuous physical presence. *See* section 244(a)(2) of the Act. The then new section 244(a)(1) established, *inter alia*, the "extreme hardship" standard for all other applicants for suspension who only needed to show 7 years of continuous physical presence. Congress' intent was to lessen the degree of hardship required of applicants for suspension under section 244(a)(1). *See Matter of Hwang, supra*, at 452. The shifts in legislation regarding this forth of relief reflect something of the ebb and flow of Congress' reaction to immigration over the last century.

qualifying relative before a respondent can be found eligible for cancellation of removal under section 240A(b) of the present Act. The legislative history of the 1952 Act referencing such hardship is nearly 50 years old and arose in a different statutory context. Moreover, although the hardship term used then is the same as the one we consider now, there is nothing in the legislative history of the current cancellation statute to suggest that such an extreme standard should be applied. In fact, as discussed above, that history suggests a standard that, although high, is clearly less than "unconscionable." Furthermore, 50 years of case law regarding the meaning of both "extreme hardship" and "exceptional and extremely unusual hardship" have intervened since the legislative history of the 1952 Act was promulgated. Finally, the Board case law that immediately followed the 1952 Act adopted the "unconscionable" standard, but found that the standard was met in circumstances that arguably would not now be deemed "truly exceptional." *See, e.g., Matter of H-,* 5 I&N Dec. 416 (BIA 1953) (focusing principally on long residence and an inability to return to the United States). Therefore, we do not find that an "unconscionable" standard is an appropriate one to apply in evaluating a respondent's eligibility for cancellation of removal under section 240A(b) of the Act.

Similarly, we do not find determinative guidance from the series of cases dating from 1953 to 1957, which applied the "exceptional and extremely unusual hardship standard" in the suspension of deportation context prior to the amendments to section 244 of the Act in 1962. *Matter of U-,* 5 I&N Dec. 413 (BIA 1953); *Matter of S-,* 5 I&N Dec. 409 (BIA 1953) [numerous other citations omitted—eds.].[2]

This case law covers only that period of time when the "exceptional and extremely unusual hardship" standard was applied to all applicants for suspension of deportation, predating the period during which the standard was required principally for criminal aliens. Furthermore, in many of these cases the focus was on hardship to the alien, a hardship element that cannot even be considered under the present statute. *See, e.g., Matter of S-,* 5 I&N Dec. 409 (setting out the factors to consider in evaluating the necessary degree of hardship for suspension of deportation eligibility). Finally, all of this case law arose in a different overall statutory context and obviously significantly predated the decades of interpretation of the "extreme hardship" standard that culminated in Congress' enactment in 1996 of the cancellation of removal provisions in section 240A(b) of the Act. *See, e.g., Cortes-Castillo v. INS,* [997 F.2d 1199, 1204 (7th Cir.1993)] ("The definition of 'exceptional and extremely unusual hardship', now applied only to aliens seeking relief under section 244(a)(2), has become more stringent in the forty years since the Board decided *Matter of S.* and *Matter*

---

[2] In *Matter of S-,* 5 I&N Dec. 409, we identified five factors to be considered in evaluating "exceptional and extremely unusual hardship." This decision was issued simultaneously with four other published Board decisions, * * * which applied the standard in varying factual circumstances. The approach of providing examples and discussion in published Board decisions in varying factual settings likely remains the best manner in which to provide content to the phrase "exceptional and extremely unusual hardship" in the context of applications for cancellation of removal under the present law.

of U.").[3] In view of these considerations, as well as the fact that so many years have passed and so much intervening (and not necessarily consistent) case law has developed regarding the term "extreme hardship" since these cases were decided, we do not find that any determinative guidance considering the phrase "exceptional and extremely unusual hardship" in the cancellation of removal context arises from these early suspension of deportation cases.

Thus, although both the relevant legislative history from the 1952 Act and the old case law discussed above provide an historical context for evaluating the "exceptional and extremely unusual hardship" standard in applications for cancellation of removal, our principal focus is on the statutory language itself and the legislative history of the revisions that were enacted in 1996. What is clear is that the term "exceptional and extremely unusual hardship" is a more restrictive standard than the "extreme hardship" standard applied in section 244(a)(1) suspension of deportation cases, particularly as it was applied in *Matter of 0-J-0-, supra*. The new standard requires a showing of hardship beyond that which has historically been required in suspension of deportation cases involving the "extreme hardship" standard. As the legislative history indicates, the hardship to an alien's relatives, if the alien is obliged to leave the United States, must be "substantially" beyond the ordinary hardship that would be expected when a close family member leaves this country. Cancellation of removal under section 240A(b) of the Act is to be limited to "truly exceptional" situations. H.R. Conf. Rep. No. 104-828.

At the same time, we recognize that some cases in which this Board or the Immigration Judges have found "extreme hardship" under the suspension statute may also have presented facts and circumstances that rose to the level of "exceptional and extremely unusual hardship." Moreover, although guidance as to this term's meaning can be provided, each case must be assessed and decided on its own facts.

III. FACTORS TO CONSIDER

We do find it appropriate and useful to look to the factors that we have considered in the past in assessing "extreme hardship" for purposes of adjudicating suspension of deportation applications, as set forth in our decision in *Matter of Anderson*, 16 I&N Dec. 596 (BIA 1978). That is, many of the factors that should be considered in assessing "exceptional and extremely unusual hardship" are essentially the same as those that have been considered for

---

[3] A more recent Board precedent, *Matter of Pena-Diaz*, 20 I&N Dec. 841 (BIA 1994), involved a respondent who was required to meet the more exacting exceptional and extremely unusual hardship standard for suspension of deportation because he had been convicted of a controlled substance violation. Under the particular circumstances of that case, we found that the respondent had shown a prima facie case of exceptional and extremely unusual hardship where he had been in the United States for more than 20 years, and where the Service had "affirmatively permitted" him to remain here for many years by granting his request for deferred action. *Id.* at 846. However, that case did not provide a discussion of the exceptional and extremely unusual hardship standard and involved a motion to reopen where only a prima facie showing of the requisite hardship had to be made. Thus, it is of limited value to us today.

many years in assessing "extreme hardship," but they must be weighed according to the higher standard required for cancellation of removal. However, insofar as some of the factors set forth in *Matter of Anderson* may relate only to the applicant for relief, they cannot be considered under the cancellation statute, where only hardship to qualifying relatives, and not to the applicant, may be considered. Factors relating to the applicant himself or herself can only be considered insofar as they may affect the hardship to a qualifying relative.

In *Matter of Anderson, supra,* we stated that such factors as the age of a respondent, both at the time of entry and at the time of the application for relief, family ties in the United States and abroad, length of residence in this country, the health of the respondent and qualifying family members, the political and economic conditions in the country of return, the possibility of other means of adjusting status in the United States, the alien's involvement and position in his or her community here, and his or her immigration history are all proper factors to be considered. *Id.* at 597.

For cancellation of removal, we consider the ages, health, and circumstances of qualifying lawful permanent resident and United States citizen relatives. For example, an applicant who has elderly parents in this country who are solely dependent upon him for support might well have a strong case. Another strong applicant might have a qualifying child with very serious health issues, or compelling special needs in school. A lower standard of living or adverse country conditions in the country of return are factors to consider only insofar as they may affect a qualifying relative, but generally will be insufficient in themselves to support a finding of exceptional and extremely unusual hardship. As with extreme hardship, all hardship factors should be considered in the aggregate when assessing exceptional and extremely unusual hardship.

IV. APPLICATION OF THE EXCEPTIONAL AND EXTREMELY UNUSUAL HARDSHIP STANDARD TO THE RESPONDENT

This case presents a good example of the difference between the "extreme hardship" and the "exceptional and extremely unusual hardship" standards. Were this a suspension of deportation case, where only extreme hardship is required and where hardship to the respondent himself could be considered, the respondent might well have been found eligible for that relief. The hardship to the respondent, particularly in view of his 20 years of residence after his entry at age 14, his loss of long-standing employment, the adverse effect of his forced departure from this country on his two school-age United States citizen children, and the separation from his lawful permanent resident parents would likely have been found to rise to the level of "extreme" hardship by a majority of this Board. However, under the cancellation of removal requirements, we cannot conclude that the respondent has established that the hardship to his citizen children or lawful permanent resident parents rises to the higher level of "exceptional and extremely unusual hardship."

The respondent's two oldest children will likely relocate to Mexico with him. However, although he has lived here for many years, the respondent is 34 years old and is apparently in good health and able to work. There is nothing to show that he would be unable to work and support his United States citizen children in Mexico. His wife is also from Mexico and, as indicated above, departed the United States shortly before the respondent's hearing, taking their infant child back to Mexico with her. Therefore, should the children go to Mexico with their father, the family will be reunited. The respondent testified that his children are in good health.

The respondent's oldest child is 12 years old. He testified at the hearing that he has classes in both English and Spanish and can speak, read, and write in both languages. He testified that although he is close to his grandparents in the United States, if his father leaves this country, he will go with him. He stated that he is doing well in school, where he has friends. Asked if he would prefer to stay in the United States or go to Mexico, the child replied that he would like to stay here, "because I think it's better here than in Mexico."

The respondent's parents have been lawful permanent residents since 1995. His father still works, but his mother is not employed. The respondent did not present any evidence to show that they have any particular health problems or that there are any other unusual factors that might make it an exceptional and extremely unusual hardship for them if the respondent is returned to Mexico. The record does not reflect the ages of the respondent's parents. We note that the respondent testified that he has siblings who also live in the Dallas area, and presumably they could help their parents, should that become necessary.

Even considering all of the factors presented cumulatively, we find that the respondent has not met his burden of establishing that either his children or his parents would suffer exceptional and extremely unusual hardship if he is deported. The respondent has not provided evidence to establish that his qualifying relatives would suffer hardship that is substantially different from, or beyond, that which would normally be expected from the deportation of an alien with close family members here.

We recognize that the respondent's children will suffer some hardship, and likely will have fewer opportunities, should they go to Mexico, and we further recognize that the respondent's parents will suffer some hardship from having their son living farther away. We have no doubt that if the respondent were eligible for cancellation of removal, we would grant such relief in the exercise of discretion. However, Congress has established an "exceptional and extremely unusual hardship" standard of eligibility for cancellation of removal, and we cannot find that the evidence presented in this case rises to the high level of hardship required under section 240A(b)(1)(D) of the Act. Accordingly, the respondent's appeal must be dismissed.

ROSENBERG, BOARD MEMBER, concurring and dissenting.

I respectfully concur in part and dissent in part.

I concur with the majority's conclusion that in enacting section 240A(b)(1)(D) of the Immigration and Nationality Act, Congress foreclosed certain aliens from eligibility for relief from removal based on long-term residence in the United States. I also agree that while the plain meaning of the individual words in the standard "exceptional and extremely unusual hardship" may be commonly understood to refer to some type of difficulty or burden that is uncommon, rare, or different from the norm, these are not terms of "fixed and inflexible content or meaning." *Matter of Hwang*, 10 I&N Dec. 448, 451 (BIA 1964).

As the majority acknowledges, our interpretation of this standard, even as defined by the plain meaning of the words used, tends to be subjective in nature and is largely dependent on definition through case-by-case application. Therefore, I believe that the critical elements in any cancellation of removal adjudication always will be the evidentiary factors and how they are presented.

* * * I am not comfortable with the majority's attempt to distinguish the meaning of the language of this standard, as a matter of law, from the very same language that has existed and been applied in the Act since 1952. In light of the fact that we are pronouncing a different interpretation of this standard in the context of cancellation of removal for the first time, I believe it more prudent to remand this case to give the respondent an opportunity to submit evidence that might allow him to satisfy the standard that we have articulated today.

I. EXCEPTIONAL AND EXTREMELY UNUSUAL HARDSHIP

The majority's effort to justify our giving a different meaning to Congress' repeated use of the phrase "exceptional and extremely unusual hardship" as the standard for certain cancellation of removal applications is simply unpersuasive. I find no basis for invoking an exception to the principle that "Congress normally can be presumed to have had knowledge of the interpretation given to the incorporated law," merely because Congress adopted only a phrase and not a whole section of prior law. *Lorillard v. Pons*, 434 U.S. 5 75, 5 81 (1978). More specifically, "Congress is presumed to be aware of an administrative or judicial interpretation of a statute and to adopt that interpretation when it re-enacts a statute without change." *Lorillard v. Pons, supra*, at 580-81.

The "exceptional and extremely unusual" language was not only the hardship standard that applied to all suspension of deportation applications under the Act between 1952 and 1962, but represents the standard that, until 1996, continued to govern our hardship adjudications in suspension of deportation claims presented by aliens who were subject to deportation for criminal, fraud, or security violations of the Act. The legislative history reflects that in enacting this form of cancellation of removal, Congress apparently examined closely the historical underpinnings and application of the suspension of deportation provisions. Indeed, Congress not only explicitly adopted the stricter hardship standard, which had existed all along, but also eliminated altogether access to this form of relief for individuals convicted of criminal offenses and incorporated across the board the requirement that an individual have 10 years of continuous physical presence to qualify for relief.

Each of the changes reflects Congress' awareness of the prior 10-year suspension of deportation provision, including the specific hardship standard that had been applied over the years. Surely, by virtue of making these changes, Congress must be deemed to have considered how we had interpreted and applied that standard. Therefore, I cannot agree with the majority's wholesale rejection of our case law addressing the "exceptional and extremely unusual hardship" standard as providing nothing more than an "historical context." Rather, it provides the context that gives this phrase meaning.

Similarly, I do not agree that we somehow are being evenhanded in rejecting this case law, while also rejecting a statement in the legislative history of the 1952 Act that the hardship must rise to an "unconscionable" level before it will meet the standard. It is the case law that interprets the legislative provisions, and not a prior legislative statement intended to guide that interpretation, that makes up our jurisprudence as to what constitutes exceptional and extremely unusual hardship. It is that jurisprudence of which Congress is presumed to be aware when it legislates anew and uses the same language. Therefore, I believe that the existing body of our prior case law does provide useful guidance in determining whether a showing of exceptional and extremely unusual hardship has been made.

II. Due Process and Evidentiary Factors

* * *

The majority contends that "[t]his case presents a good example of the difference between the 'extreme hardship' and the 'exceptional and extremely unusual hardship' standards. Were this a suspension of deportation case, . . . the respondent might well have been found eligible for that relief." However, we are not considering only the hardship to the respondent or an aggregate of the hardship to the respondent and his qualifying family members. We are considering only the hardship to his United States citizen children and his lawful permanent resident parents.

The significance of the respondent's 8- and 12-year old children's acculturation as United States citizens in an American family is very likely far greater than what is suggested by the minimal amount of evidence that was presented at the hearing or considered by the Immigration Judge. Specifically, the children's birthright citizenship status, their ties to their grandparents and extended family in the United States, the substantial amount of time they have been schooled in the United States educational system, and their socialization in the United States generally, are all factors that are unique to these children. The potential value of these United States citizen children's ties certainly is in the "parking lot" or a "ball park," not out of it, as the Immigration Judge put it. Consequently, with a proper and extensive evidentiary presentation, it is possible that the children's loss and the nature of the hardship they would suffer if their father is removed and those ties are severed may very well be "exceptional and extremely unusual."

* * *

Unquestionably, the children face a dramatic change in their day-to-day lives. Even putting the potential change in their economic circumstances and standard of living aside, they face a change of geography, climate, cuisine, culture, language, and social mores. They face a loss of their home, their childhood roots, their friends, and their customary family circle. They face separation from their grandparents. They face a completely different school system and classes taught in a completely different language. Are the hardships resulting from these involuntary changes "truly exceptional"?

The legislative history emphasizes that the ordinary results of a parent's removal are not to be considered in determining the existence of exceptional and extremely unusual hardship to qualifying family members. The ordinary results of a parent's deportation relative to his or her United States citizen children may well be leaving one's home and friends for another country and possibly having to adapt to a new school system or a reduced standard of living.

However, not every United States citizen child of a parent who is subject to removal has spent his or her whole life in this country, maintaining no ties to his father's homeland. Just as the respondent's arrival as a teenager and lengthy residence here make it more likely that he also is assimilated to the United States, these children very likely lit sparklers on the Fourth of July, marched in the Columbus Day parade, and cheered as loudly as any other American during the World Series. Not every child has a parent subject to removal who has lived here since his formative years. Not every child of a removable parent is approaching his or her teenage years. Not every child has grandparents who have immigrated here from their home country. Not every child would have to readjust to a society and a school system where classes are conducted in a different language.

Moreover, the Immigration Judge grossly erred in his assumption that it would be "counterproductive" to grant cancellation because the respondent's wife had returned to Mexico. Amazingly, the majority seems to accept the notion that under the circumstances of the children's mother having had to return to Mexico, their having to accompany the respondent upon his removal would likely be the occasion for a family reunion, rather than an exile. To the contrary, the fact that their mother was forced to leave them and go back to Mexico with their little brother is more than likely an exacerbating condition that makes the potential hardship faced by these children even greater. Their mother's departure with their infant sibling was not a joyful or desired event, but one that the family was required to face owing to her lack of lawful immigration status in the United States.

* * *

Although I believe that some of my suppositions regarding the extraordinary nature of the ties that the children will be forced to sever and the hardship they will have to endure may well be correct, they are not substantiated in the record. The deficiency in the record before us is the lack of corroborating and supporting evidence that forcefully demonstrates that the hardships to the children truly will be of a level that meets the exceptional and extremely unusual hardship standard.

Such evidence might include a professional evaluation of the children's language capabilities; individual medical and psychological reports by expert witnesses indicating the potential impact of relocation to Mexico on the children's development and ability to flourish; authoritative documentation indicating the similarities and differences between the United States and Mexican school systems; recognized sociological studies reflecting the ability of United States citizen children to adapt to different cultures and countries; economic studies indicating the likely employment prospects for the respondent and the resulting effect on the children's standard of living; reports regarding the anticipated ease or difficulty of later adjustment to United States social and educational standards, should the children wish to return when they reach college age; and any information concerning the children's ability to maintain contacts with their aunts, uncles, grandparents, friends, teachers, or other influential figures in the United States. In all cases, were evidence of this type to be presented, it must be specifically linked to these individual children, in terms of their gender, age, level of development, level of achievement, and any special problems or needs that they may have. Any reports should be authenticated. Any evaluations should be attested to under oath, with a recitation of the qualifications of the maker of the document. All expert witnesses should be available to appear in court, give direct testimony, and be cross-examined.

    * * * [I]n light of the fact that neither the parties nor the Immigration Judge had the benefit of our interpretation of the statutory standard at the time of the hearing, I would remand the record for further proceedings. This will give all the opportunity to present any available evidence that may better substantiate the respondent's claim and will allow the Immigration Judge to make a decision consistent with our interpretation of the statute. Accordingly, I concur in part and dissent in part.

777: Discretion in Cancellation Cases (add to note 3)

In *Matter of C-V-T-*, Int.Dec. 3342 (BIA 1998), the Board held that the general standards for the exercise of discretion developed in *Matter of Marin*, 16 I&N Dec. 581 (BIA 1978) (relating to now-repealed INA § 212(c)) are applicable in cancellation cases under § 240A(a).

783: Section 212(h) Waiver (add new note 5)

    5. Section 212(h) includes language stating the waiver is not available "to an alien who has previously been admitted to the United States as an alien lawfully admitted for permanent residence if ... since the date of such admission the alien has been convicted of an aggravated felony." Does this mean that an alien who has been convicted of an aggravated felony but *is not* an LPR may be eligible for 212(h) relief? The Board has answered that question in the affirmative. *Matter of Michel*, Int.Dec. 3335 (BIA 1998) (involving an alien who had not been lawfully admitted to the U.S. and who was the beneficiary of an immediate relative petition filed by his citizen father). But can *that* distinction—granting greater rights to a non-LPR than an LPR—withstand constitutional scrutiny? In *Lara-Ruiz v. INS*, 241 F.3d 934 (7th Cir.2001), the court rejected an equal protection challenge to the statute brought by a permanent resident alien. Said the court:

> We find that a rational basis exists for Congress' decision to declare only those aggravated felons who have previously been admitted as LPRs ineligible for § 212(h) relief. One of Congress' purposes in enacting reforms to the INA through IIRIRA was to expedite the removal of criminal aliens from the United States. Eliminating the availability of § 212(h) relief for LPR aggravated felons would eradicate one source of delay that might thwart this effort .... Moreover, LPRs enjoy rights and privileges by virtue of

their status which are not shared by non-LPRs, and they typically
have closer and long-standing ties to the United States through
employment and family relationships. Therefore, Congress may
rationally have concluded that LPRs who commit serious crimes
despite these factors are uniquely poor candidates for relief from
removal through the "backdoor" of waiver of inadmissibility . . . .
In banning only LPR aggravated felons from waiver eligibility,
Congress might well have found it significant that, unlike non-LPR
aggravated felons, such aliens have already demonstrated that
closer ties to the United States and all of the benefits attending LPR
status were insufficient to deter them from committing serious
crimes. Therefore Congress might have reasoned that LPR
aggravated felons were a higher risk of recidivism, and were
generally less deserving of a second chance than were non-LPR
aggravated felons.

Id. at 947-48. Are you persuaded? Is it likely that Congress considered this
issue at all? If it had, what decision do you think it would have reached? Two
federal district courts have concluded that the provision violates equal
protection. *See Jankowski v. INS*, 138 F.Supp.2d 269 (D.Conn.2001); *Song v.
INS*, 82 F.Supp.2d 1121, 1133 (C.D.Cal. 2000) (statute is irrational because
"Congress has created a distinction which rewards those necessarily guilty of at
least two crimes, illegal entry and the 'aggravated felony,' by treating them
better than individuals guilty only of the same 'aggravated *felony*.'")

783: *INS v. Yang* [Note to users of the first printing of the Fourth Edition]

INS v. Yang considers relief under what is now INA § 237(a)(1)(H)—not
§ 212(h) as indicated. This mistake has been corrected in the second printing of
the Fourth Edition.

786: *INS v. Yang* (substitute for note 1)

1. After *Yang*, the BIA rejected the INS policy of disregarding the initial
fraud when deciding on a discretionary waiver in such cases. *Matter of Tijam*,
Int.Dec. 3372 (BIA 1998).

Chapter Eight: Removal Procedures

834: Right to Counsel (add before *Aguilera-Enriquez*)

Under an emerging model for providing basic legal representation to detained aliens, outside advocacy organizations provide pre-hearing "rights presentations" to all detainees in a given facility, in cooperation with INS and EOIR officials. Many respondents then decide not to contest removal, and their cases are usually completed that day at a master calendar hearing before the immigration judge. Others are then usually able to meet privately after the presentation with lawyers or paralegals from the organization to discuss the case. With this further advice, some choose not to contest, others are given written materials and counseling that will help them to pursue their claims themselves, and still others are selected by the organization for full pro bono representation. This approach was first adopted at the detention facility in Florence, Arizona, and is now coming into widespread use at detention facilities around the country. *See* Nugent, *Strengthening Access to Justice: Prehearing Rights Presentations for Detained Respondents*, 76 Interp.Rel. 1077 (1999).

870: Expedited Removal (add after carryover paragraph)

The independent Expedited Removal Study, based at the University of California, Hastings College of Law, has gathered data on the implementation of expedited removal and raised a number of points of concern, regarding both implementation and access to information. *See* Musalo et al., *The Expedited Removal Study: Report on the First Three Years of Implementation of Expedited Removal*, <http://www.uchastings.edu/ers/reports/2000/2000%20Report.pdf> (2000). For an assessment of expedited removal concluding that it should be retained but with modifications, see Martin, *Two Cheers for Expedited Removal Under the New Immigration Laws*, 40 Va. J. Int'l L. 673 (2000). In 2000, the Senate considered but did not pass Senate Bill 1940, which, among other provisions, would have limited the use of expedited removal procedures to immigration emergencies and add due process safeguards. Meanwhile, in December 2000 the INS issued a memorandum introducing new procedures designed to streamline the "credible fear" process, see 78 Interp.Rel. 337 (2001).

870-71: Note on Judicial Review of Expedited Removal

The two pending cases mentioned in the text, *Liberians United v. Reno* and *Wood v. Reno*, were consolidated with and decided under the caption, *American Immigration Lawyers Association v. Reno*, 18 F.Supp.2d 38 (D.D.C. 1998). The district court first ruled that it lacked jurisdiction over several of the claims for failure to comply with deadlines for filing, and that the plaintiffs lacked standing to bring certain other claims. The court then rejected the remaining statutory and constitutional claims on the merits. On appeal, the D.C. Circuit affirmed. *See American Immigration Lawyers Association v. Reno*, 199 F.3d 1352 (D.C.Cir.2000).

871: Expedited Removal of Aliens in the United States

In September 1999, the INS published a Federal Register notice announcing its intent—after a public comment period—to apply expedited removal procedures on a pilot basis to certain criminal aliens detained in three correctional facilities in Texas. The pilot program would cover only a limited class: aliens convicted in a criminal proceeding of illegal entry, where the court record establishes the time, place, and manner of entry. This would be the first time that expedited removal would be applied outside the port of entry context. *See* 64 Fed.Reg. 51338 (1999); 76 Interp.Rel. 1416 (1999). The INS did not announce an implementation date, and there have been no further developments.

872: Reinstatement of Removal Orders

The Ninth Circuit recently decided a case that challenged reinstatement of removal on procedural due process and other grounds. The court did not reach the constitutional issues, deciding instead that INA § 241(a)(5) does not apply to reentries before the statute's enactment date. On this basis, § 241(a)(5) applied to none of the five plaintiffs. *See Castro-Cortez v. INS*, 239 F.3d 1037 (9th Cir.2001).

874: Removal of Terrorists (add before section 4)

In *Kiareldeen v. Reno*, 71 F.Supp.2d 402 (D.N.J. 1999), a federal district court held that it violated due process to detain an alien based on secret evidence pending removal proceedings. According to the court:

> To assay the constitutionality of the INS procedures applied to the petitioner, the court considers the three factors enunciated in *Mathews v. Eldridge*, 424 U.S. 319, 96 S.Ct. 893, 47 L.Ed.2d 18 (1976). The first, the petitioner's private interest in his physical liberty, must be accorded the utmost weight. Kiareldeen has been removed from his community, his home, and his family, and has been denied rights that "[rank] high among the interests of the individual." *Landon v. Plasencia*, 459 U.S. 21, 32, 103 S.Ct. 321, 74 L.Ed.2d 21 (1982). The second, the risk of erroneous deprivation, also militates in the petitioner's favor. Use of secret evidence creates a one-sided process by which the protections of our adversarial system are rendered impotent. The petitioner has been compelled by the government to attempt to prove the negative in the face of anonymous "slurs of unseen and unsworn informers." *Jay [v. Boyd]*, 351 U.S. [345], 365, 76 S.Ct. 919 (Warren, J., dissenting). As the District Court wrote in the *AADC* case, "[o]ne would be hard pressed to design a procedure more likely to result in erroneous deprivations." Quoted in *AADC v. Reno*, 70 F.3d [1045,] 1069 [(9th Cir.1995)].
>
> Finally, the court considers the government's interest in relying on secret evidence. Even if the interest is deemed to be the unarguably weighty one of national security, as the government maintains, the court must inquire "whether that interest is so all-encompassing that it requires that [the petitioner] be denied

virtually every fundamental feature of due process." *Rafeedie,* 795 F.Supp. [13,] 19 [(D.D.C. 1992)].

The court does not, however, necessarily accept at face value the government's contentions that the national security is implicated by the petitioner's alleged misdeeds. The court has considered the government's unclassified "summary" evidence and finds it lacking in either detail or attribution to reliable sources which would shore up its credibility. More important, however, is the apparent conclusion that even the government does not find its own allegations sufficiently serious to commence criminal proceedings. The petitioner asserts, unchallenged, that the FBI recently closed its criminal investigation of Kiareldeen, and does not intend to reopen the investigation unless it receives new information that he is involved in terrorist activity. Under these circumstances, the government's claimed interest in detaining the petitioner cannot be said to outweigh the petitioner's interest in returning to freedom.

Here, the government's reliance on secret evidence violates the due process protections that the Constitution directs must be extended to all persons within the United States, citizens and resident aliens alike. The INS procedures patently failed the *Mathews* test of constitutional sufficiency. And the court finds this failure to be sufficient basis to grant the petitioner's writ of habeas corpus and direct his release from custody.

Id. at 413-14. For a similar analysis, see *Najjar v. Reno,* 97 F.Supp.2d 1329 (S.D.Fla. 2000).

In 2000, Congress considered but did not pass legislation, the Secret Evidence Repeal Act, H.R. 2121, that would prohibit the use of secret evidence in a number of contexts. It would repeal INA §§ 501-507. It would also amend INA § 240(b)(4)(B) in several ways: (1) to require that removal proceedings provide "a reasonable opportunity to examine all of the evidence against the alien," (2) to allow aliens to present evidence on their behalf, and (3) to cross-examine the government's witnesses. *See* 77 Interp.Rel. 697 (2000). For discussions of the use of secret evidence in immigration proceedings, see Akram, *Scheherezade Meets Kafka: Two Dozen Sordid Tales of Ideological Exclusion,* 14 Geo. Immig. L.J. 51 (1999); Frenzen, *National Security and Procedural Fairness: Secret Evidence and the Immigration Laws,* 76 Interp.Rel. 1677 (1999).

874-75: Removal of Aliens With Criminal Convictions

In July 1999, the INS published a proposed rule that would allow the government to remove nonviolent offenders in state custody before they complete their sentences, implementing INA § 241(a)(4)(B). *See* 64 Fed.Reg. 37461 (1999), *corrected* 64 Fed.Reg. 39560 (1999); 75 Interp.Rel. 1092 (1999).

876-77: Administrative Removal

In *United States v. Benitez-Villafuerte*, 186 F.3d 651 (5th Cir.1999), *cert. denied*, 528 U.S. 1097, 120 S.Ct. 838, 145 L.Ed. 2d 704 (2000), the Fifth Circuit considered and rejected a procedural due process challenge to administrative removal under INA § 238. The case was a criminal prosecution of an alien for illegal reentry under § 276. One of the elements of the offense was prior removal, which in this case had occurred under § 238. The alien defendant collaterally attacked the prior removal on procedural due process grounds. The court rejected this argument, finding that § 238 satisfies the requirements of notice of charges, a hearing before an executive or administrative tribunal, and a fair opportunity to be heard. *Id.* at 657.

880-81: Linking Immigration Law and Criminal Law

For critical discussions of the principle that immigration proceedings are civil, not criminal, see Kanstroom, *Deportation, Social Control, and Punishment: Some Thoughts About Why Hard Laws Make Bad Cases*, 113 Harv. L. Rev. 1889 (2000); Pauw, *A New Look at Deportation As Punishment: Why At Least Some of the Constitution's Criminal Procedure Protections Must Apply*, 52 Admin. L. Rev. 305 (2000).

885: A Statutory Overview (add after carryover paragraph)

The Transition Period Custody Rules expired without being extended, and the mandatory detention provisions in INA § 236(c) took effect on October 9, 1998. They were challenged on constitutional grounds in a number of lawsuits, with varying outcomes. Several of these courts did not reach the constitutional issue, finding instead that § 236(c) does not apply to aliens who completed their criminal sentences before October 9, 1998. *See, e.g., Alwaday v. Beebe*, 43 F.Supp.2d 1130 (D.Or. 1999). In July 1999, the INS adopted this interpretation of § 236(c). *See* 76 Interp.Rel. 1082 (1999). Aliens who completed their criminal sentences before October 9, 1998, may apply for release from detention. If the INS does not release them, they may apply for a bond redetermination hearing before an immigration judge, and they may appeal any negative determination to the BIA.

887: A Statutory Overview (add after carryover paragraph)

In June 1999, a settlement was reached in litigation challenging INS practices at the San Pedro Service Processing Center. It requires the INS to follow its national standards at the San Pedro facility with regard to visitation, telephone access, access to legal materials, and group legal rights presentation. The settlement is significant because there is otherwise no formal enforcement mechanism for the national standards. *See* 76 Interp.Rel. 1327 (1999). The INS has now completed the full set of national standards, which will apply to state and county jails, phased in over a two-year period. 77 Interp.Rel. 1637 (2000).

889-900: Mandatory Detention (substitute for material starting with first full paragraph ("In contrast to *Carlson*") on 889 through end of section (i) on 900)

In contrast to *Carlson*, INA § 236(c) requires detention for certain categories of aliens in removal proceedings—including some permanent residents. Are these mandatory provisions in the 1996 Act constitutional?

A more recent Supreme Court decision that bears on this question involved detention of juveniles. *Reno v. Flores*, 507 U.S. 292, 113 S.Ct. 1439, 123 L.Ed.2d 1 (1993), was a class action that challenged INS policy regarding detention of minor children pending deportation. Under former 8 C.F.R. § 242.24, detained minors in deportation proceedings could normally be released only to their parents, close relatives, or legal guardians. If none of these was available, minors were detained in juvenile care facilities, rather than released to the custody of "other responsible adults," as plaintiffs sought. The Court majority rejected the suit's facial challenge to the regulation as violating substantive and procedural due process, and as exceeding the Attorney General's statutory authority.

Key to the majority's constitutional holding was its characterization of the right at issue not as freedom from detention, but merely the right "to be placed in the custody of a willing-and-able private custodian rather than that of a government-operated or government-selected child-care institution." 507 U.S. at 302, 113 S.Ct. at 1447. According to the Court, that right did not amount to a constitutional imperative, especially given the traditional deference to the political branches in immigration law. 507 U.S. at 300-09, 113 S.Ct. at 1446-51. Justices O'Connor and Souter concurred, finding that there is "a constitutionally protected interest in freedom from institutional confinement," 507 U.S. at 315, 113 S.Ct. at 1454, but that INS policy satisfied due process. Justices Stevens and Blackmun dissented, arguing that Congress did not authorize a presumption that all unrelated adults are unsuitable custodians. They would have struck down the regulation; the right at stake was the "not the right of detained juveniles to be released to one particular custodian rather than another, but the right not to be detained in the first place." 504 U.S. at 341, 113 S.Ct. at 1468.

A number of courts have explored the constitutionality of INA § 236(c). Consider the following two decisions. As we go to press, the first remains the only federal appellate decision on the constitutionality of § 236(c). The other is a district court decision that goes the other way; it is now on appeal.

PARRA v. PERRYMAN
United States Court of Appeals, Seventh Circuit, 1999.
172 F.3d 954.

F. EASTERBROOK, CIRCUIT JUDGE.

Manuel Parra, a citizen of Mexico, is confined by the federal government pending the conclusion of removal proceedings. Parra was convicted in 1996 of aggravated criminal sexual assault, a felony that by virtue of INA § 237(a)(2)(A)(iii) requires his removal from the United States. On December 7, 1998, Parra was taken into federal custody and ordered to show cause why he

100

should not be removed. Because this proceeding began after April 1, 1997, it is governed by the Illegal Immigration Reform and Immigrant Responsibility Act of 1996 (IIRIRA), Division C of Pub.L. 104-208, 110 Stat. 3009-546 (Sept. 30, 1996). We therefore use the new statutory terminology of "removal" rather than "deportation" and cite to the current provisions of Title 8, avoiding the complex transition issues that affect some older cases.

Section 236(c)(1) of the Immigration and Nationality Act says that the Attorney General "shall take into custody any alien who" is removable as an aggravated felon under § 237(a)(2)(A)(iii) (or a number of other sections). A person taken into custody under § 236(c)(1) may be released under § 236(c)(2) [which ties release to 18 U.S.C. § 3521] * * *. Section 3521 is the witness protection program, and Parra is not eligible for its benefits. Nor is he eligible for another safety valve, a transition rule that permitted release on bail until October 9, 1998. See IIRIRA § 303(b)(3). An immigration judge ordered Parra released on bond, despite the expiration of § 303(b)(3), but an administrative appeal automatically stayed the release order. 8 C.F.R. § 3.19(*i*)(2). In consequence, Parra is being held without possibility of bail. He sought a writ of habeas corpus under 28 U.S.C. § 2241, contending that the amended § 236(c) violates the due process clause of the fifth amendment, but the district court dismissed his petition for want of jurisdiction. Parra asks us for release pending appeal of that decision; the INS, by contrast, seeks summary affirmance.

LaGuerre v. Reno, 164 F.3d 1035 (7th Cir.1998), holds that the IIRIRA channels most claims concerning removal to the court of appeals, and forecloses the use of § 2241 to obtain review either of contentions that will be heard by the court of appeals, or that Congress has determined may not be heard by any court. Accord, *Richardson v. Reno,* 162 F.3d 1338 (11th Cir.1998). One line of argument that cannot be made at any time, in any court, is that a person with a conviction for an aggravated felony is entitled to discretionary relief permitting him to remain in the United States. *Yang v. INS,* 109 F.3d 1185, 1190-92 (7th Cir.1997). For someone in Parra's position, then, removal is overwhelmingly likely. He concedes that he is an alien and that he has been convicted (on his plea of guilty) of a crime meeting the statutory definition of an aggravated felony. On March 3, 1999, an immigration judge concluded that Parra is deportable and ineligible for any relief from removal; his motions papers in this court do not even hint at a substantive argument that he is entitled to remain in the United States. The question at hand therefore is where he passes the time while waiting for the order to become final. He says that he wants to spend it at home, with his family (he has three children who are U.S. citizens); the Department of Justice fears that if released on bail Parra will go into hiding in order to stay in the United States indefinitely. According to the Department, approximately 90% of persons in Parra's situation absconded when released on bail before the IIRIRA. 62 Fed.Reg. 10,312, 10,323 (1997). But we oughtn't get ahead of things; jurisdiction is the first issue.

[The court found the district court had jurisdiction under 28 U.S.C. § 2241.]

Although the district court should have addressed Parra's claim on the merits, a remand is unnecessary. Section 236(c) plainly is within the power of

Congress. *Martinez v. Greene,* 28 F.Supp.2d 1275 (D.Colo. 1998), which held the statute unconstitutional, is unpersuasive. Persons subject to § 236(c) have forfeited any *legal* entitlement to remain in the United States and have little hope of clemency. (One is tempted to say "no" hope, but life is full of surprises, and a last-minute amendment of the immigration laws or change in policy has kept many an immigrant in this country. For current purposes "little" hope will do.) Before the IIRIRA bail was available to persons in Parra's position as a corollary to the possibility of discretionary relief from deportation; now that this possibility is so remote, so too is any reason for release pending removal. Parra's legal right to remain in the United States has come to an end. An alien in Parra's position can withdraw his defense of the removal proceeding and return to his native land, thus ending his detention immediately. He has the keys in his pocket. A criminal alien who insists on postponing the inevitable has no constitutional right to remain at large during the ensuing delay, and the United States has a powerful interest in maintaining the detention in order to ensure that removal actually occurs.

The due process calculus under *Mathews v. Eldridge,* 424 U.S. 319, 335, 96 S.Ct. 893, 47 L.Ed.2d 18 (1976), requires the court to evaluate the private interest, the probability of error (and the effect of additional safeguards on the rate of error), and the government's interest in dispensing with those safeguards, with a thumb on the scale in favor of the statute's constitutionality. The private interest here is not liberty in the abstract, but liberty *in the United States* by someone no longer entitled to remain in this country but eligible to live at liberty in his native land; the probability of error is zero when the alien *concedes* all elements that require removal (as Parra has done); and the public interest is substantial given the high flight rate of those released on bail. The Supreme Court held in *United States v. Salerno,* 481 U.S. 739, 107 S.Ct. 2095, 95 L.Ed.2d 697 (1987), that pretrial detention in criminal prosecutions (a parallel to pre-removal detention) comports with the Constitution even though the private interest is greater, the likelihood of error must be deemed significant given the prosecutor's high burden at a criminal trial, and the public interest is less (for the skip rate on bond in criminal prosecutions is well under 90%). Given the sweeping powers Congress possesses to prescribe the treatment of aliens, see *Fiallo v. Bell,* 430 U.S. 787, 792, 97 S.Ct. 1473, 52 L.Ed.2d 50 (1977), the constitutionality of § 236(c) is ordained.

Well before the IIRIRA we stated that once deportation proceedings have begun an alien's detention is constitutional. *Arias v. Rogers,* 676 F.2d 1139, 1143-44 (7th Cir.1982). Both *Reno v. Flores,* 507 U.S. 292, 113 S.Ct. 1439, 123 L.Ed.2d 1 (1993), and *Carlson v. Landon,* 342 U.S. 524, 72 S.Ct. 525, 96 L.Ed. 547 (1952), hold that under pre-IIRIRA law an alien had no entitlement to release pending the conclusion of deportation proceedings. If this was so even when the Attorney General had open-ended authority to grant discretionary relief from deportation—and thus to render the imprisonment gratuitous—then there can be no doubt about the constitutionality of § 236(c) now that these powers to forego removal have been curtailed.

The judgment of the district court is vacated, and the case is remanded with instructions to deny the petition on the merits.

KIM v. SCHILTGEN
United States District for the Northern District of California, 1999,
1999 U.S. Dist. LEXIS 12511, appeal pending.

S. ILLSTON, DISTRICT JUDGE.

On August 6, 1999, the Court heard argument on Hyung Joon Kim's petition for a writ of habeas corpus challenging the constitutionality of the mandatory detention provisions of INA § 236(c). Having carefully considered the arguments of the parties and the papers submitted, the Court GRANTS Kim's petition and orders the government to provide a bail hearing as specified herein. To the extent that Kim seeks immediate release from INS detention during the pendency of his deportation proceedings, Kim's petition is DENIED.

BACKGROUND

Petitioner Hyung J. Kim ("Kim"), a citizen of Korea, is confined by the federal government pending the conclusion of his removal proceedings. Kim was born in Seoul, Korea, on December 10, 1977, and entered the United States as a non-immigrant on March 10, 1984 at the age of six. He became a legal permanent resident of the United States on March 26, 1986 at age 8. He is now twenty-one, and has lived in the United States for fifteen years.

On July 8, 1996, at age 18, Kim was convicted in California state court of first degree burglary. On April 23, 1997, at age 19, he was convicted in California state court of petty theft with priors, and on October 8, 1997, he was sentenced to three years in state prison. His estimated release date was February 1, 1999.

On December 16, 1998, the Immigration and Naturalization Service ("INS") issued a notice to appear, placing Kim in removal proceedings under the Immigration and Nationality Act ("INA" or "the Act"). The notice to appear charged Kim with deportability pursuant to § 237(a)(2)(A)(iii) of the INA, as an alien convicted of an aggravated felony as defined in § 101(a)(43) of the Act. Under this section, theft offenses for which the sentence is to at least one year imprisonment are defined as aggravated felonies. Kim's conviction for petty theft with priors, for which he received a three-year sentence, thus met the definition of an aggravated felony.

At the same time the notice to appear was issued, the INS determined that Kim would be held without a bond hearing, because the INA prohibited his release from custody. The notice to appear was served on Kim on February 2, 1999, after he had completed his prison sentence, and Kim was accordingly taken into INS custody. Kim remains a legal permanent resident until a final finding of his deportability is made.

* * * A person taken into custody under § 236(c)(1) may only be released if the person is a participant in the federal witness protection program and can show that he is not a flight risk or a danger to the community. As Kim is not a member of the witness protection program, § 236(c)(1) results in his mandatory detention pending his deportation proceedings. Because under the statute he cannot be released on bail, he has not been granted a bail hearing.

Kim filed this petition for a writ of habeas corpus on May 17, 1999. Kim asserts that by mandating his detention without a bail hearing, § 236(c)(1) violates his constitutional right to due process as guaranteed by the Fifth Amendment to the United States Constitution. Kim seeks a declaration of this Court that § 236(c)(1) of the INA is unconstitutional on its face as violative of procedural and substantive due process rights. Kim also requests an order directing Thomas Schiltgen, District Director of the San Francisco INS, to release Kim from custody.

LEGAL STANDARD

* * *

A federal statute is presumed constitutional unless shown otherwise. *Martinez v. Greene*, 28 F.Supp.2d 1275, 1281 (D.Colo. 1998). To prevail on a facial challenge to the constitutionality of a statute, the petitioner "must establish that no set of circumstances exists under which the [statute] would be valid." *United States v. Salerno*, 481 U.S. 739, 745, 107 S.Ct. 2095, 95 L.Ed. 2d 697 (1987).

DISCUSSION

* * *

Kim claims that he has been denied due process of law, in violation of the Fifth Amendment, because he has not had, and in fact by statute cannot have, a bail hearing to determine whether he is a suitable candidate for release pending his removal proceedings.[4] Kim argues that this mandatory detention under § 236(c) violates criminal aliens' rights to both substantive and procedural due process.

a. Substantive due process.

A petitioner's right to substantive due process prevents the government from conduct that "shocks the conscience." *Rochin v. California*, 342 U.S. 165, 172, 72 S.Ct. 205, 96 L.Ed. 183 (1952). Violations of substantive due process occur when the government interferes with rights "implicit in the concept of ordered liberty." *Palko v. Connecticut*, 302 U.S. 319, 325-26, 58 S.Ct. 149, 82 L.Ed. 288 (1937).

In evaluating whether § 236(c) violates aliens' substantive due process rights, Kim argues this Court should adopt the standard of review delineated in *United States v. Salerno*, 481 U.S. 739, 107 S.Ct. 2095, 95 L.Ed. 2d 697 (1987). The *Salerno* standard involves a two step analysis. First, the court determines whether the statute at issue is "impermissible punishment or permissible regulation." *Salerno*, 481 U.S. at 747. If it qualifies as a permissible regulation, the court then examines whether the statute is an excessive means of achieving the permissible goal. If it is excessive, then the statute violates the petitioner's substantive due process rights. See *id.* Kim argues this standard should govern this Court's examination of § 236(c).

---

[4] From Kim's moving papers, the Court has been unable to determine if Kim is contesting the applicability of § 236(c)(1) to him. However, as Kim argues that § 236(c) is facially unconstitutional the Court need not examine the particulars of Kim's own case.

Respondents contend that the *Salerno* test is overly strict and therefore inappropriate. Citing Congress' broad authority over immigration, respondents argue the Court must defer to Congress' judgment, and restrict its examination of § 236(c) to the rational review test. Respondents suggest the "(unexacting) standard of rationally advancing some legitimate governmental purpose," a standard applied in *Reno v. Flores*, 507 U.S. 292, 305, 113 S.Ct. 1439, 123 L.Ed. 2d 1 (1993).

It is clear that lawful resident aliens possess substantive due process rights during deportation proceedings. See *Landon v. Plasencia*, 459 U.S. 21, 33, 103 S.Ct. 321, 74 L.Ed. 2d 21 (1982) ("Once an alien gains admission to our country and begins to develop the ties that go with permanent residence, his constitutional status changes accordingly."); see also *Flores*, 507 U.S. at 306 ("It is well established that the Fifth Amendment entitles aliens to due process of law in deportation proceedings."); *Mathews v. Diaz*, 426 U.S. 67, 96 S.Ct. 1883, 48 L.Ed. 2d 478 (1976).

While lawful resident aliens do enjoy substantive due process rights, Congress has the power to limit those rights. Congress' power over immigration is plenary, and it may accordingly promulgate rules for aliens "that would be unacceptable if applied to citizens." *Fiallo v. Bell*, 430 U.S. 787, 792, 97 S.Ct. 1473, 52 L.Ed. 2d 50 (1977). It has been stated that "over no conceivable subject is the legislative power of Congress more complete" than over immigration. *Id.* The effect of this extraordinary breadth of Congressional power is to curtail judicial review of immigration policy. As the Supreme Court has stated, "our cases have long recognized the power to expel or exclude aliens as a fundamental sovereign attribute exercised by the Government's political departments, largely immune from judicial control." *Shaughnessy v. Mezei*, 345 U.S. 206, 210, 73 S.Ct. 625, 97 L.Ed. 956 (1953).

Despite Congress' plenary authority over immigration, however, there is a distinction between substantive immigration policy and the procedures by which that policy is implemented. While courts must defer to Congress' authority when reviewing substantive immigration policy, there is no such restriction to their review of the rules that implement or enforce that policy. Specifically, Congress' decisions about the admissibility and deportability of aliens must be accorded deference by the courts, but the courts may require Congress to "respect the procedural safeguards of due process" in the *implementation* of those decisions. *Fiallo*, 430 U.S. at 792 n.4. The Supreme Court has recognized this distinction between the level of review appropriate for substantive versus procedural immigration legislation. In *INS v. Chadha*, 462 U.S. 919, 103 S.Ct. 2764, 77 L.Ed. 2d 317 (1983), for example, the Court, while reviewing a challenge to the constitutionality of a section of the INA, stated that

> the plenary authority of Congress over aliens under Art. I, § 8, cl. 4 is not open to question, but what is challenged here is *whether Congress has chosen a constitutionally permissible means of implementing that power.* As we made clear in *Buckley v. Valeo*: "Congress has plenary authority in all cases in which it has substantive legislative jurisdiction, *so long as the exercise of that authority does not offend some other constitutional restriction.*"

Chadha, 462 U.S. at 940-41 (emphasis added) (internal citations omitted). Courts therefore may examine the procedural means by which Congress reaches its substantive immigration ends under a stricter standard than pure deference.

Several courts have recently held that § 236(c) is a procedural statute, rather than one embodying substantive immigration policy. "Indefinite detention of aliens ordered deported is not a matter of immigration policy; it is only a means by which the government implements Congress' directives." *Phan v. Reno*, 56 F.Supp.2d 1149 (W.D.Wash. 1999). The court in *Martinez v. Greene*, 28 F.Supp.2d 1275, 1281 (D.Colo. 1998), in examining a facial challenge to § 236(c) identical to the case at bar, characterized the petitioner's case as "challenging the method by which the immigration statutes are implemented," rather than implicating Congress' plenary authority over substantive immigration policy.

The Court agrees that § 236(c) is not substantive immigration legislation. The statute does not determine which aliens are deportable and which are not, nor does it confer or deny entitlements. Such determinations and categorical "line-drawing" are the hallmarks of immigration policy legislation. See *Fiallo*, 430 U.S. at 797-98. In contrast, § 236(c) simply delineates the procedure for detaining aliens already determined by Congress to be deportable. As Judge Smith stated in *Danh v. Demore*, 59 F.Supp.2d 994 (N.D.Cal. 1999), "mandatory detention with no possibility of bond is not a simple . . . policy decision that a system of ordered liberty can entrust solely to the political branches of government. It is only ancillary to substantive immigration policy and, as such, does not escape searching judicial review." *Danh*, 59 F.Supp.2d at 1000. Since § 236(c) is only "a method by which the immigration statutes are implemented," and accordingly not entitled to deferential review, the Court applies the *Salerno* standard. *Martinez*, 28 F.Supp.2d at 1281.

Respondents' reliance on the standard used in *Flores* is accordingly inapposite. In *Flores*, juvenile aliens brought a class action suit against the INS for violations of substantive due process. The juvenile aliens were detained under INS regulations preventing their release unless they could show they could be released to the custody of a parent or legal guardian. *Flores*, 507 U.S. at 294-98. In determining which standard of review to apply, the Supreme Court rejected a strict scrutiny standard because a fundamental liberty interest was not at stake. See *id.* at 299-300, 305-306. First, as juveniles, the petitioners were always in some form of custody, and accordingly had no fundamental right to be released into a non-custodial setting. See *id.* at 301-03. Second, the petitioners were not being detained in jail or prison, but in low-security facilities meeting "state licensing requirements for shelter care, foster care . . . and related services to dependent children." *Id.* at 298. Finally, as aliens, the petitioners were subject to Congress' plenary authority over immigration, and accordingly possessed a lesser right to substantive due process.

Flores is distinguishable from the present case. Unlike the juvenile aliens in *Flores*, criminal aliens detained by § 236(c) are adults, with a full interest in being free from custody, and are in fact detained in jail, rather than in surroundings approximating foster care. Nor is Congress' plenary authority over immigration dispositive, since the regulations at issue here reflect not substantive immigration policy, but rather procedural implementation of it.

Respondents also contend that since *Salerno* was a criminal case, and deportation proceedings are classified as civil proceedings, the *Salerno* standard is inapposite. Respondents argue that as criminal defendants are afforded procedural safeguards to which aliens are not entitled, such as the presumption of innocence and the right to a speedy trial, a standard of review that evolved from a criminal case cannot be applicable to aliens. The Court finds this argument unpersuasive. What is at stake is not the presumption of innocence or right to a speedy trial, but the right to be free from bodily restraint. While aliens may not possess rights to the former, they certainly enjoy a right to the latter. See *Wong Wing v. United States*, 163 U.S. 228, 238, 16 S.Ct. 977, 41 L.Ed. 140 (1896) ("all persons within the territory of the United States are entitled to the protection guaranteed by [the Fifth and Sixth] amendments."); see also *Harisiades v. Shaughnessy*, 342 U.S. 580, 586-87 n.9, 72 S.Ct. 512, 96 L.Ed. 586 (1952) (immigrants stand "on an equal footing with citizens" under the Constitution with respect to protection of personal liberty). As the court stated in *Danh*, "it strains the imagination that individuals detained because of criminal activity should have more rights than those held simply for regulatory purposes." *Danh*, 59 F.Supp.2d at 1001. The fact that the *Salerno* standard emerged from a criminal case does not obviate its relevance here. Indeed, the *Salerno* test has been used by all courts reviewing the constitutionality of § 236(c) but one. See *Diaz-Zaldierna v. Fasano*, 43 F.Supp.2d 1114 (S.D.Cal. 1999), *Van Eeton v. Beebe*, 49 F.Supp.2d 1186 (D.Or. 1999), *Martinez*, 28 F.Supp.2d 1275, *Danh*, 59 F.Supp.2d 994; but see *Parra*, 172 F.3d 954.

In applying the *Salerno* test, a court must first determine whether the infringement on liberty at issue is "impermissible punishment or permissible regulation." *Salerno*, 481 U.S. at 747. The Supreme Court has held that deportation is regulatory, not punitive. See *INS v. Lopez-Mendoza*, 468 U.S. 1032, 1038, 104 S.Ct. 3479, 82 L.Ed. 2d 778 (1984); see also *Carlson v. Landon*, 342 U.S. 524, 537, 72 S.Ct. 525, 96 L.Ed. 547 (1952). As for the legitimacy of the regulation, in its enactment of IIRIRA, which amended the INA to include § 236(c), Congress referred to several valid motivations. Congress wished to prevent criminal aliens from absconding during their removal proceedings, as at the time twenty percent of criminal aliens released on bond did not return for deportation. Congress was also motivated by the need to protect the public from potentially dangerous criminal aliens, and to restore public confidence in the immigration system. See S. Rep. No. 48, 104th Cong., 1st Sess. (1995) (1995 WL 170285 (Leg. Hist.) at 1-6, 9, 18-23). These are legitimate and permissible goals, well within Congress' plenary power over immigration policy. Accordingly, § 236(c) passes the first prong of the *Salerno* test as permissible regulation.

The next step is to determine whether the infringement on liberty is "excessive in relation to the regulatory goal Congress sought to achieve." *Salerno*, 481 U.S. at 747. Respondents argue that in light of a twenty percent abscondence rate, mandatory detention for all criminal aliens pending deportation is not excessive. The Court disagrees. To obtain its goals regarding a relatively small minority of criminal aliens, section 236(c) applies to *every* criminal alien an irrebuttable presumption that they pose a flight risk and/or a danger to the community. In *Carlson*, the Supreme Court stated that such blanket presumptions, with no safeguards to protect due process rights, are impermissible. In that case, the Supreme Court affirmed the detention of Communist aliens, but specifically cited the Attorney General's discretion to grant bond as a factor in its decision. The Court stated, "of course purpose to injure *could not be imputed generally to all aliens subject to deportation.*" *Carlson*, 342 U.S. at 538 (emphasis added). Yet this is precisely what § 236(c) does. While the government's goals are valid, § 236(c) simply paints with too broad a brush. That twenty percent of criminal aliens do not return for deportation cannot justify mandatory detention without a bail hearing for the remaining eighty percent. As the *Martinez* court stated, "Due process demands more." *Martinez*, 28 F.Supp.2d at 1283. Less excessive means exist for accomplishing Congress' goals, such as having individualized bail hearings. Section 236(c) accordingly fails the second prong of the *Salerno* test, as an excessive infringement of criminal aliens' rights to substantive due process.

Salerno and *Carlson* both support this result. In *Salerno*, the Supreme Court upheld the Bail Reform Act's pretrial detention measures, in part because "the arrestee [was] entitled to a prompt detention hearing" and the Attorney General had discretion to grant bail. *Salerno*, 481 U.S. at 747. In contrast, the Attorney General has no discretion to grant either bail or a bail hearing under § 236(c), as the statute requires mandatory detention. In the absence of that discretion, § 236(c)'s infringement on the aliens' liberty interest becomes excessive. In *Carlson*, the Attorney General had discretion to release Communist aliens on bail pending their deportation, but chose to deny bail. The Supreme Court upheld the Attorney General's decision as falling within his discretion, but pointed out that the *existence* of that discretion was crucial. *Carlson*, 342 U.S. at 538. Again, § 236(c) contains no discretionary provisions. Instead, a purpose to injure is imputed generally to all aliens subject to deportation, in direct contradiction to the Supreme Court's admonition in *Carlson*. This blanket presumption is simply excessive in relation to Congress' goals.

Other district courts have granted petitions for writs of habeas corpus based on § 236(c), but have generally restricted their analysis to the constitutionality of § 236(c) as applied to individual petitioners. See, e.g., *Van Eeton*, 49 F.Supp.2d 1186, *Danh*, 59 F.Supp.2d 994, *Phan*, 56 F.Supp.2d 1149. The district court in *Diaz-Zaldierna* found that § 236(c) was not unconstitutional as applied to the petitioner, in part because the petitioner had a hearing scheduled to determine whether § 236(c) even applied to his case. *Diaz-Zaldierna*, 43 F.Supp.2d at 1120. Because these courts conducted as-applied analysis, they did not reach the question now before this Court, whether § 236(c) is facially unconstitutional.

The two courts that have addressed this facial issue have reached different conclusions. *Martinez* held that the mandatory detention strictures of § 236(c) are excessive in light of Congress' goals, and accordingly that they violate substantive due process. *Martinez*, 28 F.Supp.2d at 1282. In *Parra*, the Seventh

Circuit applied a purely deferential standard to its review of § 236(c), and found that it "plainly is within the power of Congress." *Parra*, 172 F.3d at 958. *Parra*'s result, however, is distinguishable. The *Parra* court did not apply the *Salerno* test, as the court deferred to Congress' plenary power over immigration and accordingly did not look beyond the rational review test.[6] As explained above, this Court has determined that § 236(c) is a procedural implementation of immigration policy, and so examination of the statute under the *Salerno* test is appropriate. Under the second prong of that test, § 236(c) is excessive in light of its goals.

For the reasons stated above, the Court finds that § 236(c) is unconstitutional on its face, having failed the second prong of the *Salerno* test. Mandatory detention of all criminal aliens under § 236(c) is plainly excessive in light of Congress' goals, and therefore violates substantive due process.

b. Procedural due process.

Kim also argues that § 236(c)(1) violates criminal aliens' rights to procedural due process.[7] "Procedural due process requires that [a] restriction [on liberty] be implemented fairly." *Salerno*, 481 U.S. at 746. To determine whether a given procedure, statute, or governmental conduct violates a petitioner's right to due process, courts apply the three-step analysis from *Mathews v. Eldridge*, 424 U.S. 319, 335, 96 S.Ct. 893, 47 L.Ed. 2d 18 (1976). The court must evaluate the private interest that will be affected by the official action; the risk of erroneous deprivation of the private interest, and the effect of any additional safeguards on that risk; and the government's interest in maintaining the current procedures. See id.

Despite respondents' contentions to the contrary, resident legal aliens are entitled to procedural due process protection under *Mathews*. Respondents argue that "because of Congress' plenary power over immigration and its right to detain aliens as part of the removal process, all that procedural due process requires is 'some level of individualized determination' to ensure that the alien's detention pending his removal is not arbitrary." Respondents' Return and Opposition to Petition for Writ of Habeas Corpus, 15:3-6. Respondents' assertion is misplaced, as § 236(c), a procedural implementation of Congress' immigration policy, does not merit this kind of deferential review. The Court also notes that many courts have applied *Mathews* when reviewing both § 236(c)

---

[6] In addition, the *Parra* court analyzed the constitutionality of § 236(c) in reference to an abscondence rate of 90%. *Parra*, 172 F.3d at 956. The Congressional records, however, indicate a 20% abscondence rate. See S.Rep. No. 48, 104th Cong., 1st Sess., (1995) (1995 WL 170285 (Leg Hist.) At 1-6, 9, 18-23. Respondents refer to the 20% abscondence rate, as did the court in *Danh*. See * * * *Danh*, 59 F.Supp.2d 994.

[7] Once a court finds that a petitioner's substantive due process rights have been violated, it is not strictly necessary to evaluate possible violation of his or her procedural due process rights. "Only when a restriction on liberty survives substantive due process scrutiny does the further question of whether the restriction is implemented in a procedurally fair manner become ripe for consideration." *Danh*, 59 F.Supp.2d at 1004. However, the Court will consider petitioner's procedural due process claim, should it later be determined that § 236(c) does not violate substantive due process.

and its predecessor, ADAA § 7343(a). See, e.g., *Van Eeton*, 49 F.Supp.2d 1186; *Martinez*, 28 F.Supp.2d at 1282; *Leader v. Blackman*, 744 F.Supp. 500, 508 (S.D.N.Y. 1990); *Paxton v. INS*, 745 F.Supp. 1261, 1266 (E.D.Mich. 1990). Respondents' position seems particularly untenable since *Parra*, the case upon which respondents heavily rely for many of their arguments, also applied the *Mathews* test to determine the petitioner's procedural due process rights. Accordingly, the procedural due process rights of aliens under § 236(c) must be evaluated under the *Mathews* test.

The private interest at stake here is "great—the right to be free of indefinite and possible long-term detention pending a deportability determination." *Martinez*, 28 F.Supp.2d at 1283. The *Danh* court called the private interest "fundamental to any democratic society: the right to freedom from arbitrary detention." *Danh*, 59 F.Supp.2d at 1004. The risk of erroneous deprivation of that interest is substantial, since under § 236(c) no procedures exist to determine whether the given individual merits release on bond. Additional safeguards are readily available, as for example the bond hearing procedures which were in place during the transitional period under IIRIRA § 303(b)(3). Finally, the burden on the government in changing its procedures is minimal. Since criminal aliens already must come before an Immigration Judge for a determination of whether § 236(c) applies to them, the government could reinstitute bond hearings at that same time. While the government's interest in preventing alien abscondence and protecting the public is strong, it is insufficient to overrule the stronger private interest and high risk of erroneous deprivation of that private interest. Accordingly, the Court finds that § 236(c) violates criminal aliens' rights to procedural due process.

CONCLUSION

For the foregoing reasons, the Court finds and declares that § 236(c) violates criminal aliens' rights to substantive and procedural due process. The mandatory detention provision of § 236(c) fails to provide any meaningful procedure to detained aliens; accordingly, there are no circumstances under which § 236(c) could be valid. It is therefore unconstitutional on its face. Kim's application for a writ of habeas corpus is granted to the extent that respondents shall promptly provide Kim with an individualized bond hearing, pursuant to IIRIRA's Transition Custody Rules, IIRIRA § 303(b)(3), or otherwise as respondents may elect, to determine whether Kim is a flight risk or a danger to the community.

It is so ordered.

Notes

1. Which case, *Parra* or *Kim*, more accurately reads *Carlson*, *Salerno*, and *Flores*? Which decision more persuasively applies the *Mathews v. Eldridge* balancing test?

2. *Kim* involved a permanent resident. *Parra* did, too (although the court's opinion omits this fact). How should a court respond to a constitutional challenge to mandatory detention of an alien who is *not* a permanent resident?

3. Over 50 district court decisions have addressed the constitutionality of § 236(c). About two-thirds have struck down the statute, almost all of them sustaining as-applied challenges. Many of these decisions have emphasized that the noncitizen in question had some basis for challenging removal. *See, e.g., Danh v. Demore*, 59 F.Supp.2d 994, 1002-03 (N.D.Cal. 1999); *Van Eeton v. Beebe*, 49 F.Supp.2d 1186, 1190 (D.Or. 1999) . Many of the decisions upholding the constitutionality of § 236(c) against as-applied challenges emphasized that the noncitizen had little or no chance of avoiding removal. *See, e.g., Avramenkov v. INS*, 99 F.Supp.2d 210, 215-16 (D.Conn.2000) ; *Reyes v. Underdown*, 73 F.Supp.2d 653, 658 (W.D.La.1999);; *Alikhani v. Fasano*, 70 F.Supp.2d 1124, 1135 (S.D.Cal.1999) . How persuasive is this distinction? If the question is whether mandatory detention implicates a liberty interest, should the answer depend on the likelihood of removal? If the answer to this question is yes, is the Kim decision wrong in sustaining a facial challenge to § 236(c)?

4. What will happen at a hearing to determine if Kim should be released? Won't his criminal record be considered in deciding whether he is likely to abscond or presents a threat to the community? Does due process require an independent decisionmaker, not an INS hearing officer?

916-25: Detention After a Removal Order: Indefinite Detention (substitute for *Barrera-Echavarria* and notes 1-6 on 924-25)

In 1995, the Ninth Circuit decided *Barrera-Echavarria v. Rison*, 44 F.3d 1441 (9th Cir.) (en banc), *cert. denied*, 516 U.S. 976, 116 S.Ct. 479, 133 L.Ed.2d 407 (1995) . The case involved a Mariel Cuban who arrived in the United States in 1980 and was ordered excluded in 1985. He could not be repatriated, however, and except for a brief period on immigration parole in 1992, Barrera had been in detention since 1985, with no end to confinement in sight. The court first rejected his argument that the government lacked the statutory authority to detain him indefinitely. The court held that such authority existed (under a pre-1996 version of the relevant INA section):

> A judicial decision requiring that excludable aliens be released into American society when neither their countries of origin nor any third country will admit them might encourage the sort of intransigence Cuba has exhibited in the negotiations over the Mariel refugees. *See, e.g., Jean v. Nelson*, 727 F.2d 957, 975 (11th Cir.1984) *(en banc)* ("[T]his approach would ultimately result in our losing control over our borders. A foreign leader could eventually compel us to grant physical admission via parole to any aliens he wished by the simple expedient of sending them here and then refusing to take them back."), *aff'd*, 472 U.S. 846, 105 S.Ct. 2992, 86 L.Ed.2d 664 (1985). In an area with sensitive foreign policy implications, we must hesitate to interpret an ambiguous statutory scheme as requiring such a result. We therefore hold that the Attorney General's detention of Barrera has been authorized by statute.

The court then rejected Barrera's constitutional argument. Relying heavily on his status as an excludable alien and on the Supreme Court's decision in *Shaughnessy v. United States ex rel. Mezei*, 345 U.S. 206, 73 S.Ct. 625, 97 L.Ed. 956 (1953) , the Ninth Circuit concluded:

> While excludable aliens might * * * enjoy some constitutional protections, we find that applicable Supreme Court precedent squarely precludes a conclusion that they have a constitutional right to be free from detention, even for an extended time. * * * Because excludable aliens are deemed under the entry doctrine not to be present on United States territory, a holding that they have no substantive right to be free from immigration detention reasonably follows.

The court noted that Barrera's detention was not "indefinite" or "permanent" as long as he received annual reviews to determine whether he met established criteria for release on parole—as he was receiving under a longstanding INS detention review program for Mariel Cuban detainees.. The court also rejected arguments that Barrera's detention violated international law. In contrast, the Sixth Circuit held in *Rosales-Garcia v. Holland*, 238 F.3d 704 (6th Cir.2001), that detention of a paroled-in Mariel Cuban was indefinite and violated Fifth Amendment due process rights. *Id.*, at 725.

In August 1999, the INS issued a memorandum setting out interim review procedures for other persons in long-term detention. *See* 76 Interp.Rel. 1285 (1999). The memorandum's announced intent was to implement interim procedures pending the adoption of a permanent program based loosely on the review process for Mariel Cubans who have final removal orders but whom the Cuban government will not accept. In December 2000, the INS adopted a final rule establishing a post-order custody review procedure for aliens (other than Mariel Cubans) detained beyond the 90-day period in INA § 241(a)(1). *See* 65 Fed.Reg. 80281 (2000).

What if person initially admitted as a lawful *permanent resident* becomes removable but cannot be removed because his country of nationality will not accept him, or because he is stateless? Several federal courts of appeals considered whether indefinite detention of permanent residents is authorized by statute and consistent with the Constitution. A conflict in the circuits resulted, and in 2001 the case went to the Supreme Court.

ZADVYDAS v. DAVIS
Supreme Court of the United States, 2001.
121 S.Ct. 2491.

JUSTICE BREYER delivered the opinion of the Court.

When an alien has been found to be unlawfully present in the United States and a final order of removal has been entered, the Government ordinarily secures the alien's removal during a subsequent 90-day statutory "removal period," during which time the alien normally is held in custody.

A special statute authorizes further detention if the Government fails to remove the alien during those 90 days. It says:

> An alien ordered removed [1] who is inadmissible . . . [2] [or] removable [as a result of violations of status requirements or entry conditions, violations of criminal law, or reasons of security or

foreign policy] or [3] who has been determined by the Attorney General to be a risk to the community or unlikely to comply with the order of removal, may be detained beyond the removal period and, if released, shall be subject to [certain] terms of supervision .... INA § 241(a)(6).

In these cases, we must decide whether this post-removal-period statute authorizes the Attorney General to detain a removable alien *indefinitely* beyond the removal period or only for a period *reasonably necessary* to secure the alien's removal. We deal here with aliens who were admitted to the United States but subsequently ordered removed. Aliens who have not yet gained initial admission to this country would present a very different question. Based on our conclusion that indefinite detention of aliens in the former category would raise serious constitutional concerns, we construe the statute to contain an implicit "reasonable time" limitation, the application of which is subject to federal court review.

I

A

The post-removal-period detention statute is one of a related set of statutes and regulations that govern detention during and after removal proceedings. While removal proceedings are in progress, most aliens may be released on bond or paroled. After entry of a final removal order and during the 90-day removal period, however, aliens must be held in custody. INA § 241(a)(2). Subsequently, as the post-removal-period statute provides, the Government "may" continue to detain an alien who still remains here or release that alien under supervision. INA § 241(a)(6).

Related Immigration and Naturalization Service (INS) regulations add that the INS District Director will initially review the alien's records to decide whether further detention or release under supervision is warranted after the 90-day removal period expires. 8 CFR §§ 241.4(c)(1), (h), (k)(1)(i) (2001). If the decision is to detain, then an INS panel will review the matter further, at the expiration of a 3-month period or soon thereafter. § 241.4(k)(2)(ii). And the panel will decide, on the basis of records and a possible personal interview, between still further detention or release under supervision. § 241.4(i). In making this decision, the panel will consider, for example, the alien's disciplinary record, criminal record, mental health reports, evidence of rehabilitation, history of flight, prior immigration history, and favorable factors such as family ties. § 241.4(f). To authorize release, the panel must find that the alien is not likely to be violent, to pose a threat to the community, to flee if released, or to violate the conditions of release. § 241.4(e). And the alien must demonstrate "to the satisfaction of the Attorney General" that he will pose no danger or risk of flight. § 241.4(d)(1). If the panel decides against release, it must review the matter again within a year, and can review it earlier if conditions change. §§ 241.4(k)(2)(iii), (v).

B

1

We consider two separate instances of detention. The first concerns Kestutis Zadvydas, a resident alien who was born, apparently of Lithuanian parents, in a displaced persons camp in Germany in 1948. When he was eight years old, Zadvydas immigrated to the United States with his parents and other family members, and he has lived here ever since.

Zadvydas has a long criminal record, involving drug crimes, attempted robbery, attempted burglary, and theft. He has a history of flight, from both criminal and deportation proceedings. Most recently, he was convicted of possessing, with intent to distribute, cocaine; sentenced to 16 years' imprisonment; released on parole after two years; taken into INS custody; and, in 1994, ordered deported to Germany.

In 1994, Germany told the INS that it would not accept Zadvydas because he was not a German citizen. Shortly thereafter, Lithuania refused to accept Zadvydas because he was neither a Lithuanian citizen nor a permanent resident. In 1996, the INS asked the Dominican Republic (Zadvydas' wife's country) to accept him, but this effort proved unsuccessful. In 1998, Lithuania rejected, as inadequately documented, Zadvydas' effort to obtain Lithuanian citizenship based on his parents' citizenship; Zadvydas' reapplication is apparently still pending.

The INS kept Zadvydas in custody after expiration of the removal period. In September 1995, Zadvydas filed a petition for a writ of habeas corpus under 28 U.S.C. § 2241 challenging his continued detention. In October 1997, a Federal District Court granted that writ and ordered him released under supervision. In its view, the Government would never succeed in its efforts to remove Zadvydas from the United States, leading to his permanent confinement, contrary to the Constitution.

The Fifth Circuit reversed this decision. *Zadvydas v. Underdown*, 185 F.3d 279 (1999). It concluded that Zadvydas" detention did not violate the Constitution because eventual deportation was not "impossible," good faith efforts to remove him from the United States continued, and his detention was subject to periodic administrative review. *Id.*, at 294, 297. The Fifth Circuit stayed its mandate pending potential review in this Court.

2

The second case is that of Kim Ho Ma. Ma was born in Cambodia in 1977. When he was two, his family fled, taking him to refugee camps in Thailand and the Philippines and eventually to the United States, where he has lived as a resident alien since the age of seven. In 1995, at age 17, Ma was involved in a gang-related shooting, convicted of manslaughter, and sentenced to 38 months' imprisonment. He served two years, after which he was released into INS custody.

In light of his conviction of an "aggravated felony," Ma was ordered removed. The 90-day removal period expired in early 1999, but the INS continued to keep Ma in custody, because, in light of his former gang membership, the nature of his crime, and his planned participation in a prison hunger strike, it was "unable to conclude that Mr. Ma would remain nonviolent and not violate the conditions of release." App. to Pet. for Cert. in No. 00-38, p. 87a.

In 1999 Ma filed a petition for a writ of habeas corpus under 28 U.S.C. § 2241. A panel of five judges in the Federal District Court for the Western District of Washington, considering Ma's and about 100 similar cases together, issued a joint order holding that the Constitution forbids post-removal-period detention unless there is "a realistic chance that [the] alien will be deported" (thereby permitting classification of the detention as "in aid of deportation"). *Binh Phan v. Reno*, 56 F.Supp.2d 1149, 1156 (1999). The District Court then held an evidentiary hearing, decided that there was no "realistic chance" that Cambodia (which has no repatriation treaty with the United States) would accept Ma, and ordered Ma released.

The Ninth Circuit affirmed Ma's release. *Kim Ho Ma v. Reno*, 208 F.3d 815 (2000). It concluded, based in part on constitutional concerns, that the statute did not authorize detention for more than a "reasonable time" beyond the 90-day period authorized for removal. *Id.*, at 818. And, given the lack of a repatriation agreement with Cambodia, that time had expired upon passage of the 90 days. *Id.*, at 830-831.

3

Zadvydas asked us to review the decision of the Fifth Circuit authorizing his continued detention. The Government asked us to review the decision of the Ninth Circuit forbidding Ma's continued detention. We granted writs in both cases, agreeing to consider both statutory and related constitutional questions. We consolidated the two cases for argument; and we now decide them together.

II

We note at the outset that the primary federal habeas corpus statute, 28 U.S.C. § 2241, confers jurisdiction upon the federal courts to hear these cases. * * *

* * *

III

The post-removal-period detention statute applies to certain categories of aliens who have been ordered removed, namely inadmissible aliens, criminal aliens, aliens who have violated their nonimmigrant status conditions, and aliens removable for certain national security or foreign relations reasons, as well as any alien "who has been determined by the Attorney General to be a risk to the community or unlikely to comply with the order of removal." INA § 241(a)(6); see also 8 CFR § 241.4(a) (2001). It says that an alien who falls into one of these categories "may be detained beyond the removal period and, if released, shall be subject to [certain] terms of supervision." INA § 241(a)(6).

The Government argues that the statute means what it literally says. It sets no "limit on the length of time beyond the removal period that an alien who falls within one of the Section 241(a)(6) categories may be detained." Hence, "whether to continue to detain such an alien and, if so, in what circumstances and for how long" is up to the Attorney General, not up to the courts.

"[I]t is a cardinal principle" of statutory interpretation, however, that when an Act of Congress raises "a serious doubt" as to its constitutionality, "this Court will first ascertain whether a construction of the statute is fairly possible by which the question may be avoided." *Crowell v. Benson*, 285 U.S. 22, 62 (1932). We have read significant limitations into other immigration statutes in order to avoid their constitutional invalidation. For similar reasons, we read an implicit limitation into the statute before us. In our view, the statute, read in light of the Constitution's demands, limits an alien's post-removal-period detention to a period reasonably necessary to bring about that alien's removal from the United States. It does not permit indefinite detention.

A

A statute permitting indefinite detention of an alien would raise a serious constitutional problem. The Fifth Amendment's Due Process Clause forbids the Government to "depriv[e]" any "person . . . of . . . liberty . . . without due process of law." Freedom from imprisonment—from government custody, detention, or other forms of physical restraint—lies at the heart of the liberty that Clause protects. And this Court has said that government detention violates that Clause unless the detention is ordered in a *criminal* proceeding with adequate procedural protections, see *United States v. Salerno*, 481 U.S. 739, 746 (1987), or, in certain special and "narrow" non-punitive "circumstances," *Foucha* [*v. Louisiana*, 504 U.S. 71, 80 (1992)], where a special justification, such as harm-threatening mental illness, outweighs the "individual's constitutionally protected interest in avoiding physical restraint." *Kansas v. Hendricks*, 521 U.S. 346, 356 (1997). The proceedings at issue here are civil, not criminal, and we assume that they are nonpunitive in purpose and effect. There is no sufficiently strong special justification here for indefinite civil detention—at least as administered under this statute. The statute, says the Government, has two regulatory goals: "ensuring the appearance of aliens at future immigration proceedings" and "[p]reventing danger to the community." But by definition the first justification—preventing flight—is weak or nonexistent where removal seems a remote possibility at best. As this Court said in *Jackson v. Indiana*, 406 U.S. 715 (1972), where detention's goal is no longer practically attainable, detention no longer "bear[s] [a] reasonable relation to the purpose for which the individual [was] committed." *Id.*, at 738.

The second justification—protecting the community—does not necessarily diminish in force over time. But we have upheld preventive detention based on dangerousness only when limited to specially dangerous individuals and subject to strong procedural protections. [Citing *Hendricks*, *Salerno*, and *Foucha*]. In cases in which preventive detention is of potentially *indefinite* duration, we have also demanded that the dangerousness rationale be accompanied by some other special circumstance, such as mental illness, that helps to create the danger.

The civil confinement here at issue is not limited, but potentially permanent. The provision authorizing detention does not apply narrowly to "a small segment of particularly dangerous individuals," *Hendricks, supra,* at 368, say suspected terrorists, but broadly to aliens ordered removed for many and various reasons, including tourist visa violations. And, once the flight risk justification evaporates, the only special circumstance present is the alien's removable status itself, which bears no relation to a detainee's dangerousness.

Moreover, the sole procedural protections available to the alien are found in administrative proceedings, where the alien bears the burden of proving he is not dangerous, without (in the Government's view) significant later judicial review. This Court has suggested, however, that the Constitution may well preclude granting "an administrative body the unreviewable authority to make determinations implicating fundamental rights." *Superintendent, Mass. Correctional Institution at Walpole v. Hill,* 472 U.S. 445, 450 (1985) (O'Connor, J.). The Constitution demands greater procedural protection even for property. The serious constitutional problem arising out of a statute that, in these circumstances, permits an indefinite, perhaps permanent, deprivation of human liberty without any such protection is obvious.

The Government argues that, from a constitutional perspective, alien status itself can justify indefinite detention, and points to *Shaughnessy v. United States ex rel. Mezei,* 345 U.S. 206 (1953), as support. That case involved a once lawfully admitted alien who left the United States, returned after a trip abroad, was refused admission, and was left on Ellis Island, indefinitely detained there because the Government could not find another country to accept him. The Court held that Mezei's detention did not violate the Constitution. *Id.,* at 215-216.

Although *Mezei,* like the present cases, involves indefinite detention, it differs from the present cases in a critical respect. As the Court emphasized, the alien's extended departure from the United States required him to seek entry into this country once again. His presence on Ellis Island did not count as entry into the United States. Hence, he was "treated," for constitutional purposes, "as if stopped at the border." *Id.,* at 213, 215. And that made all the difference.

The distinction between an alien who has effected an entry into the United States and one who has never entered runs throughout immigration law. See *Kaplan v. Tod,* 267 U.S. 228, 230 (1925) (despite nine years' presence in the United States, an "excluded" alien "was still in theory of law at the boundary line and had gained no foothold in the United States"); *Leng May Ma v. Barber,* 357 U.S. 185, 188-190 (1958) (alien "paroled" into the United States pending admissibility had not effected an "entry"). It is well established that certain constitutional protections available to persons inside the United States are unavailable to aliens outside of our geographic borders. See *United States v. Verdugo-Urquidez,* 494 U.S. 259, 269 (1990) (Fifth Amendment's protections do not extend to aliens outside the territorial boundaries); *Johnson v. Eisentrager,* 339 U.S. 763, 784 (1950) (same). But once an alien enters the country, the legal circumstance changes, for the Due Process Clause applies to all "persons" within the United States, including aliens, whether their presence here is lawful, unlawful, temporary, or permanent. See *Plyler v. Doe,* 457 U.S. 202, 210 (1982); *Mathews v. Diaz,* 426 U.S. 67, 77 (1976); *Kwong Hai Chew v. Colding,* 344 U.S. 590, 596-598, and n.5 (1953); *Yick Wo v. Hopkins,* 118 U.S.

356, 369 (1886); cf. *Mezei, supra,* at 212 ("[A]liens who have once passed through our gates, even illegally, may be expelled only after proceedings conforming to traditional standards of fairness encompassed in due process of law"). Indeed, this Court has held that the Due Process Clause protects an alien subject to a final order of deportation, see *Wong Wing v. United States,* 163 U.S. 228, 238 (1896), though the nature of that protection may vary depending upon status and circumstance, see *Landon v. Plasencia,* 459 U.S. 21, 32-34 (1982); *Johnson, supra,* at 770.

In *Wong Wing, supra,* the Court held unconstitutional a statute that imposed a year of hard labor upon aliens subject to a final deportation order. That case concerned substantive protections for aliens who had been ordered removed, not procedural protections for aliens whose removability was being determined. The Court held that punitive measures could not be imposed upon aliens ordered removed because "all persons within the territory of the United States are entitled to the protection" of the Constitution. 163 U.S., at 238 (citing *Yick Wo, supra,* at 369 (holding that equal protection guarantee applies to Chinese aliens)). And contrary to Justice Scalia's characterization, in *Mezei* itself, both this Court's rejection of Mezei's challenge to the procedures by which he was deemed excludable and its rejection of his challenge to continued detention rested upon a basic territorial distinction.

In light of this critical distinction between *Mezei* and the present cases, *Mezei* does not offer the Government significant support, and we need not consider the aliens' claim that subsequent developments have undermined Mezei's legal authority. Nor are we aware of any other authority that would support Justice Kennedy's limitation of due process protection for removable aliens to freedom from detention that is arbitrary or capricious.

The Government also looks for support to cases holding that Congress has "plenary power" to create immigration law, and that the judicial branch must defer to executive and legislative branch decisionmaking in that area. Brief for Respondents in No. 99-7791, at 17, 20 (citing *Harisiades v. Shaughnessy,* 342 U.S. 580, 588-589 (1952)). But that power is subject to important constitutional limitations. See *INS v. Chadha,* 462 U.S. 919, 941-942 (1983) (Congress must choose "a constitutionally permissible means of implementing" that power); *The Chinese Exclusion Case,* 130 U.S. 581, 604 (1889) (congressional authority limited "by the Constitution itself and considerations of public policy and justice which control, more or less, the conduct of all civilized nations"). In these cases, we focus upon those limitations. In doing so, we nowhere deny the right of Congress to remove aliens, to subject them to supervision with conditions when released from detention, or to incarcerate them where appropriate for violations of those conditions. The question before us is not one of "'confer[ring] on those admitted the right to remain against the national will'" or "'sufferance of aliens'" who should be removed. Rather, the issue we address is whether aliens that the Government finds itself unable to remove are to be condemned to an indefinite term of imprisonment within the United States.

Nor do the cases before us require us to consider the political branches' authority to control entry into the United States. Hence we leave no "unprotected spot in the Nation's armor." *Kwong Hai Chew, supra,* at 602.

Neither do we consider terrorism or other special circumstances where special arguments might be made for forms of preventive detention and for heightened deference to the judgments of the political branches with respect to matters of national security. The sole foreign policy consideration the Government mentions here is the concern lest courts interfere with "sensitive" repatriation negotiations. But neither the Government nor the dissents explain how a habeas court's efforts to determine the likelihood of repatriation, if handled with appropriate sensitivity, could make a significant difference in this respect.

Finally, the Government argues that, whatever liberty interest the aliens possess, it is "greatly diminished" by their lack of a legal right to "liv[e] at large in this country." The choice, however, is not between imprisonment and the alien "living at large." It is between imprisonment and supervision under release conditions that may not be violated. And, for the reasons we have set forth, we believe that an alien's liberty interest is, at the least, strong enough to raise a serious question as to whether, irrespective of the procedures used, the Constitution permits detention that is indefinite and potentially permanent.

B

Despite this constitutional problem, if "Congress has made its intent" in the statute "clear, 'we must give effect to that intent.'" *Miller v. French*, 530 U.S. 327, 336 (2000) (quoting *Sinclair Refining Co. v. Atkinson*, 370 U.S. 195, 215 (1962)). We cannot find here, however, any clear indication of congressional intent to grant the Attorney General the power to hold indefinitely in confinement an alien ordered removed. And that is so whether protecting the community from dangerous aliens is a primary or (as we believe) secondary statutory purpose. After all, the provision is part of a statute that has as its basic purpose effectuating an alien's removal. Why should we assume that Congress saw the alien's dangerousness as unrelated to this purpose?

The Government points to the statute's word "may." But while "may" suggests discretion, it does not necessarily suggest unlimited discretion. In that respect the word "may" is ambiguous. Indeed, if Congress had meant to authorize long-term detention of unremovable aliens, it certainly could have spoken in clearer terms. Compare INA § 507(b)(2)(C) ("If no country is willing to receive" a terrorist alien ordered removed, "the Attorney General may, notwithstanding any other provision of law, retain the alien in custody" and must review the detention determination every six months).

The Government points to similar related statutes that *require* detention of criminal aliens during removal proceedings and the removal period, and argues that these show that mandatory detention is the rule while discretionary release is the narrow exception. But the statute before us applies not only to terrorists and criminals, but also to ordinary visa violators; and, more importantly, post-removal-period detention, unlike detention pending a determination of removability or during the subsequent 90-day removal period, has no obvious termination point.

* * *

We have found nothing in the history of these statutes [that are precursors of § 241(a)(6)] that clearly demonstrates a congressional intent to authorize indefinite, perhaps permanent, detention. Consequently, interpreting the statute to avoid a serious constitutional threat, we conclude that, once removal is no longer reasonably foreseeable, continued detention is no longer authorized by statute. See 1 E. Coke, Institutes *70b ("*Cessante ratione legis cessat ipse lex*") (the rationale of a legal rule no longer being applicable, that rule itself no longer applies).

IV

The Government seems to argue that, even under our interpretation of the statute, a federal habeas court would have to accept the Government's view about whether the implicit statutory limitation is satisfied in a particular case, conducting little or no independent review of the matter. In our view, that is not so. Whether a set of particular circumstances amounts to detention within, or beyond, a period reasonably necessary to secure removal is determinative of whether the detention is, or is not, pursuant to statutory authority. The basic federal habeas corpus statute grants the federal courts authority to answer that question. See 28 U.S.C. § 2241(c)(3) (granting courts authority to determine whether detention is "in violation of the . . . laws . . . of the United States"). In doing so the courts carry out what this Court has described as the "historic purpose of the writ," namely "to relieve detention by executive authorities without judicial trial." *Brown v. Allen*, 344 U.S. 443, 533 (1953) (Jackson, J., concurring in result).

In answering that basic question, the habeas court must ask whether the detention in question exceeds a period reasonably necessary to secure removal. It should measure reasonableness primarily in terms of the statute's basic purpose, namely assuring the alien's presence at the moment of removal. Thus, if removal is not reasonably foreseeable, the court should hold continued detention unreasonable and no longer authorized by statute. In that case, of course, the alien's release may and should be conditioned on any of the various forms of supervised release that are appropriate in the circumstances, and the alien may no doubt be returned to custody upon a violation of those conditions. And if removal is reasonably foreseeable, the habeas court should consider the risk of the alien's committing further crimes as a factor potentially justifying confinement within that reasonable removal period.

We recognize, as the Government points out, that review must take appropriate account of the greater immigration-related expertise of the Executive Branch, of the serious administrative needs and concerns inherent in the necessarily extensive INS efforts to enforce this complex statute, and the Nation's need to "speak with one voice" in immigration matters. But we believe that courts can take appropriate account of such matters without abdicating their legal responsibility to review the lawfulness of an alien's continued detention.

Ordinary principles of judicial review in this area recognize primary Executive Branch responsibility. They counsel judges to give expert agencies decisionmaking leeway in matters that invoke their expertise. See *Pension Benefit Guaranty Corporation v. LTV Corp.*, 496 U.S. 633, 651-652 (1990). They recognize Executive Branch primacy in foreign policy matters. See *Container Corp. of America v. Franchise Tax Bd.*, 463 U.S. 159, 196 (1983).

And they consequently require courts to listen with care when the Government's foreign policy judgments, including, for example, the status of repatriation negotiations, are at issue, and to grant the Government appropriate leeway when its judgments rest upon foreign policy expertise.

We realize that recognizing this necessary Executive leeway will often call for difficult judgments. In order to limit the occasions when courts will need to make them, we think it practically necessary to recognize some presumptively reasonable period of detention. We have adopted similar presumptions in other contexts to guide lower court determinations. See *Cheff v. Schnackenberg*, 384 U.S. 373, 379-380 (1966) (plurality opinion) (adopting rule, based on definition of "petty offense" in United States Code, that right to jury trial extends to all cases in which sentence of six months or greater is imposed); *County of Riverside v. McLaughlin*, 500 U.S. 44, 56-58 (1991) (O'Connor, J.) (adopting presumption, based on lower court estimate of time needed to process arrestee, that 48-hour delay in probable cause hearing after arrest is reasonable, hence constitutionally permissible).

While an argument can be made for confining any presumption to 90 days, we doubt that when Congress shortened the removal period to 90 days in 1996 it believed that all reasonably foreseeable removals could be accomplished in that time. We do have reason to believe, however, that Congress previously doubted the constitutionality of detention for more than six months. See Juris. Statement of United States in *United States v. Witkovich*, O. T. 1956, No. 295, pp. 8-9. Consequently, for the sake of uniform administration in the federal courts, we recognize that period. After this 6-month period, once the alien provides good reason to believe that there is no significant likelihood of removal in the reasonably foreseeable future, the Government must respond with evidence sufficient to rebut that showing. And for detention to remain reasonable, as the period of prior post-removal confinement grows, what counts as the "reasonably foreseeable future" conversely would have to shrink. This 6-month presumption, of course, does not mean that every alien not removed must be released after six months. To the contrary, an alien may be held in confinement until it has been determined that there is no significant likelihood of removal in the reasonably foreseeable future.

V

The Fifth Circuit held Zadvydas' continued detention lawful as long as "good faith efforts to effectuate . . . deportation continue" and Zadvydas failed to show that deportation will prove "impossible." 185 F.3d, at 294, 297. But this standard would seem to require an alien seeking release to show the absence of *any* prospect of removal—no matter how unlikely or unforeseeable—which demands more than our reading of the statute can bear. The Ninth Circuit held that the Government was required to release Ma from detention because there was no reasonable likelihood of his removal in the foreseeable future. 208 F.3d, at 831. But its conclusion may have rested solely upon the "absence" of an "extant or pending" repatriation agreement without giving due weight to the likelihood of successful future negotiations. See *id.*, at 831, and n.30.

Consequently, we vacate the decisions below and remand both cases for further proceedings consistent with this opinion.

It is so ordered.

JUSTICE SCALIA, with whom JUSTICE THOMAS joins, dissenting.

I join Part I of Justice Kennedy's dissent, which establishes the Attorney General's clear statutory authority to detain criminal aliens with no specified time limit. I write separately because I do not believe that, as Justice Kennedy suggests in Part II of his opinion, there may be some situations in which the courts can order release. I believe that * * * a "careful description" of the substantive right claimed, *Reno v. Flores*, 507 U.S. 292, 302 (1993), suffices categorically to refute its existence. A criminal alien under final order of removal who allegedly will not be accepted by any other country in the reasonably foreseeable future claims a constitutional right of supervised release into the United States. This claim can be repackaged as freedom from "physical restraint" or freedom from "indefinite detention," but it is at bottom a claimed right of release into this country by an individual who *concededly* has no legal right to be here. There is no such constitutional right.

Like a criminal alien under final order of removal, an inadmissible alien at the border has no right to be in the United States. *The Chinese Exclusion Case*, 130 U.S. 581, 603 (1889). In *Shaughnessy v. United States ex rel. Mezei*, 345 U.S. 206 (1953), we upheld potentially indefinite detention of such an inadmissible alien whom the Government was unable to return anywhere else. We said that "we [did] not think that respondent's continued exclusion deprives him of any statutory or constitutional right." *Id.*, at 215. While four members of the Court thought that Mezei deserved greater procedural protections (the Attorney General had refused to divulge any information as to why Mezei was being detained, *id.*, at 209), no Justice asserted that Mezei had a substantive constitutional right to release into this country. And Justice Jackson's dissent, joined by Justice Frankfurter, affirmatively asserted the opposite, with no contradiction from the Court: "Due process does not invest any alien with a right to enter the United States, *nor confer on those admitted the right to remain against the national will*. Nothing in the Constitution requires admission *or sufferance* of aliens hostile to our scheme of government." *Id.*, at 222-223 (emphasis added). Insofar as a claimed legal right to release into this country is concerned, an alien under final order of removal stands on an equal footing with an inadmissible alien at the threshold of entry: He has no such right.

The Court expressly declines to apply or overrule *Mezei*, but attempts to distinguish it—or, I should rather say, to obscure it in a legal fog. First, the Court claims that "[t]he distinction between an alien who has effected an entry into the United States and one who has never entered runs throughout immigration law." True enough, but only where that distinction makes perfect sense: with regard to the question of what *procedures* are necessary to prevent entry, as opposed to what *procedures* are necessary to eject a person already in the United States. See, *e.g.*, *Landon v. Plasencia*, 459 U.S. 21, 32 (1982) ("Our cases have frequently suggested that a continuously present resident alien is entitled to a fair hearing *when threatened with deportation*" (emphasis added)). The Court's citation of *Wong Wing v. United States*, 163 U.S. 228 (1896), for the proposition that we have "held that the Due Process Clause protects an alien subject to a final order of deportation," is arguably relevant. That case at least involved aliens under final order of deportation.* But all it held is that they could not be subjected to the punishment of hard labor without a judicial trial. I am sure they cannot be tortured, as well—but neither prohibition has anything to do with their right to be released into the United States. Nor does *Wong Wing* show that the rights of detained aliens subject to final order of deportation are different from the rights of aliens arrested and detained at the border—unless the Court believes that the detained alien in *Mezei could* have been set to hard labor.

Mezei thus stands unexplained and undistinguished by the Court's opinion. We are offered no justification why an alien under a valid and final order of removal—which has *totally extinguished* whatever right to presence in this country he possessed—has any greater due process right to be released into the country than an alien at the border seeking entry. Congress undoubtedly thought that both groups of aliens—inadmissible aliens at the threshold and criminal aliens under final order of removal—could be constitutionally detained on the same terms, since it provided the authority to detain both groups in the very same statutory provision, see INA § 241(a)(6). Because I believe *Mezei* controls these cases, and, like the Court, I also see no reason to reconsider *Mezei*, I find no constitutional impediment to the discretion Congress gave to the Attorney General. Justice Kennedy's dissent explains the clarity of the detention provision, and I see no obstacle to following the statute's plain meaning.

JUSTICE KENNEDY, with whom THE CHIEF JUSTICE joins, and with whom JUSTICE SCALIA and JUSTICE THOMAS join as to Part I, dissenting.

The Court says its duty is to avoid a constitutional question. It deems the duty performed by interpreting a statute in obvious disregard of congressional intent; curing the resulting gap by writing a statutory amendment of its own; committing its own grave constitutional error by arrogating to the Judicial Branch the power to summon high officers of the Executive to assess their progress in conducting some of the Nation's most sensitive negotiations with foreign powers; and then likely releasing into our general population at least hundreds of removable or inadmissible aliens who have been found by fair procedures to be flight risks, dangers to the community, or both. Far from avoiding a constitutional question, the Court's ruling causes systemic dislocation in the balance of powers, thus raising serious constitutional concerns not just for the cases at hand but for the Court's own view of its proper authority. Any supposed respect the Court seeks in not reaching the constitutional question is outweighed by the intrusive and erroneous exercise of its own powers. In the guise of judicial restraint the Court ought not to intrude upon the other branches. The constitutional question the statute presents, it must be acknowledged, may be a significant one in some later case; but it ought not to drive us to an incorrect

---

* The Court also cites *Landon v. Plasencia*, 459 U.S. 21 (1982), as oblique support for the claim that the due process protection afforded aliens under final order of removal "may vary depending upon status and circumstance." But that case is entirely inapt because it did not involve an alien subject to a final order of deportation. * * *

interpretation of the statute. The Court having reached the wrong result for the wrong reason, this respectful dissent is required.

I

* * *

By [INA § 241(a)(6)], Congress confers upon the Attorney General discretion to detain an alien ordered removed. It gives express authorization to detain "beyond the removal period." The class of removed aliens detainable under the section includes aliens who were inadmissible and aliens subject to final orders of removal, provided they are a risk to the community or likely to flee. The issue to be determined is whether the authorization to detain beyond the removal period is subject to the implied, nontextual limitation that the detention be no longer than reasonably necessary to effect removal to another country. The majority invokes the canon of constitutional doubt to read that implied term into the statute. One can accept the premise that a substantial constitutional question is presented by the prospect of lengthy, even unending, detention in some instances; but the statutory construction the Court adopts should be rejected in any event. The interpretation has no basis in the language or structure of the INA and in fact contradicts and defeats the purpose set forth in the express terms of the statutory text.

The Court, it is submitted, misunderstands the principle of constitutional avoidance which it seeks to invoke. The majority gives a brief bow to the rule that courts must respect the intention of Congress, *ante*, at 16, but then waltzes away from any analysis of the language, structure, or purpose of the statute. Its analysis is not consistent with our precedents explaining the limits of the constitutional doubt rule. The rule allows courts to choose among constructions which are "fairly possible," *Crowell v. Benson*, 285 U.S. 22, 62 (1932), not to "'press statutory construction to the point of disingenuous evasion even to avoid a constitutional question,'" *Salinas v. United States*, 522 U.S. 52, 60 (1997) (quoting *Seminole Tribe of Fla. v. Florida*, 517 U.S. 44, 57, n.9 (1996)). Were a court to find two interpretations of equal plausibility, it should choose the construction that avoids confronting a constitutional question. The majority's reading of the statutory authorization to "detai[n] beyond the removal period," however, is not plausible. An interpretation which defeats the stated congressional purpose does not suffice to invoke the constitutional doubt rule, for it is "plainly contrary to the intent of Congress." *United States v. X-Citement Video, Inc.*, 513 U.S. 64, 78 (1994). The majority announces it will reject the Government's argument "that the statute means what it literally says," but then declines to offer any other acceptable textual interpretation. The majority does not demonstrate an ambiguity in the delegation of the detention power to the Attorney General. It simply amends the statute to impose a time limit tied to the progress of negotiations to effect the aliens' removal. The statute cannot be so construed. The requirement the majority reads into the law simply bears no relation to the text; and in fact it defeats the statutory purpose and design.

Other provisions in § 241 itself do link the requirement of a reasonable time period to the removal process [citing §§ 241(c)(1)(A), § 241(c)(3)(A)(ii)(II)]. That Congress chose to impose the limitation in these sections and not in § 241(a)(6) is evidence of its intent to measure the detention period by other standards. When Congress has made express provisions for the contingency that repatriation might be difficult or prolonged in other portions of the statute, it should be presumed that its omission of the same contingency in the detention section was purposeful. * * *

The 6-month period invented by the Court, even when modified by its sliding standard of reasonableness for certain repatriation negotiations, makes the statutory purpose to protect the community ineffective. The risk to the community exists whether or not the repatriation negotiations have some end in sight; in fact, when the negotiations end, the risk may be greater. The authority to detain beyond the removal period is to protect the community, not to negotiate the aliens' return. The risk to the community survives repatriation negotiations. To a more limited, but still significant, extent, so does the concern with flight. It is a fact of international diplomacy that governments and their policies change; and if repatriation efforts can be revived, the Attorney General has an interest in ensuring the alien can report so the removal process can begin again.

* * * The risk to the community posed by a removable alien is a function of a variety of circumstances, circumstances that do not diminish just because the alien cannot be deported within some foreseeable time. Those circumstances include the seriousness of the alien's past offenses, his or her efforts at rehabilitation, and some indication from the alien that, given the real prospect of detention, the alien will conform his or her conduct. This is the purpose for the periodic review of detention status provided for by the regulations. The Court's amendment of the statute reads out of the provision the congressional decision that dangerousness alone is a sufficient basis for detention, and reads out as well any meaningful structure for supervised release.

* * *

The majority's unanchored interpretation ignores another indication that the Attorney General's detention discretion was not limited to this truncated period. Section 241(a)(6) permits continued detention not only of removable aliens but also of inadmissible aliens, for instance those stopped at the border before entry. Congress provides for detention of both categories within the same statutory grant of authority. Accepting the majority's interpretation, then, there are two possibilities, neither of which is sustainable. On the one hand, it may be that the majority's rule applies to both categories of aliens, in which case we are asked to assume that Congress intended to restrict the discretion it could confer upon the Attorney General so that all inadmissible aliens must be allowed into our community within six months. On the other hand, the majority's logic might be that inadmissible and removable aliens can be treated differently. Yet it is not a plausible construction of § 241(a)(6) to imply a time limit as to one class but not to another. The text does not admit of this possibility. As a result, it is difficult to see why "[a]liens who have not yet gained initial admission to this country would present a very different question."

Congress' power to detain aliens in connection with removal or exclusion, the Court has said, is part of the Legislature's considerable authority over immigration matters. See, *e.g., Wong Wing v. United States*, 163 U.S. 228, 235 (1896) ("Proceedings to exclude or expel would be vain if those accused could not be held in custody pending the inquiry into their true character, and while arrangements were being made for their deportation"). It is reasonable to assume, then, and it is the proper interpretation of the INA and § 241(a)(6), that when Congress provided for detention "beyond the removal period," it exercised its considerable power over immigration and delegated to the Attorney General the discretion to detain inadmissible and other removable aliens for as long as they are determined to be either a flight risk or a danger to the Nation.

The majority's interpretation, moreover, defeats the very repatriation goal in which it professes such interest. The Court rushes to substitute a judicial judgment for the Executive's discretion and authority. As the Government represents to us, judicial orders requiring release of removable aliens, even on a temporary basis, have the potential to undermine the obvious necessity that the Nation speak with one voice on immigration and foreign affairs matters. The result of the Court's rule is that, by refusing to accept repatriation of their own nationals, other countries can effect the release of these individuals back into the American community. If their own nationals are now at large in the United States, the nation of origin may ignore or disclaim responsibility to accept their return. The interference with sensitive foreign relations becomes even more acute where hostility or tension characterizes the relationship, for other countries can use the fact of judicially mandated release to their strategic advantage, refusing the return of their nationals to force dangerous aliens upon us. One of the more alarming aspects of the Court's new venture into foreign affairs management is the suggestion that the district court can expand or contract the reasonable period of detention based on its own assessment of the course of negotiations with foreign powers. The Court says it will allow the Executive to perform its duties on its own for six months; after that, foreign relations go into judicially supervised receivership.

* * *

In addition to weakening the hand of our Government, court ordered release cannot help but encourage dilatory and obstructive tactics by aliens who, emboldened by the Court's new rule, have good reason not to cooperate by making their own repatriation or transfer seem foreseeable. An alien ordered deported also has less incentive to cooperate or to facilitate expeditious removal when he has been released, even on a supervised basis, than does an alien held at an Immigration and Naturalization Service (INS) detention facility. Neither the alien nor his family would find any urgency in assisting with a petition to other countries to accept the alien back if the alien could simply remain in the United States indefinitely.

The risk to the community posed by the mandatory release of aliens who are dangerous or a flight risk is far from insubstantial; the motivation to protect the citizenry from aliens determined to be dangerous is central to the immigration power itself. The Government cites statistical studies showing high recidivism rates for released aliens. One Government Accounting Office study cited by Congress in floor debates on the Antiterrorism and Effective Death Penalty Act of 1996, 110 Stat. 1214, put the figure as high as 77 percent. 142 Cong. Rec. 7972 (1996); Brief for Respondents in No. 99-7791, at 27, n.13. It seems evident a criminal record accumulated by an admitted alien during his or her time in the United States is likely to be a better indicator of risk than factors relied upon during the INS's initial decision to admit or exclude. Aliens ordered deported as the result of having committed a felony have proved to be dangerous.

Any suggestion that aliens who have completed prison terms no longer present a danger simply does not accord with the reality that a significant risk may still exist, as determined by the many factors set forth in the regulations. See 8 CFR § 241.4(f) (2001). Underworld and terrorist links are subtle and may be overseas, beyond our jurisdiction to impose felony charges. Furthermore, the majority's rationale seems to apply to an alien who flees prosecution or escapes from custody in some other country. The fact an alien can be deemed inadmissible because of fraud at the time of entry does not necessarily distinguish his or her case from an alien whose entry was legal. Consider, for example, a fugitive alien who enters by fraud or stealth and resides here for five years with significant ties to the community, though still presenting a danger; contrast him with an alien who entered lawfully but a month later committed an act making him removable. Why the Court's rationale should apply to the second alien but not the first is not apparent.

The majority cannot come to terms with these distinctions under its own rationale. The rule the majority creates permits consideration of nothing more than the reasonable foreseeability of removal. That standard is not only without sound basis in the statutory structure, but also is not susceptible to customary judicial inquiry. * * *

This rule of startling breadth invites potentially perverse results. Because other nations may refuse to admit aliens who have committed certain crimes often the aliens who have committed the most serious crimes will be those who may be released immediately under the majority's rule. * * * Today's result will ensure these dangerous individuals, and hundreds more like them, will remain free while the Executive Branch tries to secure their removal. By contrast, aliens who violate mere tourist visa requirements, can in the typical case be held pending deportation on grounds that a minor offender is more likely to be removed. There is no reason to suppose Congress intended this odd result.

The majority's rule is not limited to aliens once lawfully admitted. Today's result may well mandate the release of those aliens who first gained entry illegally or by fraud, and, indeed, is broad enough to require even that inadmissible and excludable aliens detained at the border be set free in our community. In *Rosales-Garcia v. Holland*, 238 F.3d 704, 725 (CA6 2001), for example, Rosales, a Cuban citizen, arrived in this country during the 1980 Mariel boatlift. Upon arrival in the United States, Rosales was released into the custody of a relative under the Attorney General's authority to parole illegal aliens, see INA § 212(d)(5)(A), and there he committed multiple crimes for which he was convicted and imprisoned. While serving a sentence for burglary and grand larceny, Rosales escaped from prison, another of the offenses for which he ultimately served time. The INS eventually revoked Rosales' immigration parole, ordered him deported, and held him pending deportation, subject to periodic consideration for parole under the Cuban Review Plan. In reasoning remarkably similar to the majority's, the Court of Appeals for the Sixth Circuit held that the indefinite detention of Rosales violated Fifth

Amendment due process rights, because "the government offered . . . no credible proof that there is any possibility that Cuba may accept Rosales's return anytime in the foreseeable future." 238 F.3d, at 725. This result—that Mariel Cubans and other illegal, inadmissible aliens will be released notwithstanding their criminal history and obvious flight risk—would seem a necessary consequence of the majority's construction of the statute.

* * *

It is curious that the majority would approve of continued detention beyond the 90-day period, or, for that matter, during the 90-day period, where deportation is not reasonably foreseeable. If the INS cannot detain an alien because he is dangerous, it would seem irrelevant to the Constitution or to the majority's presumption that the INS has detained the alien for only a little while. The reason detention is permitted at all is that a removable alien does not have the same liberty interest as a citizen does. The Court cannot bring itself to acknowledge this established proposition. Likewise, it is far from evident under the majority's theory why the INS can condition and supervise the release of aliens who are not removable in the reasonably foreseeable future, or why "the alien may no doubt be returned to custody upon a violation of those conditions." It is true that threat of revocation of supervised release is necessary to make the supervised release itself effective, a fact even counsel for Zadvydas acknowledged. If that is so, however, the whole foundation for the Court's position collapses.

* * *

II

The aliens' claims are substantial; their plight is real. They face continued detention, perhaps for life, unless it is shown they no longer present a flight risk or a danger to the community. In a later case the specific circumstances of a detention may present a substantial constitutional question. That is not a reason, however, for framing a rule which ignores the law governing alien status.

As persons within our jurisdiction, the aliens are entitled to the protection of the Due Process Clause. Liberty under the Due Process Clause includes protection against unlawful or arbitrary personal restraint or detention. The liberty rights of the aliens before us here are subject to limitations and conditions not applicable to citizens, however. See, *e.g., Mathews v. Diaz*, 426 U.S. 67, 79-80 (1976) ("In the exercise of its broad power over naturalization and immigration, Congress regularly makes rules that would be unacceptable if applied to citizens"). No party to this proceeding contests the initial premise that the aliens have been determined to be removable after a fair hearing under lawful and proper procedures. Section 240 sets forth the proceedings required for deciding the inadmissibility or removability of an alien, including a hearing before an immigration judge, at which the INS carries "the burden of establishing by clear and convincing evidence that . . . the alien is deportable." INA § 240(c)(3)(A). Aliens ordered removed pursuant to these procedures are given notice of their right to appeal the decision, INA § 240(c)(4), may move the immigration judge to reconsider, § 240(c)(5), can seek discretionary cancellation of removal, § 240A, and can obtain habeas review of the Attorney General's decision not to consider waiver of deportation. As a result, aliens like Zadvydas and Ma do not arrive at their removable status without thorough, substantial procedural safeguards.

The majority likely is correct to say that the distinction between an alien who entered the United States, as these aliens did, and one who has not, "runs throughout immigration law." The distinction is not so clear as it might seem, however, and I doubt it will suffice to confine the rationale adopted by the majority. The case which often comes to mind when one tests the distinction is *Shaughnessy v. United States ex rel. Mezei*, 345 U.S. 206 (1953), where the Court considered the situation of an alien denied entry and detained on Ellis Island. The detention had no foreseeable end, for though Mezei was inadmissible to the United States it seemed no other country would have him. The case presented a line-drawing problem, asking whether the alien was in our country; or whether his situation was the same as if he were still on foreign shores; or whether he fell in a legal category somewhere in between, though if this were true, it still would not be clear how to resolve the case. The Court held the alien had no right to a hearing to secure his release. (Approximately 17 months after this Court denied Mezei relief, the Attorney General released him on parole. It appears Mezei never returned to INS custody, though he was not admitted to the United States as a citizen or lawful permanent resident. See Weisselberg, The Exclusion and Detention of Aliens: Lessons From the Lives of Ellen Knauff and Ignatz Mezei, 143 U. Pa. L. Rev. 933, 979-984 (1995)).

Here the majority says the earlier presence of these aliens in the United States distinguishes the cases from *Mezei*. For reasons given here it is submitted the majority is incorrect in its major conclusions in all events, so even if it were assumed these aliens are in a class with more rights than *Mezei*, it makes no difference. For purposes of this dissent it is not necessary to rely upon *Mezei*.

That said, it must be made clear these aliens are in a position far different from aliens with a lawful right to remain here. They are removable, and their rights must be defined in accordance with that status. The due process analysis must begin with a "careful description of the asserted right." *Reno v. Flores*, 507 U.S. 292, 302 (1993). We have "long held that an alien seeking initial admission to the United States requests a privilege and has no constitutional rights regarding his application, for the power to admit or exclude aliens is a sovereign prerogative." *Landon v. Plasencia*, 459 U.S. 21, 32 (1982). The same is true for those aliens like Zadvydas and Ma, who face a final order of removal. When an alien is removable, he or she has no right under the basic immigration laws to remain in this country. The removal orders reflect the determination that the aliens' ties to this community are insufficient to justify their continued presence in the United States. An alien's admission to this country is conditioned upon compliance with our laws, and removal is the consequence of a breach of that understanding.

It is true the Court has accorded more procedural protections to those aliens admitted to the country than those stopped at the border, observing that "a continuously present alien is entitled to a fair hearing when threatened with deportation." *Ibid.*; *Mezei, supra*, at 212 ("[A]liens who have once passed through our gates, even illegally, may be expelled only after proceedings conforming to traditional standards of fairness encompassed in due process of law . . . . But an alien on the threshold of initial entry stands on a different footing: 'Whatever the procedure authorized by Congress is, it is due process as far as an alien denied entry is concerned'" (quoting *United States ex rel. Knauff v. Shaughnessy*, 338 U.S. 537, 544 (1950))). Removable and excludable aliens are situated differently before an order of removal is entered; the removable alien, by virtue of his continued presence here, possesses an interest in remaining, while the excludable alien seeks only the privilege of entry.

Still, both removable and inadmissible aliens are entitled to be free from detention that is arbitrary or capricious. Where detention is incident to removal, the detention cannot be justified as punishment nor can the confinement or its conditions be designed in order to punish. See *Wong Wing v. United States*, 163 U.S. 228 (1896). This accords with international views on detention of refugees and asylum seekers. See Report of the United Nations Working Group on Arbitrary Detention, U.N. Doc. E/CN.4/2000/4 (Dec. 28, 1999); United Nations High Commissioner for Refugees, Guidelines on Applicable Criteria and Standards Relating to the Detention on Asylum-Seekers (Feb. 10, 1999). It is neither arbitrary nor capricious to detain the aliens when necessary to avoid the risk of flight or danger to the community.

Whether a due process right is denied when removable aliens who are flight risks or dangers to the community are detained turns, then, not on the substantive right to be free, but on whether there are adequate procedures to review their cases, allowing persons once subject to detention to show that through rehabilitation, new appreciation of their responsibilities, or under other standards, they no longer present special risks or danger if put at large. The procedures to determine and to review the status-required detention go far toward this objective.

By regulations, promulgated after notice and comment, the Attorney General has given structure to the discretion delegated by the INA in order to ensure fairness and regularity in INS detention decisions. [Justice Kennedy described the postcustody review procedures.] * * *

In this context the proper analysis can be informed by our cases involving parole-eligibility or parole-revocation determinations. In *Morrissey v. Brewer*, 408 U.S. 471 (1972), for example, we held some amount of process was due an individual whose parole was revoked, for "the liberty of a parolee, although indeterminate, includes many of the core values of unqualified liberty." *Id.*, at 482; see also *Board of Pardons v. Allen*, 482 U.S. 369 (1987). We rejected in *Morrissey* the suggestion that the State could justify parole revocation "without some informal procedural guarantees," 408 U.S., at 483, but "[g]iven the previous conviction and the proper imposition of conditions," we recognized that "the State has an overwhelming interest in being able to return the individual to imprisonment without the burden of a new adversary criminal trial." *Ibid.* We held the review process need not include a judicial officer or formal court proceeding, but could be conducted by a neutral administrative official.

While the majority expresses some concern that the regulations place the burden on the alien to show he is no longer dangerous, that question could be adjudicated in a later case raising the issue. It should be noted the procedural protection here is real, not illusory; and the criteria for obtaining release are far from insurmountable. Statistics show that between February 1999 and mid-November 2000 some 6,200 aliens were provided custody reviews before expiration of the 90-day removal period, and of those aliens about 3,380 were released. As a result, although the alien carries the burden to prove detention is no longer justified, there is no showing this is an unreasonable burden.

Like the parolee in *Morrissey*, who was aware of the conditions of his release, the aliens in the instant cases have notice, constructive or actual, that the INA imposes as a consequence of the commission of certain crimes not only deportation but also the possibility of continued detention in cases where deportation is not immediately feasible. And like the prisoner in *Board of Pardons v. Allen*, who sought federal-court review of the discretionary decision denying him parole eligibility, removable aliens held pending deportation have a due process liberty right to have the INS conduct the review procedures in place. Were the INS, in an arbitrary or categorical manner, to deny an alien access to the administrative processes in place to review continued detention, habeas jurisdiction would lie to redress the due process violation caused by the denial of the mandated procedures under 8 CFR § 241.4 (2001).

This is not the posture of the instant cases, however. Neither Zadvydas nor Ma argues that the Attorney General has applied the procedures in an improper manner; they challenge only the Attorney General's authority to detain at all where removal is no longer foreseeable. The Government has conceded that habeas jurisdiction is available under 28 U.S.C. § 2241 to review an alien's challenge to detention following entry of a final order of deportation, although it does not detail what the nature of the habeas review would be. As a result, we need not decide today whether, and to what extent, a habeas court could review the Attorney General's determination that a detained alien continues to be dangerous or a flight risk. Given the undeniable deprivation of liberty caused by the detention, there might be substantial questions concerning the severity necessary for there to be a community risk; the adequacy of judicial review in specific cases where it is alleged there is no justification for concluding an alien is dangerous or a flight risk; and other issues. These matters are not presented to us here.

In all events, if judicial review is to be available, the inquiry required by the majority focuses on the wrong factors. Concepts of flight risk or future dangerousness are manageable legal categories. See, *e.g., Kansas v. Hendricks*, 521 U.S. 346 (1997); *Foucha v. Louisiana*, 504 U.S. 71 (1992). The majority instead would have the Judiciary review the status of repatriation negotiations, which, one would have thought, are the paradigmatic examples of nonjusticiable inquiry. The inquiry would require the Executive Branch to surrender its primacy in foreign affairs and submit reports to the courts respecting its ongoing negotiations in the international sphere. High officials of the Department of State could be called on to testify as to the status of these negotiations. The Court finds this to be a more manageable, more appropriate role for the Judiciary than to review a single, discrete case deciding whether there were fair procedures and adequate judicial safeguards to determine whether an alien is dangerous to the community so that long-term detention is justified. The Court's rule is a serious misconception of the proper judicial function, and it is not what Congress enacted.

* * *

Notes

1. How plausible is the Court's reading of the statute (and legislative history)? If you find it unconvincing, what explains the Court's ultimate conclusion?

2. After *Zadvydas*, what is the statutory authority for the prolonged or indefinite detention of excludable aliens such as the Marielitos? Is there no longer any such authority, even though the Court's invocation of the canon to avoid serious constitutional doubt focused only on aliens who had once been admitted to the United States? And what is the statutory authority for the prolonged or indefinite detention of an alien who was initially admitted as a permanent resident, then ordered removed after returning from a trip outside the United States?

3. Justice Breyer's opinion for the Court observes: "The provision authorizing detention does not apply narrowly to 'a small segment of particularly dangerous individuals,' [citing *Hendricks*] say suspected terrorists, but broadly to aliens ordered removed for many and various reasons, including tourist visa violations." Is Justice Breyer suggesting there is an exception to the *Zadvydas* holding for "terrorists"? What would be the basis for this exception?

4. After *Zadvydas*, how robust is *Mezei* as precedent? Does *Zadvydas* endorse *Mezei*? Does *Zadvydas* endorse the basic distinction, based on some definition of the border, between aliens outside and inside the United States?

5. What if any bearing does *Zadvydas* have on the mandatory detention cases, *Parra* and *Kim* (see material for pp. 889-90 *supra*)?

942-57: Habeas Corpus Review (substitute for *Mbiya*, *Mojica*, and Notes 1-4 on 955-57)

INS v. ST. CYR
Supreme Court of the United States, 2001.
121 S.Ct. 2271.

JUSTICE STEVENS delivered the opinion of the Court.

* * *

Respondent, Enrico St. Cyr, is a citizen of Haiti who was admitted to the United States as a lawful permanent resident in 1986. Ten years later, on March 8, 1996, he pled guilty in a state court to a charge of selling a controlled substance in violation of Connecticut law. That conviction made him deportable. Under pre-AEDPA law applicable at the time of his conviction, St. Cyr would have been eligible for a waiver of deportation at the discretion of the Attorney General. However, removal proceedings against him were not commenced until April 10, 1997, after both AEDPA and IIRIRA became effective, and, as the Attorney General interprets those statutes, he no longer has discretion to grant such a waiver.

* * *

I

[The Court summarized the history of former INA § 212(c), which allowed any permanent resident with "a lawful unrelinquished domicile of seven consecutive years" to apply for a discretionary waiver from deportation. If relief was granted, the deportation proceeding was terminated and the alien remained a permanent resident. The Court noted "the class of aliens whose continued residence in this country has depended on their eligibility for § 212(c) relief is extremely large, and not surprisingly, a substantial percentage of their applications for § 212(c) relief have been granted. Consequently, in the period between 1989 and 1995 alone, § 212(c) relief was granted to over 10,000 aliens." The Court further explained that two sets of amendments to the INA in 1996 limited eligibility for § 212(c) relief. (For more on § 212(c) and its successor provision, cancellation of removal in § 240A, see Casebook pp. 771-73.)]

In the Attorney General's opinion, these amendments have entirely withdrawn his § 212(c) authority to waive deportation for aliens previously convicted of aggravated felonies. Moreover, as a result of other amendments adopted in AEDPA and IIRIRA, the Attorney General also maintains that there is no judicial forum available to decide whether these statutes did, in fact, deprive him of the power to grant such relief. As we shall explain below, we disagree on both points. In our view, a federal court does have jurisdiction to decide the merits of the legal question, and the District Court and the Court of Appeals decided that question correctly in this case.

II

The first question we must consider is whether the District Court retains jurisdiction under the general habeas corpus statute, 28 U.S.C. § 2241, to entertain St. Cyr's challenge. His application for a writ raises a pure question of law. He does not dispute any of the facts that establish his deportability or the conclusion that he is deportable. Nor does he contend that he would have any right to have an unfavorable exercise of the Attorney General's discretion reviewed in a judicial forum. Rather, he contests the Attorney General's conclusion that, as a matter of statutory interpretation, he is not eligible for discretionary relief.

The District Court held, and the Court of Appeals agreed, that it had jurisdiction to answer that question in a habeas corpus proceeding. The INS argues, however, that four sections of the 1996 statutes—specifically, § 401(e) of AEDPA and three sections of IIRIRA (INA §§ 242(a)(1), 242(a)(2)(C), and 242(b)(9))—stripped the courts of jurisdiction to decide the question of law presented by respondent's habeas corpus application.

For the INS to prevail it must overcome both the strong presumption in favor of judicial review of administrative action and the longstanding rule requiring a clear statement of congressional intent to repeal habeas jurisdiction. See *Ex parte Yerger*, 8 Wall. 85, 102 (1869) ("We are not at liberty to except from [habeas corpus jurisdiction] any cases not plainly excepted by law"); *Felker v. Turpin*, 518 U.S. 651, 660-661 (1996) (noting that "[n]o provision of Title I mentions our authority to entertain original habeas petitions," and the statute "makes no mention of our authority to hear habeas petitions filed as original matters in this Court"). Implications from statutory text or legislative history are not sufficient to repeal habeas jurisdiction; instead, Congress must articulate specific and unambiguous statutory directives to effect a repeal.

In this case, the plain statement rule draws additional reinforcement from other canons of statutory construction. First, as a general matter, when a particular interpretation of a statute invokes the outer limits of Congress' power, we expect a clear indication that Congress intended that result. See *Edward J. DeBartolo Corp. v. Florida Gulf Coast Building & Constr. Trades Council*, 485 U.S. 568, 575 (1988). Second, if an otherwise acceptable construction of a statute would raise serious constitutional problems, and where an alternative interpretation of the statute is "fairly possible," see *Crowell v. Benson*, 285 U.S. 22, 62 (1932), we are obligated to construe the statute to avoid such problems.

A construction of the amendments at issue that would entirely preclude review of a pure question of law by any court would give rise to substantial constitutional questions. Article I, § 9, cl. 2, of the Constitution provides: "The Privilege of the Writ of Habeas Corpus shall not be suspended, unless when in Cases of Rebellion or Invasion the public Safety may require it." Because of that Clause, some "judicial intervention in deportation cases" is unquestionably "required by the Constitution." *Heikkila v. Barber*, 345 U.S. 229, 235 (1953).

Unlike the provisions of AEDPA that we construed in *Felker v. Turpin*, 518 U.S. 651 (1996), this case involves an alien subject to a federal removal order rather than a person confined pursuant to a state-court conviction. Accordingly, regardless of whether the protection of the Suspension Clause encompasses all cases covered by the 1867 Amendment extending the protection of the writ to state prisoners, cf. *id.*, at 663-664, or by subsequent legal developments, at the absolute minimum, the Suspension Clause protects the writ "as it existed in 1789."

At its historical core, the writ of habeas corpus has served as a means of reviewing the legality of executive detention, and it is in that context that its protections have been strongest. In England prior to 1789, in the Colonies, and in this Nation during the formative years of our Government, the writ of habeas corpus was available to nonenemy aliens as well as to citizens. It enabled them to challenge executive and private detention in civil cases as well as criminal. Moreover, the issuance of the writ was not limited to challenges to the jurisdiction of the custodian, but encompassed detentions based on errors of law, including the erroneous application or interpretation of statutes. It was used to command the discharge of seamen who had a statutory exemption from impressment into the British Navy, to emancipate slaves, and to obtain the freedom of apprentices and asylum inmates. Most important, for our purposes, those early cases contain no suggestion that habeas relief in cases involving executive detention was only available for constitutional error.

Notwithstanding the historical use of habeas corpus to remedy unlawful executive action, the INS argues that this case falls outside the traditional scope of the writ at common law. It acknowledges that the writ protected an individual who was held without legal authority, but argues that the writ would not issue where "an official had statutory authorization to detain the individual but . . . the official was not properly exercising his discretionary power to determine whether the individual should be released." In this case, the INS points out, there is no dispute that the INS had authority in law to hold St. Cyr, as he is eligible for removal. St. Cyr counters that there is historical evidence of the writ issuing to redress the improper exercise of official discretion.

St. Cyr's constitutional position also finds some support in our prior immigration cases. In *Heikkila v. Barber*, the Court observed that the then-existing statutory immigration scheme "had the effect of precluding judicial intervention in deportation cases *except insofar as it was required by the Constitution*," 345 U.S., at 234-235 (emphasis added)—and that scheme, as discussed below, did allow for review on habeas of questions of law concerning an alien's eligibility for discretionary relief. Therefore, while the INS' historical arguments are not insubstantial, the ambiguities in the scope of the exercise of the writ at common law identified by St. Cyr, and the suggestions in this Court's prior decisions as to the extent to which habeas review could be limited consistent with the Constitution, convince us that the Suspension Clause questions that would be presented by the INS' reading of the immigration statutes before us are difficult and significant.

In sum, even assuming that the Suspension Clause protects only the writ as it existed in 1789, there is substantial evidence to support the proposition that pure questions of law like the one raised by the respondent in this case could have been answered in 1789 by a common law judge with power to issue the writ of habeas corpus. It necessarily follows that a serious Suspension Clause issue would be presented if we were to accept the INS's submission that the 1996 statutes have withdrawn that power from federal judges and provided no adequate substitute for its exercise. See Hart, The Power of Congress to Limit the Jurisdiction of Federal Courts: An Exercise in Dialectic, 66 Harv. L. Rev. 1362, 1395-1397 (1953). The necessity of resolving such a serious and difficult constitutional issue—and the desirability of avoiding that necessity—simply reinforce the reasons for requiring a clear and unambiguous statement of constitutional intent.

Moreover, to conclude that the writ is no longer available in this context would represent a departure from historical practice in immigration law. The writ of habeas corpus has always been available to review the legality of executive detention. Federal courts have been authorized to issue writs of habeas corpus since the enactment of the Judiciary Act of 1789, and § 2241 of the Judicial Code provides that federal judges may grant the writ of habeas corpus on the application of a prisoner held "in custody in violation of the Constitution or laws or treaties of the United States." 28 U.S.C. § 2241. Before and after the enactment in 1875 of the first statute regulating immigration, that jurisdiction was regularly invoked on behalf of noncitizens, particularly in the immigration context.

Until the enactment of the 1952 Immigration and Nationality Act, the sole means by which an alien could test the legality of his or her deportation order was by bringing a habeas corpus action in district court. In such cases, other than the question whether there was some evidence to support the order, the courts generally did not review factual determinations made by the Executive.

See *Ekiu v. United States*, 142 U.S. 651, 659 (1892). However, they did review the Executive's legal determinations. See *Gegiow v. Uhl*, 239 U.S. 3, 9 (1915) ("The statute by enumerating the conditions upon which the allowance to land may be denied, prohibits the denial in other cases. And when the record shows that a commissioner of immigration is exceeding his power, the alien may demand his release upon *habeas corpus*"); see also Neuman, Jurisdiction and the Rule of Law after the 1996 Immigration Act, 113 Harv. L. Rev. 1963, 1965-1969 (2000). In case after case, courts answered questions of law in habeas corpus proceedings brought by aliens challenging Executive interpretations of the immigration laws.

Habeas courts also regularly answered questions of law that arose in the context of discretionary relief. See, *e.g., United States ex rel. Accardi v. Shaughnessy*, 347 U.S. 260 (1954); *United States ex rel. Hintopoulos v. Shaughnessy*, 353 U.S. 72, 77 (1957). Traditionally, courts recognized a distinction between eligibility for discretionary relief, on the one hand, and the favorable exercise of discretion, on the other hand. See Neuman, 113 Harv. L. Rev., at 1991 (noting the "strong tradition in habeas corpus law . . . that subjects the legally erroneous failure to exercise discretion, unlike a substantively unwise exercise of discretion, to inquiry on the writ"). Eligibility that was "governed by specific statutory standards" provided "a right to a ruling on an applicant's eligibility," even though the actual granting of relief was "not a matter of right under any circumstances, but rather is in all cases a matter of grace." *Jay v. Boyd*, 351 U.S. 345, 353-354 (1956). Thus, even though the actual suspension of deportation authorized by § 19(c) of the Immigration Act of 1917 was a matter of grace, in *United States ex rel. Accardi v. Shaughnessy*, 347 U.S. 260 (1954), we held that a deportable alien had a right to challenge the Executive's failure to exercise the discretion authorized by the law. The exercise of the District Court's habeas corpus jurisdiction to answer a pure question of law in this case is entirely consistent with the exercise of such jurisdiction in *Accardi*.

Thus, under the pre-1996 statutory scheme—and consistent with its common-law antecedents—it is clear that St. Cyr could have brought his challenge to the Board of Immigration Appeals' legal determination in a habeas corpus petition under 28 U.S.C. § 2241. The INS argues, however, that AEDPA and IIRIRA contain four provisions that express a clear and unambiguous statement of Congress' intent to bar petitions brought under § 2241, despite the fact that none of them mention that section. The first of those provisions is AEDPA's § 401(e).

While the title of § 401(e)—"ELIMINATION OF CUSTODY REVIEW BY HABEAS CORPUS"—would seem to support the INS' submission, the actual text of that provision does not. As we have previously noted, a title alone is not controlling. The actual text of § 401(e), unlike its title, merely repeals a subsection of the 1961 statute amending the judicial review provisions of the 1952 Immigration and Nationality Act. Neither the title nor the text makes any mention of 28 U.S.C. § 2241.

* * *

The INS also relies on three provisions of IIRIRA, now codified at INA §§ 242(a)(1), 242(a)(2)(C), and 242(b)(9). As amended by § 306 of IIRIRA,

INA § 242(a)(1) now provides that, with certain exceptions, including those set out in subsection (b) of the same statutory provision, "[j]udicial review of a final order of removal . . . is governed only by" the Hobbs Act's procedures for review of agency orders in the courts of appeals. Similarly, § 242(b)(9), which addresses the "[c]onsolidation of questions for judicial review," provides that "[j]udicial review of all questions of law and fact, including interpretation and application of constitutional and statutory provisions, arising from any action taken or proceeding brought to remove an alien from the United States under this subchapter shall be available only in judicial review of a final order under this section." Finally, § 242(a)(2)(C), which concerns "[m]atters not subject to judicial review," states: "Notwithstanding any other provision of law, no court shall have jurisdiction to review any final order of removal against an alien who is removable by reason of having committed" certain enumerated criminal offenses.

The term "judicial review" or "jurisdiction to review" is the focus of each of these three provisions. In the immigration context, "judicial review" and "habeas corpus" have historically distinct meanings. In *Heikkila*, the Court concluded that the finality provisions at issue "preclud[ed] judicial review" to the maximum extent possible under the Constitution, and thus concluded that the APA was inapplicable. *Id.*, at 235. Nevertheless, the Court reaffirmed the right to habeas corpus. Noting that the limited role played by the courts in habeas corpus proceedings was far narrower than the judicial review authorized by the APA, the Court concluded that "it is the scope of inquiry on habeas corpus that differentiates" habeas review from "judicial review." *Id.*, at 236. Both §§ 242(a)(1) and (a)(2)(C) speak of "judicial review"—that is, full, nonhabeas review. Neither explicitly mentions habeas, or 28 U.S.C. § 2241. Accordingly, neither provision speaks with sufficient clarity to bar jurisdiction pursuant to the general habeas statute.

The INS also makes a separate argument based on § 242(b)(9). We have previously described § 242(b)(9) as a "zipper clause." *Reno v. American-Arab Anti-Discrimination Committee*, 525 U.S. 471, 483 (1999).[a] Its purpose is to consolidate "judicial review" of immigration proceedings into one action in the court of appeals, but it applies only "[w]ith respect to review of an order of removal under subsection (a)(1)." INA § 242(b). Accordingly, this provision, by its own terms, does not bar habeas jurisdiction over removal orders *not* subject to judicial review under § 242(a)(1)—including orders against aliens who are removable by reason of having committed one or more criminal offenses. Subsection (b)(9) simply provides for the consolidation of issues to be brought in petitions for "[j]udicial review," which, as we note above, is a term historically distinct from habeas. It follows that § 242(b)(9) does not clearly apply to actions brought pursuant to the general habeas statute, and thus cannot repeal that statute either in part or in whole.

If it were clear that the question of law could be answered in another judicial forum, it might be permissible to accept the INS' reading of § 242. But the absence of such a forum, coupled with the lack of a clear, unambiguous, and

---

[a] See material for pp. 962-75.—eds.

express statement of congressional intent to preclude judicial consideration on habeas of such an important question of law, strongly counsels against adopting a construction that would raise serious constitutional questions. Accordingly, we conclude that habeas jurisdiction under § 2241 was not repealed by AEDPA and IIRIRA.

III

[Reaching the merits, the Court concluded that "§ 212(c) relief remains available for aliens, like respondent, whose convictions were obtained through plea agreements and who, notwithstanding those convictions, would have been eligible for § 212(c) relief at the time of their plea under the law then in effect." For more on this part of the decision, see material for pp. 718-21 and 771-72 *supra*.]

JUSTICE O'CONNOR, dissenting.

I join Parts I and III of Justice Scalia's dissenting opinion in this case. I do not join Part II because I believe that, assuming, arguendo, that the Suspension Clause guarantees some minimum extent of habeas review, the right asserted by the alien in this case falls outside the scope of that review for the reasons explained by Justice Scalia in Part II-B of his dissenting opinion. The question whether the Suspension Clause assures habeas jurisdiction in this particular case properly is resolved on this ground alone, and there is no need to say more.

JUSTICE SCALIA, with whom THE CHIEF JUSTICE and JUSTICE THOMAS join, and with whom JUSTICE O'CONNOR joins as to Parts I and III, dissenting.

The Court today finds ambiguity in the utterly clear language of a statute that forbids the district court (and all other courts) to entertain the claims of aliens such as respondent St. Cyr, who have been found deportable by reason of their criminal acts. It fabricates a superclear statement, "magic words" requirement for the congressional expression of such an intent, unjustified in law and unparalleled in any other area of our jurisprudence. And as the fruit of its labors, it brings forth a version of the statute that affords *criminal* aliens *more* opportunities for delay-inducing judicial review than are afforded to non-criminal aliens, or even than were afforded to criminal aliens prior to this legislation concededly designed to *expedite* their removal. Because it is clear that the law deprives us of jurisdiction to entertain this suit, I respectfully dissent.

I

In categorical terms that admit of no exception, the Illegal Immigration Reform and Immigrant Responsibility Act of 1996 (IIRIRA), unambiguously repeals the application of 28 U.S.C. § 2241 (the general habeas corpus provision), and of all other provisions for judicial review, to deportation challenges brought by certain kinds of criminal aliens. This would have been readily apparent to the reader, had the Court at the outset of its opinion set forth the relevant provisions of IIRIRA and of its statutory predecessor, the Antiterrorism and Effective Death Penalty Act of 1996 (AEDPA), 110 Stat.

1214. I will begin by supplying that deficiency, and explaining IIRIRA's jurisdictional scheme. It begins with what we have called a channeling or "'zipper' clause," *Reno v. American-Arab Anti-Discrimination Comm.*, 525 U.S. 471, 483 (1999)—namely, § 242(b)(9). This provision, entitled "Consolidation of questions for judicial review," provides as follows:

> Judicial review of *all* questions of law and fact, including interpretation and application of constitutional and statutory provisions, arising from *any action taken or proceeding brought to remove an alien* from the United States under this subchapter shall be available *only* in judicial review of a final order under this section.

(Emphases added.)

In other words, *if* any review is available of any "questio[n] of law ... arising from any action taken or proceeding brought to remove an alien from the United States under this subchapter," it is available "only in judicial review of a final order under this section [§ 242]." What kind of review does that section provide? That is set forth in § 242(a)(1), which states:

> Judicial review of a final order of removal (other than an order of removal without a hearing pursuant to [the expedited-removal provisions for undocumented aliens arriving at the border found in] section 235(b)(1) of this title) is governed only by chapter 158 of title 28 [the Hobbs Act], except as provided in subsection (b) of this section [which modifies some of the Hobbs Act provisions] and except that the court may not order the taking of additional evidence under section 2347(c) of [Title 28].

In other words, *if* judicial review is available, it consists *only* of the modified Hobbs Act review specified in § 242(a)(1).

In some cases (including, as it happens, the one before us), there can be no review at all, because IIRIRA categorically and unequivocally rules out judicial review of challenges to deportation brought by certain kinds of criminal aliens. Section 242(a)(2)(C) provides:

> Notwithstanding *any* other provision of law, *no court* shall have jurisdiction to review any final order of removal against an alien who is removable by reason of having committed [one or more enumerated] criminal offense[s] [including drug-trafficking offenses of the sort of which respondent had been convicted].

(Emphases added.)

Finally, the pre-IIRIRA antecedent to the foregoing provisions—AEDPA § 401(e)—and the statutory background against which that was enacted, confirm that § 2241 habeas review, in the district court or elsewhere, has been unequivocally repealed. In 1961, Congress amended the Immigration and Nationality Act of 1952 (INA), by directing that the procedure for Hobbs Act review in the courts of appeals "shall apply to, and shall be the *sole and exclusive procedure* for, the judicial review of all final orders of deportation" under the INA. INA § 106(a) (repealed Sept. 30, 1996) (emphasis added). Like § 242(a)(2)(C), this provision squarely prohibited § 2241 district-court habeas review. At the same time that it enacted this provision, however, the 1961

Congress enacted a specific exception: "any alien held in custody pursuant to an order of deportation may obtain judicial review thereof by habeas corpus proceedings," INA § 106(a)(10). (This would of course have been surplusage had § 2241 habeas review not been covered by the "sole and exclusive procedure" provision.)   Section 401(e) of AEDPA repealed this narrow exception, and there is no doubt what the repeal was thought to accomplish: the provision was entitled "ELIMINATION OF CUSTODY REVIEW BY HABEAS CORPUS."   It gave universal preclusive effect to the "sole and exclusive procedure" language of § 106(a).   And it is this regime that IIRIRA has carried forward.

The Court's efforts to derive ambiguity from this utmost clarity are unconvincing.   First, the Court argues that §§ 242(a)(2)(C) and 242(b)(9) are not as clear as one might think—that, even though they are sufficient to repeal the jurisdiction of the courts of appeals, they do not cover habeas jurisdiction in the district court, since, "[i]n the immigration context, 'judicial review' and 'habeas corpus' have historically distinct meanings."   Of course § 242(a)(2)(C) does not even *use* the term "judicial review" (it says "jurisdiction to review")—but let us make believe it does.   The Court's contention that in *this* statute it does not include habeas corpus is decisively refuted by the language of § 242(e)(2), enacted along with §§ 242(a)(2)(C) and 242(b)(9): "*Judicial review* of any determination made under section 235(b)(1) of this title [governing review of expedited removal orders against undocumented aliens arriving at the border] is available in *habeas corpus* proceedings . . . ." (Emphases added.)   It is hard to imagine how Congress could have made it any clearer that, when it used the term "judicial review" in IIRIRA, it included judicial review through habeas corpus.   Research into the "historical" usage of the term "judicial review" is thus quite beside the point.

But the Court is demonstrably wrong about that as well.   Before IIRIRA was enacted, from 1961 to 1996, the governing immigration statutes unquestionably treated "judicial review" as encompassing review by habeas corpus. * * *

The *only* support the Court offers in support of the asserted "longstanding distinction between 'judicial review' and 'habeas'" is language from a single opinion of this Court, *Heikkila v. Barber*, 345 U.S. 229 (1953).   There, we "differentiate[d]" "habeas corpus" from "judicial review *as that term is used in the Administrative Procedure Act.*" *Id.*, at 236 (emphasis added).   But that simply asserts that habeas corpus review is different from ordinary APA review, which no one doubts.   It does *not* assert that habeas corpus review is not judicial review *at all*.   Nowhere does *Heikkila* make such an implausible contention.

The Court next contends that the zipper clause, § 242(b)(9), "by its own terms, does not bar" § 2241 district-court habeas review of removal orders, because the opening sentence of subsection (b) states that "[w]ith respect to review of an order of removal *under subsection (a)(1) of this section*, the following requirements apply . . . ." (Emphasis added.)   But in the broad sense, § 242(b)(9) *does* "apply" "to review of an order of removal under subsection (a)(1)," because it mandates that "review of all questions of law and fact . . . arising from any action taken or proceeding brought to remove an alien from the

United States under this subchapter" must take place *in connection with* such review. This is "application" enough—and to insist that subsection (b)(9) be given effect only *within* the review of removal orders that takes place under subsection (a)(1), is to render it meaningless. * * *

Unquestionably, unambiguously, and unmistakably, IIRIRA expressly supersedes § 2241's general provision for habeas jurisdiction. The Court asserts that *Felker v. Turpin*, 518 U.S. 651 (1996), and *Ex parte Yerger*, 8 Wall. 85 (1869), reflect a "longstanding rule requiring a clear statement of congressional intent to repeal habeas jurisdiction." They do no such thing. Those cases simply applied the general principle—not unique to habeas—that "[r]epeals by implication are not favored." *Felker, supra*, at 660; *Yerger, supra*, at 105. * * * In the present case, unlike in *Felker* and *Yerger*, none of the statutory provisions relied upon—§ 242(a)(2)(C), § 242(b)(9), or INA § 106(a) (1994 ed.)—requires us to imply from one statutory provision the repeal of another. All *by their terms* prohibit the judicial review at issue in this case.

The Court insists, however, that since "[n]either [§ 242(a)(1) nor § 242(a)(2)(C)] explicitly mentions habeas, or 28 U.S.C. § 2241," "neither provision speaks with sufficient clarity to bar jurisdiction pursuant to the general habeas statute." Even in those areas of our jurisprudence where we *have* adopted a "clear statement" rule (notably, the sovereign immunity cases to which the Court adverts), clear statement has never meant the kind of magic words demanded by the Court today—explicit reference to habeas or to § 2241—rather than reference to "judicial review" in a statute that explicitly calls habeas corpus a form of judicial review. * * *

* * *

It has happened before—too frequently, alas—that courts have distorted plain statutory text in order to produce a "more sensible" result. The unique accomplishment of today's opinion is that the result it produces is as far removed from what is sensible as its statutory construction is from the language of the text. One would have to study our statute books for a long time to come up with a more unlikely disposition. By authorizing § 2241 habeas review in the district court but foreclosing review in the court of appeals, the Court's interpretation routes all legal challenges to removal orders brought by criminal aliens to the district court, to be adjudicated under that court's § 2241 habeas authority, which specifies no time limits. After review by that court, criminal aliens will presumably have an appeal as of right to the court of appeals, and can then petition this Court for a writ of certiorari. In contrast, noncriminal aliens seeking to challenge their removal orders—for example, those charged with having been inadmissible at the time of entry, with having failed to maintain their nonimmigrant status, with having procured a visa through a marriage that was not bona fide, or with having become, within five years after the date of entry, a public charge, see §§ 237(a)(1)(A), (a)(1)(C), (a)(1)(G), (a)(5)—will still presumably be required to proceed directly to the court of appeals by way of petition for review, under the restrictive modified Hobbs Act review provisions set forth in § 242(a)(1), including the 30-day filing deadline, see § 242(b)(1). In fact, prior to the enactment of IIRIRA, criminal aliens also had to follow this procedure for immediate modified Hobbs Act review in the court of appeals.

See § 106(a). The Court has therefore succeeded in perverting a statutory scheme designed to *expedite* the removal of criminal aliens into one that now affords them *more* opportunities for (and layers of) judicial review (and hence more opportunities for delay) than are afforded *non*-criminal aliens—and more than were afforded criminal aliens prior to the enactment of IIRIRA. This outcome speaks for itself; no Congress ever imagined it.

To excuse the violence it does to the statutory text, the Court invokes the doctrine of constitutional doubt, which it asserts is raised by the Suspension Clause, U.S. Const., Art. I, § 9, cl. 2. This uses one distortion to justify another, transmogrifying a doctrine designed to maintain "a just respect for the legislature," *Ex parte Randolph*, 20 F. Cas. 242, 254 (No. 11,558) (CC Va. 1833) (Marshall, on circuit), into a means of thwarting the clearly expressed intent of the legislature. The doctrine of constitutional doubt is meant to effectuate, not to subvert, congressional intent, by giving *ambiguous* provisions a meaning that will avoid constitutional peril, and that will conform with Congress's presumed intent not to enact measures of dubious validity. The condition precedent for application of the doctrine is that the statute can *reasonably be construed* to avoid the constitutional difficulty. It is a device for interpreting what the statute says—not for *ignoring* what the statute says in order to avoid the trouble of determining whether what it says is unconstitutional. For the reasons I have set forth above, it is crystal clear that the statute before us here bars criminal aliens from obtaining judicial review, including § 2241 district-court review, of their removal orders. It is therefore also crystal clear that the doctrine of constitutional doubt has no application.

In the remainder of this opinion I address the question the Court *should* have addressed: Whether these provisions of IIRIRA are unconstitutional.

II

A

The Suspension Clause of the Constitution, Art. I, § 9, cl. 2, provides as follows:

The Privilege of the Writ of Habeas Corpus shall not be suspended,
unless when in Cases of Rebellion or Invasion the public Safety
may require it.

A straightforward reading of this text discloses that it does not guarantee any content to (or even the existence of) the writ of habeas corpus, but merely provides that the writ shall not (except in case of rebellion or invasion) be suspended. Indeed, that was precisely the objection expressed by four of the state ratifying conventions—that the Constitution failed affirmatively to guarantee a right to habeas corpus.

To "suspend" the writ was not to fail to enact it, much less to refuse to accord it particular content. Noah Webster, in his American Dictionary of the English Language, defined it—with patriotic allusion to the constitutional text—as "[t]o cause to cease for a time from operation or effect; as, to *suspend* the habeas corpus act." Vol. 2, p. 86 (1828 ed.). This was a distinct abuse of majority power, and one that had manifested itself often in the Framers' experience: temporarily but entirely eliminating the "Privilege of the Writ" for a certain geographic area or areas, or for a certain class or classes of individuals. Suspension Acts had been adopted (and many more proposed) both in this country and in England during the late 18th century—including a 7-month suspension by the Massachusetts Assembly during Shay's Rebellion in 1787. Typical of the genre was the prescription by the Statute of 1794, 34 Geo. 3, c. 54, § 2, that "'. . . [An Act for preventing wrongous imprisonment, and against undue delays in trials], insofar as the same may be construed to relate to the cases of Treason and suspicion of Treason, be suspended [for one year] . . . .'"

In the present case, of course, Congress has not temporarily withheld operation of the writ, but has permanently altered its content. That is, to be sure, an act subject to majoritarian abuse, as is Congress's framing (or its determination not to frame) a habeas statute in the first place. But that is not the majoritarian abuse against which the Suspension Clause was directed. It is no more irrational to guard against the common and well known "suspension" abuse, without guaranteeing any particular habeas right that enjoys immunity from suspension, than it is, in the Equal Protection Clause, to guard against unequal application of the laws, without guaranteeing any particular law which enjoys *that* protection. And it is no more acceptable for this Court to write a habeas law, in order that the Suspension Clause might have some effect, than it would be for this Court to write other laws, in order that the Equal Protection Clause might have some effect.

* * *

B

Even if one were to assume that the Suspension Clause, despite its text * * * , guarantees some constitutional minimum of habeas relief, that minimum would assuredly not embrace the rarified right asserted here: the right to judicial compulsion of the exercise of Executive *discretion* (which may be exercised favorably or unfavorably) regarding a prisoner's release. If one reads the Suspension Clause as a guarantee of habeas relief, the obvious question presented is: *What* habeas relief? There are only two alternatives, the first of which is too absurd to be seriously entertained. It could be contended that Congress "suspends" the writ whenever it eliminates *any* prior ground for the writ that it adopted. Thus, if Congress should ever (in the view of this Court) have authorized immediate habeas corpus—without the need to exhaust administrative remedies—for a person arrested as an illegal alien, Congress would *never* be able (in the light of sad experience) to revise that disposition. The Suspension Clause, in other words, would be a one-way ratchet that enshrines in the Constitution every grant of habeas jurisdiction. This is, as I say, too absurd to be contemplated, and I shall contemplate it no further.

The other alternative is that the Suspension Clause guarantees the common-law right of habeas corpus, as it was understood when the Constitution was ratified. There is no doubt whatever that this did not include the right to obtain discretionary release. The Court notes with apparent credulity respondent's contention "that there is historical evidence of the writ issuing to redress the improper exercise of official discretion." The only Framing-era or earlier cases it alludes to in support of that contention, establish no such thing. * * *

All the other Framing-era or earlier cases cited in the Court's opinion—indeed, *all the later Supreme Court cases until United States ex rel. Accardi v. Shaughnessy*, 347 U.S. 260, *in 1954*—provide habeas relief from executive detention only when the custodian had no legal authority to detain. The fact is that, far from forming a traditional basis for issuance of the writ of habeas corpus, the whole "concept of 'discretion' was not well developed at common law," Hafetz, The Untold Story of Noncriminal Habeas Corpus and the 1996 Immigration Acts, 107 Yale L. J. 2509, 2534 (1998), quoted in Brief for Respondent in *Calcano-Martinez v. INS*, O.T. 2000, No. 00-1011, p. 37. An exhaustive search of cases antedating the Suspension Clause discloses few instances in which courts even discussed the concept of executive discretion; and on the rare occasions when they did, they simply confirmed what seems obvious from the paucity of such discussions—namely, that courts understood executive discretion as lying entirely beyond the judicial ken. That is precisely what one would expect, since even the executive's evaluation of the *facts*—a duty that was a good deal *more* than discretionary—was not subject to review on habeas. Both in this country, until passage of the Habeas Corpus Act of 1867, and in England, the longstanding rule had been that the truth of the custodian's return *could not be controverted*. And, of course, going beyond inquiry into the legal authority of the executive to detain would have been utterly incompatible with the well-established limitation upon habeas relief for a convicted prisoner * * * .

In sum, there is no authority whatever for the proposition that, at the time the Suspension Clause was ratified—or, for that matter, even for a century and a half thereafter—habeas corpus relief was available to compel the Executive's allegedly wrongful refusal to exercise discretion. * * *

III

Given the insubstantiality of the due process and Article III arguments against barring judicial review of respondent's claim (the Court does not even bother to mention them, and the Court of Appeals barely acknowledges them), I will address them only briefly.

The Due Process Clause does not "[r]equir[e] [j]udicial [d]etermination [o]f" respondent's claim. Respondent has no legal entitlement to suspension of deportation, no matter how appealing his case. "[T]he Attorney General's suspension of deportation [is] "an act of grace" which is accorded pursuant to her 'unfettered discretion,' *Jay v. Boyd*, 351 U.S. 345, 354 (1956) . . . , and [can be likened, as Judge Learned Hand observed,] to "a judge's power to suspend the execution of a sentence, or the President's to pardon a convict," 351 U.S., at 354, n.16 . . . ." *INS v. Yueh-Shaio Yang*, 519 U.S. 26, 30 (1996). The furthest our cases have gone in imposing due process requirements upon analogous exercises of executive discretion is the following. (1) We have required *"minimal procedural safeguards"* for death-penalty clemency proceedings, to prevent them from becoming so capricious as to involve "a state official flipp[ing] a coin to determine whether to grant clemency," *Ohio Adult Parole Authority v. Woodard*, 523 U.S. 272, 289 (1998) (O'Connor, J., concurring in part and concurring in judgment). Even assuming that this holding is not part of our "death-is-different" jurisprudence, Shafer v. South Carolina, 532 U.S. ___, ___ (2001) (slip op., at 1) (Scalia, J., dissenting) (citation omitted), respondent here is not complaining about the absence of procedural safeguards; he disagrees with the Attorney General's judgment on a point of law. (2) We have recognized the existence of a due process liberty interest when a State's statutory parole procedures prescribe that a prisoner "shall" be paroled if certain conditions are satisfied, see *Board of Pardons v. Allen*, 482 U.S. 369, 370-371, 381 (1987); *Greenholtz v. Inmates of Neb. Penal and Correctional Complex*, 442 U.S. 1, 12 (1979). There is no such statutory *entitlement* to suspension of deportation, no matter what the facts. Moreover, in neither *Woodard*, nor *Allen*, nor *Greenholtz* did we intimate that the Due Process Clause conferred jurisdiction of its own force, without benefit of statutory authorization. All three cases were brought under 42 U.S.C. § 1983.

Article III, § 1's investment of the "judicial Power of the United States" in the federal courts does not prevent Congress from committing the adjudication of respondent's legal claim wholly to "non-Article III federal adjudicative bodies," Brief for Petitioners in *Calcano-Martinez v. INS*, O.T. 2000, No. 00-1011, p. 38. The notion that Article III requires every Executive determination, on a question of law or of fact, to be subject to judicial review has no support in our jurisprudence. Were it correct, the doctrine of sovereign immunity would not exist, and the APA's general permission of suits challenging administrative action, see 5 U.S.C. § 702, would have been superfluous. Of its own force, Article III does no more than commit to the courts matters that are "the stuff of the traditional actions at common law tried by the courts at Westminster in 1789," *Northern Pipeline Constr. Co. v. Marathon Pipe Line Co.*, 458 U.S. 50, 90 (1982) (Rehnquist, J., concurring in judgment)—which (as I have discussed earlier) did not include supervision of discretionary executive action.

* * *

The Court has created a version of IIRIRA that is not only unrecognizable to its framers (or to anyone who can read) but gives the statutory scheme precisely the *opposite* of its intended effect, affording criminal aliens *more* opportunities for delay-inducing judicial review than others have, or even than criminal aliens had prior to the enactment of this legislation. Because § 2241's exclusion of judicial review is unmistakably clear, and unquestionably constitutional, both this Court and the courts below were without power to entertain respondent's claims. I would set aside the judgment of the court below and remand with instructions to have the District Court dismiss for want of jurisdiction. I respectfully dissent from the judgment of the Court.

Notes

1. Recall that *Zadvydas* (see material for pp. 916-25 *supra*) also interpreted a statute in the alien's favor applying the canon to avoid serious constitutional doubt. Does the Court make a convincing case that none of the statutes cited by the government repealed habeas review under § 2241? Of what relevance is the legislative history quoted at Casebook p. 935? If you find the Court's reading of the statutes unconvincing, what explains the Court's ultimate conclusion?

2. *See generally* Legomsky, *Fear and Loathing in Congress and the Courts: Immigration and Judicial Review*, 78 Tex. L. Rev. 1615 (2000); Neuman, *Federal Courts Issues in Immigration Law*, 76 Tex. L. Rev. 1661 (2000) ; Neuman, *Jurisdiction and the Rule of Law After the 1996 Immigration Act*, 113 Harv. L. Rev. 1963 (2000) .

962-75: Consolidating Issues for Judicial Review (substitute for first full paragraph on 962, *Ramallo, American-Arab Anti-Discrimination Committee*, and notes 1, 2, and 3 on 971-73)

With this background on former INA § 106, now consider the following Supreme Court decision on the timing and consolidation issues raised by the 1996 Act.

RENO v. AMERICAN-ARAB ANTI-DISCRIMINATION COMMITTEE
Supreme Court of the United States, 1999.
525 U.S. 471, 119 S.Ct. 936, 142 L.Ed.2d 940.

JUSTICE SCALIA delivered the opinion of the Court.[*]

Respondents sued petitioners for allegedly targeting them for deportation because of their affiliation with a politically unpopular group. While their suit was pending, Congress passed the Illegal Immigration Reform and Immigrant Responsibility Act of 1996 (IIRIRA), which contains a provision restricting judicial review of the Attorney General's "decision or action" to "commence proceedings, adjudicate cases, or execute removal orders against any alien under this Act." INA § 242(g). The issue before us is whether, as petitioners contend, this provision deprives the federal courts of jurisdiction over respondents' suit.

I

The Immigration and Naturalization Service (INS), a division of the Department of Justice, instituted deportation proceedings in 1987 against Bashar Amer, Aiad Barakat, Julie Mungai, Amjad Obeid, Ayman Obeid, Naim Sharif, Khader Hamide, and Michel Shehadeh, all of whom belong to the Popular Front for the Liberation of Palestine (PFLP), a group that the Government characterizes as an international terrorist and communist organization. The INS charged all eight under the McCarran-Walter Act, which, though now repealed, provided at the time for the deportation of aliens who "advocate . . . world communism." See 8 U.S.C. §§ 1251(a)(6)(D), (G)(v), and (H) (1982 ed.). In addition, the INS charged the first six, who were only temporary residents, with routine status violations such as overstaying a visa and failure to maintain student status.[1]

Almost immediately, the aliens filed suit in District Court, challenging the constitutionality of the anti-communism provisions of the McCarran-Walter Act and seeking declaratory and injunctive relief against the Attorney General, the INS, and various immigration officials in their personal and official capacities.

---

[*] JUSTICE BREYER joins Parts I and II of this opinion.

[1] Respondents Barakat and Sharif were subsequently granted legalization and are no longer deportable based on the original status violations.

The INS responded by dropping the advocacy-of-communism charges, but it retained the technical violation charges against the six temporary residents and charged Hamide and Shehadeh, who were permanent residents, under a different section of the McCarran-Walter Act, which authorized the deportation of aliens who were members of an organization advocating "the duty, necessity, or propriety of the unlawful assaulting or killing of any [government] officer or officers" and "the unlawful damage, injury, or destruction of property."[2] INS regional counsel William Odencrantz said at a press conference that the charges had been changed for tactical reasons but the INS was still seeking respondents' deportation because of their affiliation with the PFLP. Respondents amended their complaint to include an allegation that the INS was selectively enforcing immigration laws against them in violation of their First and Fifth Amendment rights.

Since this suit seeking to prevent the initiation of deportation proceedings was filed—in 1987, during the administration of Attorney General Edwin Meese—it has made four trips through the District Court for the Central District of California and the United States Court of Appeals for the Ninth Circuit. The first two concerned jurisdictional issues not now before us. Then, in 1994, the District Court preliminarily enjoined deportation proceedings against the six temporary residents, holding that they were likely to prove that the INS did not enforce routine status requirements against immigrants who were not members of disfavored terrorist groups and that the possibility of deportation, combined with the chill to their First Amendment rights while the proceedings were pending, constituted irreparable injury. With regard to Hamide and Shehadeh's claims, however, the District Court granted summary judgment to the federal parties for reasons not pertinent here.

American-Arab Anti-Discrimination Committee v. Reno, 70 F.3d 1045 (C.A.9 1995), a case that we shall call "*AADC I*" was the Ninth Circuit's first merits determination in this case, upholding the injunction as to the six and reversing the District Court with regard to Hamide and Shehadeh.[a] The opinion rejected the Attorney General's argument that selective-enforcement claims are inappropriate in the immigration context, and her alternative argument that the special statutory-review provision of the Immigration and Nationality Act (INA), § 106, precluded review of such a claim until a deportation order issued. The Ninth Circuit remanded the case to the District Court, which entered an injunction in favor of Hamide and Shehadeh and denied the Attorney General's request that the existing injunction be dissolved in light of new evidence that all respondents participated in fundraising activities of the PFLP.

While the Attorney General's appeal of this last decision was pending, Congress passed IIRIRA which, *inter alia*, repealed the old judicial-review scheme set forth in § 106 and instituted a new (and significantly more

---

[2] When the McCarran-Walter Act was repealed, a new "terrorist activity" provision was added by the Immigration Act of 1990. See 8 U.S.C. § 1227(a)(4)(B). The INS charged Hamide and Shehadeh under this, but it is unclear whether that was in addition to, or in substitution for, the old McCarran-Walter charges.

[a] This decision is discussed in Chapter Seven of the Casebook, pp. 712-16.—eds.

restrictive) one in INA § 242. The Attorney General filed motions in both the District Court and Court of Appeals, arguing that § 242(g) deprived them of jurisdiction over respondents' selective-enforcement claim. The District Court denied the motion, and the Attorney General's appeal from that denial was consolidated with the appeal already pending in the Ninth Circuit.

It is the judgment and opinion in that appeal which is before us here: *American-Arab Anti-Discrimination Committee v. Reno*, 119 F.3d 1367 (C.A.9 1997), which we shall call "*AADC II.*" It affirmed the existence of jurisdiction under § 242, and reaching the merits of the injunctions, again affirmed the District Court. The Attorney General's petition for rehearing en banc was denied over the dissent of three judges. The Attorney General sought our review, and we granted certiorari.

II

Before enactment of IIRIRA, judicial review of most administrative action under the INA was governed by INA § 106, a special statutory-review provision directing that "the sole and exclusive procedure for . . . the judicial review of all final orders of deportation" shall be that set forth in the Hobbs Act, 28 U.S.C. § 2341 *et seq.*, which gives exclusive jurisdiction to the courts of appeals, see § 2342. Much of the Court of Appeals' analysis in *AADC I* was devoted to the question whether this pre-IIRIRA provision applied to selective-enforcement claims. Since neither the Immigration Judge nor the Board of Immigration Appeals has authority to hear such claims (a point conceded by the Attorney General in *AADC I*), a challenge to a final order of deportation based upon such a claim would arrive in the court of appeals without the factual development necessary for decision. The Attorney General argued unsuccessfully below that the Hobbs Act permits a court of appeals to remand the case to the agency, see 28 U.S.C. § 2347(c) or transfer it to a district court, see § 2347(b)(3) for further factfinding. The Ninth Circuit, believing these options unavailable, concluded that an original district-court action was respondents' only means of obtaining factual development and thus judicial review of their selective-enforcement claims. Relying on our decision in *Cheng Fan Kwok v. INS*, 392 U.S. 206, 88 S.Ct. 1970, 20 L.Ed.2d 1037 (1968), it held that the District Court could entertain the suit under either its general federal-question jurisdiction, see 28 U.S.C. § 1331, or the general jurisdictional provision of the INA, see INA § 279.

Whether we must delve further into the details of this issue depends upon whether, after the enactment of IIRIRA, § 106 continues to apply to this case. On the surface of things, at least, it does not. Although the general rule set forth in § 309(c)(1) of IIRIRA is that the revised procedures for removing aliens, including the judicial-review procedures of § 242, do not apply to aliens who were already in either exclusion or deportation proceedings on IIRIRA's effective date,[5] § 306(c)(1) of IIRIRA directs that a single provision, § 242(g),

---

[5] Section 309(c)(1) provides:
"(c) Transition for Aliens in Proceedings

shall apply "without limitation to claims arising from all past, pending, or future exclusion, deportation, or removal proceedings." Section 242(g) reads as follows:

[The Court set out the text of INA § 242(g).]

This provision seemingly governs here, depriving the federal courts of jurisdiction "[e]xcept as provided in this section." But whether it is as straightforward as that depends upon the scope of the quoted text. Here, and in the courts below, both petitioners and respondents have treated § 242(g) as covering all or nearly all deportation claims. The Attorney General has characterized it as "a channeling provision, requiring aliens to bring all deportation-related claims in the context of a petition for review of a final order of deportation filed in the court of appeals." Respondents have described it as applying to "most of what INS does." This broad understanding of § 242(g), combined with IIRIRA's effective-date provisions, creates an interpretive anomaly. If the jurisdiction-excluding provision of § 242(g) eliminates other sources of jurisdiction in *all* deportation-related cases, and if the phrase in § 242(g) "[e]xcept as provided in this section" incorporates (as one would suppose) all the other jurisdiction-related provisions of § 242, then § 309(c)(1) would be rendered a virtual nullity. To say that there is no jurisdiction in pending INS cases "except as" § 242 provides jurisdiction is simply to say that § 242's jurisdictional limitations apply to pending cases as well as future cases––which seems hardly what § 309(c)(1) is about. If, on the other hand, the phrase "[e]xcept as provided in this section" were (somehow) interpreted not to incorporate the other jurisdictional provisions of § 242—if § 242(g) stood alone, so to speak—judicial review would be foreclosed for all deportation claims in all pending deportation cases, even after entry of a final order.

The Attorney General would have us avoid the horns of this dilemma by interpreting § 242(g)'s phrase "[e]xcept as provided in this section" to mean "except as provided in § 106." Because § 106 authorizes review of only final orders, respondents must, she says, wait until their administrative proceedings come to a close and then seek review in a court of appeals. (For reasons mentioned above, the Attorney General of course rejects the Ninth Circuit's position in *AADC I* that application of § 106 would leave respondents without a judicial forum because evidence of selective prosecution cannot be introduced into the administrative record.) The obvious difficulty with the Attorney General's interpretation is that it is impossible to understand how the qualifier in § 242(g), "[e]xcept as provided in *this* section" (emphasis added), can possibly mean "except as provided in § 106." And indeed the Attorney General makes no

---

"(1) General Rule that New Rules Do Not Apply.—Subject to the succeeding provisions of this subsection [§ 309(a) carves out § 306(c) as an exception], in the case of an alien who is in exclusion or deportation proceedings before the title III-A effective date—

"(A) the amendments made by this subtitle shall not apply, and

"(B) the proceedings (including judicial review thereof) shall continue to be conducted without regard to such amendments."

attempt to explain how this can be, except to observe that what she calls a "literal application" of the statute "would create an anomalous result."

Respondents note this deficiency, but offer an equally implausible means of avoiding the dilemma. Section 309(c)(3) allows the Attorney General to terminate pending deportation proceedings and reinitiate them under § 242. They argue that § 242(g) applies only to those pending cases in which the Attorney General has made that election. That way, they claim, the phrase "[e]xcept as provided in this section" can, without producing an anomalous result, be allowed to refer (as it says) to all the rest of § 242. But this approach collides head-on with § 306(c)'s prescription that § 242(g) shall apply "*without limitation* to claims arising from *all* past, pending, or future exclusion, deportation, or removal proceedings." (Respondents argue in the alternative, of course, that if the Attorney General is right and § 106 does apply, *AADC I* is correct that their claims will be effectively unreviewable upon entry of a final order. For this reason, and because they say that habeas review, if still available after IIRIRA, will come too late to remedy this First Amendment injury, respondents contend that we must construe § 242(g) not to bar *constitutional* claims.)

The Ninth Circuit, for its part, accepted the parties' broad reading of § 242(g) and concluded, reasonably enough, that on that reading Congress could not have meant § 242(g) to stand alone:

> Divorced from all other jurisdictional provisions of IIRIRA, subsection (g) would have a more sweeping impact on cases filed before the statute's enactment than after that date. Without incorporating any exceptions, the provision appears to cut off federal jurisdiction over all deportation decisions. We do not think that Congress intended such an absurd result.

119 F.3d, at 1372. It recognized, however, the existence of the other horn of the dilemma ("that retroactive application of the entire amended version of § 242 would threaten to render meaningless section 306(c) of IIRIRA," *ibid.*), and resolved the difficulty to its satisfaction by concluding that "at least *some* of the other provisions of section 242" must be included in subsection (g) "when it applies to pending cases." *Ibid.* (emphasis added). One of those provisions, it thought, must be subsection (f), entitled "Limit on Injunctive Relief," which reads as follows:

[The Court set out the text of INA § 242(f).]

The Ninth Circuit found in this an affirmative grant of jurisdiction that covered the present case. The Attorney General argued that any such grant of jurisdiction would be limited (and rendered inapplicable to this case) by § 242(b)(9), which provides:

[The Court set out the text of INA § 242(b)(9).]

The Ninth Circuit replied that, even if § 242(b)(9) were one of those provisions incorporated into the transitional application of § 242(g), it could not preclude this suit for the same reason *AADC I* had held that § 106 could not do so— namely, the Court of Appeals' lack of access to factual findings regarding selective enforcement.

Even respondents scarcely try to defend the Ninth Circuit's reading of § 242(f) as a jurisdictional grant. By its plain terms, and even by its title, that provision is nothing more or less than a limit on injunctive relief. It prohibits federal courts from granting classwide injunctive relief against the operation of INA §§ 231-241, but specifies that this ban does not extend to individual cases. To find in this an affirmative grant of jurisdiction is to go beyond what the language will bear.

We think the seeming anomaly that prompted the parties' strained readings of § 242(g)—and that at least accompanied the Court of Appeals' strained reading—is a mirage. The parties' interpretive acrobatics flow from the belief that § 306(c)(1) cannot be read to envision a straightforward application of the "[e]xcept as provided in this section" portion of § 242(g), since that would produce in *all* pending INS cases jurisdictional restrictions identical to those that were contained in IIRIRA anyway. That belief, however, rests on the unexamined assumption that § 242(g) covers the universe of deportation claims––that it is a sort of "zipper" clause that says "no judicial review in deportation cases unless this section provides judicial review." In fact, what § 242(g) says is much narrower. The provision applies only to three discrete actions that the Attorney General may take: her "decision or action" to "*commence* proceedings, *adjudicate* cases, or *execute* removal orders." (Emphasis added.) There are of course many other decisions or actions that may be part of the deportation process—such as the decisions to open an investigation, to surveil the suspected violator, to reschedule the deportation hearing, to include various provisions in the final order that is the product of the adjudication, and to refuse reconsideration of that order.

It is implausible that the mention of three discrete events along the road to deportation was a shorthand way of referring to all claims arising from deportation proceedings. Not because Congress is too unpoetic to use synecdoche, but because that literary device is incompatible with the need for precision in legislative drafting. We are aware of no other instance in the United States Code in which language such as this has been used to impose a general jurisdictional limitation; and that those who enacted IIRIRA were familiar with the normal manner of imposing such a limitation is demonstrated by the text of § 242(b)(9), which stands in stark contrast to § 242(g).

It could be argued, perhaps, that § 242(g) is redundant if it channels judicial review of only *some* decisions and actions, since § 242(b)(9) channels judicial review of *all* of them anyway. But that is not so, since only § 242(g), and *not* § 242(b)(9) (except to the extent it is incorporated within § 242(g)), applies to what § 309(c)(1) calls "transitional cases," that is, cases pending on the effective date of IIRIRA. That alone justifies its existence. It performs the function of categorically excluding from non-final-order judicial review—even as to transitional cases otherwise governed by § 106 rather than the unmistakable "zipper" clause of § 242(b)(9)—certain specified decisions and actions of the INS. In addition, even after all the transitional cases have passed through the system, § 242(g) as we interpret it serves the continuing function of making it clear that those specified decisions and actions, which (as we shall discuss in detail below) some courts had held *not* to be included within the non-final-order review prohibition of § 106, *are* covered by the "zipper" clause of § 242(b)(9). It is rather the Court of Appeals' and the parties' interpretation which renders § 242(g) entirely redundant, adding to one "zipper" clause that does not apply to transitional cases, another one of equal scope that does apply to transitional cases. That makes it entirely inexplicable why the transitional provisions of § 306(c) refer to § 242(g) instead of § 242(b)(9)—and why § 242(g) exists at all.

There was good reason for Congress to focus special attention upon, and make special provision for, judicial review of the Attorney General's discrete acts of "commenc[ing] proceedings, adjudicat[ing] cases, [and] execut[ing] removal orders"—which represent the initiation or prosecution of various stages in the deportation process. At each stage the Executive has discretion to abandon the endeavor, and at the time IIRIRA was enacted the INS had been engaging in a regular practice (which had come to be known as "deferred action") of exercising that discretion for humanitarian reasons or simply for its own convenience. * * * [The Court quoted extensively from 6 C. Gordon, S. Mailman, & S. Yale-Loehr, Immigration Law and Procedure § 72.03[2][h](1998).] * * * Since no generous act goes unpunished, however, the INS's exercise of this discretion opened the door to litigation in instances where the INS chose *not* to exercise it. * * * Such litigation was possible because courts read § 106's prescription that the Hobbs Act shall be "the sole and exclusive procedure for the judicial review of all final orders of deportation" to be inapplicable to various decisions and actions leading up to or consequent upon final orders of deportation, and relied on other jurisdictional statutes to permit review. See, *e.g., Cheng Fan Kwok v. INS*, 392 U.S. 206, 88 S.Ct. 1970, 20 L.Ed.2d 1037 (1968) (review of refusal to stay deportation); *Ramallo v. Reno*, Civ. No. 95-01851 (D.D.C., July 23, 1996) (review of execution of removal order), described in and rev'd on other grounds, 114 F.3d 1210 (C.A.D.C.1997); *AADC I*, 70 F.3d 1045 (C.A.9 1995) (review of commencement of deportation proceedings); *Lennon v. INS*, 527 F.2d 187, 195 (C.A.2 1975) (same, dicta). Section 242(g) seems clearly designed to give some measure of protection to "no deferred action" decisions and similar discretionary determinations, providing that if they are reviewable at all, they at least will not be made the bases for separate rounds of judicial intervention outside the streamlined process that Congress has designed.

Of course *many* provisions of IIRIRA are aimed at protecting the Executive's discretion from the courts—indeed, that can fairly be said to be the theme of the legislation. It is entirely understandable, however, why Congress would want only the discretion-protecting provision of § 242(g) applied even to pending cases: because that provision is specifically directed at the deconstruction, fragmentation, and hence prolongation of removal proceedings.

Our narrow reading of § 242(g) makes sense of the statutory scheme as a whole, for it resolves the supposed tension between § 306(c)(1) and § 309(c)(1). In cases to which § 242(g) applies, the rest of § 242 is incorporated through the "[e]xcept as provided in this section" clause. This incorporation does not swallow § 309(c)(1)'s general rule that §§ 242(a)-(f) do not apply to pending cases, for § 242(g) applies to only a limited subset of deportation claims. Yet it is also faithful to § 306(c)(1)'s command that § 242(g) be applied "without limitation" (*i.e.*, including the "[e]xcept as provided" clause) to "claims arising from all past, pending, or future exclusion, deportation, or removal proceedings."

Respondents' challenge to the Attorney General's decision to "commence proceedings" against them falls squarely within § 242(g)—indeed, as we have discussed, the language seems to have been crafted with such a challenge precisely in mind—and nothing elsewhere in § 242 provides for jurisdiction. Cf. § 242(a)(1)(review of final orders); § 242(e)(2) (limited habeas review for excluded aliens); § 242(e)(3)(A) (limited review of statutes and regulations pertaining to the exclusion of aliens). As we concluded earlier, § 242(f) plainly serves as a limit on injunctive relief rather than a jurisdictional grant.

III

Finally, we must address respondents' contention that, since the lack of prior factual development for their claim will render the § 242(a)(1) exception to § 242(g) unavailing; since habeas relief will also be unavailable; and since even if one or both were available they would come too late to prevent the "chilling effect" upon their First Amendment rights; the doctrine of constitutional doubt requires us to interpret § 242(g) in such fashion as to permit immediate review of their selective-enforcement claims. We do not believe that the doctrine of constitutional doubt has any application here. As a general matter—and assuredly in the context of claims such as those put forward in the present case––an alien unlawfully in this country has no constitutional right to assert selective enforcement as a defense against his deportation.

[The Court explained its reasons for rejecting the respondents' constitutional doubt argument based on the First Amendment.[b]]

* * * When an alien's continuing presence in this country is in violation of the immigration laws, the Government does not offend the Constitution by deporting him for the additional reason that it believes him to be a member of an organization that supports terrorist activity.

Because § 242(g) deprives the federal courts of jurisdiction over respondents' claims, we vacate the judgment of the Ninth Circuit and remand with instructions for it to vacate the judgment of the District Court.

It is so ordered.

JUSTICE GINSBURG, with whom JUSTICE BREYER joins as to Part I, concurring in part and concurring in the judgment.

I agree with Justice Scalia that § 242(g) applies to this case and deprives the federal courts of jurisdiction over respondents' pre-final-order suit. Under § 242, respondents may obtain circuit court review of final orders of removal pursuant to the Hobbs Act, 28 U.S.C. § 2341 *et seq.* See § 242(a)(1). I would not prejudge the question whether respondents may assert a selective enforcement objection when and if they pursue such review. It suffices to inquire whether the First Amendment necessitates *immediate* judicial consideration of their selective enforcement plea. I conclude that it does not.

---

[b] For this part of the opinion, see this Supplement, *supra* material for p. 717.—eds.

I

Respondents argue that they are suffering irreparable injury to their First Amendment rights and therefore require instant review of their selective enforcement claims. We have not previously determined the circumstances under which the Constitution requires immediate judicial intervention in federal administrative proceedings of this order. Respondents point to our cases addressing federal injunctions that stop state proceedings, in order to secure constitutional rights. They feature in this regard *Dombrowski v. Pfister*, 380 U.S. 479, 85 S.Ct. 1116, 14 L.Ed.2d 22 (1965), as interpreted in *Younger v. Harris*, 401 U.S. 37, 47-53, 91 S.Ct. 746, 27 L.Ed.2d 669 (1971). Respondents also refer to *Oestereich v. Selective Serv. System Local Bd. No. 11*, 393 U.S. 233, 89 S.Ct. 414, 21 L.Ed.2d 402 (1968). Those cases provide a helpful framework.

In *Younger*, this Court declared that federal restraint of state prosecutions is permissible only if the state defendant establishes "great and immediate" irreparable injury, beyond "that incidental to every criminal proceeding brought lawfully and in good faith." 401 U.S., at 46, 47, 91 S.Ct. 746 (internal quotation marks omitted). A chilling effect, the Court cautioned, does not "by itself justify federal intervention." *Id.*, at 50, 91 S.Ct. 746. *Younger* recognized, however, the prospect of extraordinary circumstances in which immediate federal injunctive relief might be obtained. The Court referred, initially, to bad faith, harassing police and prosecutorial actions pursued without "any expectation of securing valid convictions." *Id.*, at 48, 91 S.Ct. 746 (internal quotation marks omitted). Further, the Court observed that there may be other "extraordinary circumstances in which the necessary irreparable injury can be shown even in the absence of the usual prerequisites of bad faith and harassment," for example, where a statute is "flagrantly and patently violative of express constitutional prohibitions in every clause, sentence and paragraph, and in whatever manner and against whomever an effort might be made to apply it." *Id.*, at 53-54, 91 S.Ct. 746 (internal quotation marks omitted).

In *Oestereich*, the Selective Service Board had withdrawn a ministry student's statutory exemption from the draft after he engaged in an act of protest. The student brought suit to restrain his induction, and this Court allowed the suit to go forward, notwithstanding a statutory bar of preinduction judicial review. Finding the Board's action "blatantly lawless," the Court concluded that to require the student to raise his claim through habeas corpus or as a defense to a criminal prosecution would be "to construe the Act with unnecessary harshness." *Id.*, at 238, 89 S.Ct. 414.

The precedent in point suggests that interlocutory intervention in Immigration and Naturalization Service (INS) proceedings would be in order, notwithstanding a statutory bar, if the INS acts in bad faith, lawlessly, or in patent violation of constitutional rights. Resembling, but more stringent than, the evaluation made when a preliminary injunction is sought, this test would demand, as an essential element, demonstration of a strong likelihood of success on the merits. The merits of respondents' objection are too uncertain to establish that likelihood. The Attorney General argued in the court below and in the petition for certiorari that the INS may select for deportation aliens who it has reason to believe have carried out fundraising for a foreign terrorist organization.

Whether the INS may do so presents a complex question in an uncharted area of the law, which we should not rush to resolve here.

Relying on *Middlesex County Ethics Comm. v. Garden State Bar Assn.*, 457 U.S. 423, 102 S.Ct. 2515, 73 L.Ed.2d 116 (1982), respondents argue that their inability to raise their selective enforcement claims during the administrative proceedings makes immediate judicial intervention necessary. As we explained in *Middlesex County*, *Younger* abstention is appropriate only when there is "an adequate opportunity in the state proceedings to raise constitutional challenges." 457 U.S., at 432, 102 S.Ct. 2515. Here, Congress has established an integrated scheme for deportation proceedings, channeling judicial review to the final order, and deferring issues outside the agency's authority until that point. Given Congress' strong interest in avoiding delay of deportation proceedings, I find the opportunity to raise a claim during the judicial review phase sufficient.

If a court of appeals reviewing final orders of removal against respondents could not consider their selective enforcement claims, the equation would be different. See *Webster v. Doe*, 486 U.S. 592, 603, 108 S.Ct. 2047, 100 L.Ed.2d 632 (1988) (a "serious constitutional question . . . would arise if a federal statute were construed to deny any judicial forum for a colorable constitutional claim" (internal quotation marks omitted)). Respondents argue that that is the case, because their claims require factfinding beyond the administrative record.

Section 242(a)(1) authorizes judicial review of "final order[s] of removal." We have previously construed such "final order" language to authorize judicial review of "all matters on which the validity of the final order is contingent, rather than only those determinations actually made at the hearing." *INS v. Chadha*, 462 U.S. 919, 938, 103 S.Ct. 2764, 77 L.Ed.2d 317 (1983) (internal quotation marks omitted). Whether there is here a need for factfinding beyond the administrative record is a matter properly postponed. I note, however, the Attorney General's position that the reviewing court of appeals may transfer a case to a district court for resolution of pertinent issues of material fact, and counsel's assurance at oral argument that petitioners will adhere to that position.

II

The petition for certiorari asked this Court to review the merits of respondents' selective enforcement objection, but we declined to do so, granting certiorari on the jurisdictional question only. We thus lack full briefing on respondents' selective enforcement plea and on the viability of such objections generally. I would therefore leave the question an open one. I note, however, that there is more to "the other side of the ledger" than the Court allows.

* * * c

[W]ere respondents to demonstrate strong likelihood of ultimate success on the merits and a chilling effect on current speech, and were we to find the agency's action flagrantly improper, precedent and sense would counsel immediate judicial intervention. But respondents have made no such

---

c For this part of the opinion, see this Supplement, *supra* material for p. 717.—eds.

demonstration. Further, were respondents to assert a colorable First Amendment claim as a now or never matter—were that claim not cognizable upon judicial review of a final order—again precedent and sense would counsel immediate resort to a judicial forum. In common with the Attorney General, however, I conclude that in the final judicial episode, factfinding, to the extent necessary to fairly address respondents' claims, is not beyond the federal judiciary's ken.

For the reasons stated, I join in Parts I and II of the Court's opinion and concur in the judgment.

JUSTICE STEVENS, concurring in the judgment.

* * *

The textual difficulty that is debated by my colleagues concerns the impact of IIRIRA on proceedings that were pending on the effective date of the Act. Putting those cases to one side for the moment, the meaning of §§ 242(b)(9) and (g) is perfectly clear. The former postpones judicial review of removal proceedings until the entry of a final order and the latter deprives federal courts of jurisdiction over collateral challenges to ongoing administrative proceedings. Thus, if § 242 applies to these respondents, the deportation proceedings pending before the Immigration and Naturalization Service (INS) are not yet ripe for review, and this collateral attack on those proceedings must be dismissed.

If we substitute the word "Act" for the word "section" in the introductory clause of § 242(g), the impact of this provision on pending proceedings is equally clear. That substitution would remove any obstacle to giving effect to the plain meaning of IIRIRA §§ 306(c)(1) and 309(c)(1). The former defines the effective date of the Act and makes § 242(g)'s prohibition against collateral attacks effective immediately; the latter makes the new rules inapplicable to aliens in exclusion or deportation proceedings pending before the INS on the effective date of the Act. Judicial review of those administrative proceedings remains available in the courts of appeal under the old statutory regime. See INA § 106.

Admittedly, there is a slight ambiguity in the text of § 309 because it refers to the "case of an alien who is in exclusion or deportation proceedings" before the effective date of the new Act. Respondents are such aliens, and therefore the word "case" arguably could be read to include their present collateral attack on the INS proceedings as well as to an eventual challenge to the final order of deportation. Because that reading would be inconsistent with § 306, however, it is clear that Congress intended § 309 to apply only to the INS "exclusion or deportation" proceedings that it expressly mentions.

To summarize, I think a fair reading of all relevant provisions in the statute makes it clear that Congress intended its prohibition of collateral attacks on ongoing INS proceedings to become effective immediately while providing that pending administrative proceedings should be completed under the scheme of judicial review in effect when they were commenced.

* * *

JUSTICE SOUTER, dissenting.

* * *

The Court's interpretation, it seems to me, parses the language of subsection (g) too finely for the business at hand. The chronological march from commencing proceedings, through adjudicating cases, to executing removal orders, surely gives a reasonable first impression of speaking exhaustively. While it is grammatically possible to read the series without total inclusion, the implausibility of doing this appears the moment one asks why Congress would have wanted to preserve interim review of the particular set of decisions by the Attorney General to which the Court adverts. It is hard to imagine that Congress meant to bar aliens already in proceedings before the effective date from challenging the commencement of proceedings against them, but to permit the same aliens to challenge, say, the decision of the Attorney General to open an investigation of them or to issue a show-cause order. Nor is there a plausible explanation of why the exclusivity provisions of subsection (g) should not apply after the effective date to review of decisions to open investigations or invite cause to be shown.

* * *

Because I cannot subscribe to the Court's attempt to render the inclusive series incomplete, I have to confront the irreconcilable contradiction between § 306(c)(1) and § 309(c)(1). Both context and principle point me to the conclusion that the latter provision must prevail over the former. First, it seems highly improbable that Congress actually intended to raise a permanent barrier to judicial review for aliens in proceedings ongoing on April 1, 1997. Judicial review was available under old INA § 106 to those aliens whose proceedings concluded before the enactment of the amended § 306(c)(1) on October 11, 1996, and judicial review of a different scope is also available under new § 242 to those whose proceedings commenced after the effective date of IIRIRA, April 1, 1997. There is no reason whatever to believe that Congress intentionally singled out for especially harsh treatment the hapless aliens who were in proceedings during the interim. This point is underscored by transitional § 309(c)(4)(A), which expressly applies subsections (a) and (c) of old INA § 106 (but not subsection (b) thereof) to judicial review of final orders of deportation or exclusion filed more than 30 days after the date of enactment. Section 309(c)(4)(A), in other words, contemplates judicial review of final orders of exclusion against aliens who were in proceedings as of the date of enactment.

Second, complete preclusion of judicial review of any kind for claims brought by aliens subject to proceedings for removal would raise the serious constitutional question whether Congress may block every remedy for enforcing a constitutional right. The principle of constitutional doubt counsels against adopting the interpretation that raises this question. "[W]here a statute is susceptible of two constructions, by one of which grave and doubtful constitutional questions arise and by the other of which such questions are avoided, our duty is to adopt the latter." *United States ex rel. Attorney General v. Delaware & Hudson Co.*, 213 U.S. 366, 408, 29 S.Ct. 527, 53 L.Ed. 836 (1909). Here, constitutional doubt lends considerable weight to the view that § 309(c)(1) ought to prevail over § 306(c)(1) and preserve judicial review under the law as it was before the enactment of IIRIRA for aliens in proceedings before April 1, 1997. While I do not lightly reach the conclusion that

§ 306(c)(1) is essentially without force, my respect for Congress's intent in enacting § 309(c)(1) is necessarily balanced by respect for Congress's intent in enacting § 306(c)(1). No canon of statutory construction familiar to me specifically addresses the situation in which two simultaneously enacted provisions of the same statute flatly contradict one another. We are, of course, bound to avoid such a dilemma if we can, by glimpsing some uncontradicted meaning for each provision. But the attempt to salvage an application for each must have some stopping place, and the Court's attempt here seems to me to go beyond that point. In this anomalous situation where the two statutory provisions are fundamentally at odds, constitutional doubt will have to serve as the best guide to breaking the tie.

Because I think that § 309(c)(1) applies to aliens in proceedings before April 1, 1997, I think it applies to respondents in this case. The law governing their proceedings and subsequent judicial review should therefore be the law prevailing before IIRIRA. That law, in my view, afforded respondents an opportunity to litigate their claims before the District Court. Former INA § 106(a) governed "judicial review of all final orders of deportation." For actions that fell outside the scope of this provision, an "alien's remedies would, of course, ordinarily lie first in an action brought in an appropriate district court." *Cheng Fan Kwok v. INS*, 392 U.S. 206, 210, 88 S.Ct. 1970, 20 L.Ed.2d 1037 (1968). In *McNary v. Haitian Refugee Center, Inc.*, 498 U.S. 479, 111 S.Ct. 888, 112 L.Ed.2d 1005 (1991), we applied this principle in finding a right of action before the district court in a constitutional challenge to procedures of the Immigration and Naturalization Service. Respondents' challenge to the constitutionality of their prosecution was filed prior to the entry of a final order of deportation, and so district court jurisdiction was appropriate here.

II

The approach I would take in this case avoids a troubling problem that the Court chooses to address despite the fact that it was not briefed before the Court: whether selective prosecution claims have vitality in the immigration context.[d]

* * *

* * * Because I am unconvinced by the Court's statutory interpretation, and because I do not think the Court should reach the selective prosecution issue, I respectfully dissent.

* * *

Notes

1. One question that had occupied federal courts before *AADC* was whether in immigration cases § 242(g) eliminates review of final removal orders by writ of habeas corpus under 28 U.S.C. § 2241. *AADC* made clear—two years before *St. Cyr* (see material for pp. 942-57 *supra*) addressed the effect of the 1996 Act on habeas corpus generally—that § 242(g) is too narrow to have that effect. *See, e.g., Mustata v. United States Dept. of Justice*, 179 F.3d 1017, 1021-23 (6th Cir.1999) ; *Mayers v. INS*, 175 F.3d 1289, 1297 (11th Cir.1999).

---

[d] For this part of the opinion, see this Supplement, *supra* material for p. 717.—eds.

2. INA § 242(b)(9) did not take effect in time to apply in *AADC* itself, but the Court refers to that subsection, calling it an "unmistakable "zipper" clause." It seems to defer judicial review until a final removal order has issued, but what does it mean when it refers to questions of law or fact "arising from any action taken or proceeding brought to remove an alien"? Does this mean that an alien detained pending removal proceedings cannot go to court to challenge that detention until after a final removal order? For discussion of this and other timing and consolidation issues raised by the 1996 Act, see Motomura, *Judicial Review in Immigration Cases After AADC: Lessons From Civil Procedure*, 14 Geo. Immig. L.J. 385 (2000).

3. How sound is the assumption that adequate administrative records will be available only when factual issues were first aired in the quasi–judicial forum of the immigration court or the BIA? What role does this assumption play—or should it play—in *AADC*? Factual issues are routinely resolved in a variety of administrative settings that do not conform to classic trial–type procedures, and the APA certainly contemplates judicial review, on the available administrative record, of much of such "informal" decisionmaking. *See* Martin, Mandel, Cheng Fan Kwok *and Other Unappealing Cases: The Next Frontier of Immigration Reform*, 27 Va. J. Int'l L. 803, 809 (1987).

The Supreme Court has emphasized exactly this possibility for courts of appeals review, but in a non–immigration setting. In *Florida Power & Light Co. v. Lorion*, 470 U.S. 729, 105 S.Ct. 1598, 84 L.Ed.2d 643 (1985) , the Nuclear Regulatory Commission had decided—without a hearing—not to initiate enforcement action requested by a petitioner. Partly for lack of a hearing, the court of appeals ruled that the petitioner must seek judicial review in the district court, notwithstanding the Hobbs Act court of appeals review that ordinarily applied to the Commission's decisions. The Supreme Court reversed, expressing concern that the lower court's approach would result in a counterproductive bifurcation of review. *Id.* at 743. The Court explained:

> Perhaps the only plausible justification for linking initial review in the court of appeals to the occurrence of a hearing before the agency would be that, absent a hearing, the reviewing court would lack an adequate agency–compiled factual basis to evaluate the agency action and a district court with factfinding powers could make up that deficiency. Such a justification cannot, however, be squared with fundamental principles of judicial review of agency action. "[T]he focal point for judicial review should be the administrative record already in existence, not some new record made initially in a reviewing court." * * *
>
> If the record before the agency does not support the agency action, if the agency has not considered all relevant factors, or if the reviewing court simply cannot evaluate the challenged agency action on the basis of the record before it, the proper course, except in rare circumstances, is to remand to the agency for additional investigation or explanation. * * * Moreover, a formal hearing before the agency is in no way necessary to the compilation of an agency record. * * * The APA specifically contemplates judicial

review on the basis of the agency record compiled in the course of informal agency action in which a hearing has not occurred.

Id. at 743-44, 105 S.Ct. at 1606-07.

4. What is the jurisdictional basis for lawsuits for which the INA neither erects a jurisdictional barrier not lays a jurisdictional basis? They may be brought in federal district court, subject to the proviso that federal courts remain courts of limited jurisdiction, and plaintiffs must plead and prove their jurisdictional basis. Recall from the beginning of this Section that the Administrative Procedure Act (APA) establishes a broad presumption that administrative actions are reviewable. However, the Supreme Court has held that the APA does not itself constitute an independent grant of jurisdiction. *Califano v. Sanders,* 430 U.S. 99, 103, 97 S.Ct. 980, 983, 51 L.Ed.2d 192 (1977) . A litigant seeking district court review must anchor her claim elsewhere.

The key jurisdictional foundation is 28 U.S.C.A. § 1331, which vests the district courts with general federal question jurisdiction (without an amount in controversy requirement). It reads: "The district courts shall have original jurisdiction of all civil actions arising under the Constitution, laws, or treaties of the United States." Note, however, that § 1331 does not override constraints on jurisdiction in other specialized arrangements for review of agency determinations—for example, former INA § 106 and new INA § 242. *See Califano v. Sanders,* 430 U.S. at 105, 97 S.Ct. at 984.

Chapter Nine: Refugees and Political Asylum

998-1007: Overseas Refugee Programs

Presidential Determinations generally follow the format of the FY 1998 document (Casebook pp. 1002-03; the most recent PD appears in the statutory supplement), but of course the annual total and allocations vary. The PD for FY 1999, 63 Fed.Reg. 55001 (1998), provided for the admission of up to 78,000 refugees. For FY 2000, President Clinton specified a ceiling of 90,000, 64 Fed.Reg. 54505 (1999), and for FY 2001, 80,000. 65 Fed.Reg. 59697 (2000). The allocations were as follows (the European allocation was subdivided more specifically, and in varying form, in FY 2000 and 2001; "NIS/Baltics" refers to the countries that emerged from what had been the Soviet Union; "NIS" means Newly Independent States):

Table 9.1A
Allocation of Refugee Admissions in Presidential Determinations

	FY 1999	FY 2000	FY 2001
Africa	12,000	18,000	20,000
East Asia	9,000	8,000	6,000
Europe	48,000		20,000
Former Yugoslavia		17,000	
Kosovo Crisis		10,000	
NIS/Baltics		20,000	
Former Soviet Union			17,000
Latin America/Caribbean	3,000	3,000	3,000
Near East/South Asia	4,000	8,000	10,000
Unallocated	2,000	6,000	4,000
Total	78,000	90,000	80,000

The Administration announced in early 2000 that FY 2000 admissions would be held to 85,000, owing to funding cuts imposed by Congress when it adopted the State Department's budget. Refugee Reports, Nov./Dec. 1999. Actual admissions totaled 76,554 for FY 1998, 85,006 for FY 1999, and 72,515 for FY 2000. Refugee Reports, Dec. 2000.

The latest refugee processing priorities used by the State Department in selecting those who will actually be admitted under the stated allocations may be found through the State Department website and are published each December in Refugee Reports. Priority One now generally covers persons in immediate danger of specified harms, and who are referred by UNHCR or, in limited circumstances, by U.S. embassies. They may be of any nationality. Priority Two focuses on groups of special concern to the United States. For FY 2001, this Priority covers refugees who meet certain specified characteristics from Burma, Cuba, the former Soviet Union, Iran, and Vietnam. On a more limited basis, it can cover refugees from Sudan, Somalia, and Togo. Priority Three essentially admits the close relatives of previously admitted refugees, and for FY 2001 this category covers refugees from Angola, Burundi, Congo (Brazzaville), Democratic Republic of Congo, Sierra Leone, and Sudan. Generally these are people who would one day qualify for a regular family-sponsored immigrant preference category; Priority Three admission allows them to avoid waiting through the regular immigrant backlog. (Those who can qualify as immediate relatives of U.S. citizens, for which there are no quotas, are required by regulation to come as immigrants, not refugees.)

When NATO forces began bombing Yugoslavia on March 24, 1999, to force an end of repression in Kosovo province, Serbian irregular forces and the Yugoslav Army intensified the ethnic cleansing of Kosovo. An estimated 860,000 Kosovars, mostly ethnic Albanians, fled over a period of eight weeks, and many thousands more were internally displaced. Albania welcomed the refugees and patched together receiving camps with aid from the international community. Macedonia was far more reluctant, keeping many thousands waiting at the border, often in conditions of great suffering. In order to induce Macedonia to permit entry, the international community pledged over 130,000 resettlement spaces in early April. The United States promised 20,000, but initially stated that the Kosovars would be brought to the U.S. military base at Guantánamo, Cuba, in order to underscore that resettlement was temporary and was not meant to advance ethnic cleansing by Serbia. (Guantánamo had been used for offshore safe haven in earlier crises, see Casebook pp. 1172-75.) On April 21, the Administration changed course and decided instead to bring its evacuees to the United States under INA § 207, giving them full refugee status and the right to adjust to permanent residence after one year. But the Administration still intended the resettlement to be temporary, and announced that it would promote the refugees' return when the war ended. By mid-2000, the United States had accepted about 14,300 Kosovars.

In early June, 1999, President Milosevic of Yugoslavia agreed to NATO terms for withdrawal from Kosovo, coupled with an international occupation of the province, and the bombing ended. A remarkably speedy voluntary repatriation began. UNHCR estimated that 740,000 Kosovars had returned by the end of July, mostly from the camps in Albania and Macedonia. Some also returned from Germany, the United States, and other evacuation sites, and the American government offered free flights home for those who signed up through May 2000. See 76 Interp.Rel. 549 (1999); *Here Come the Kosovars*, Refugee Reports, May 1999, at 1; Migration News, July/Aug. 1999. Two-thirds to three-quarters of those resettled in Canada and the United States remained in the countries of resettlement. Id., July 2000; Refugee Reports, Feb. 2001, at 8.

1011: The Lautenberg Amendment

The Lautenberg Amendment has consistently been extended, usually in one-year increments. It is currently valid until October 1, 2001.

1027: Asylum Procedures (add at end of second full paragraph)

For a revealing account of the legislative maneuvering and the work of advocates striving to preserve core asylum protections, see P.G. Schrag, A Well-Founded Fear: The Congressional Battle to Save Political Asylum in America (2000).

1030-32: Asylum Statistics

INS filings continued to decline in FY 1998 and 1999, but moved upward somewhat in 2000, and more steeply in the early months of FY 2001. Using the same counting methodology as employed for Table 9.2, INS received 54,952 applications in FY 1998, 42,350 in 1999, and 49,462 (preliminary data) in 2000. Refugee Reports, Dec. 2000, at 5, and the FY 2000 Statistical Report on the INS website, http://www.ins.usdoj.gov/graphics/aboutins/statistics/msrsep00/ASYLUM.HTM . The case-pending backlog continues to decline, to 358,376 at the end of FY 1998, 342,095 in 1999, and 328,977 (preliminary data) in 2000. Id. The pace of reductions in the backlog should pick up considerably as NACARA is used to grant most of the ABC class members permanent resident status on non-asylum grounds (see Casebook and material for pp. 1067-70 *infra*). Preliminary data for FY 2000 show a notable increase in approval rates, although the rates of course still vary greatly by nationality: 51.8 percent granted in cases decided by INS asylum officers, and 31.4 percent granted for those decided by immigration judges. In FY 2000, immigration judges received 50,838 applications. Refugee Reports, Dec. 2000, at 5-6.

An idea of the changes in source countries over the last five years can be developed by comparing the table below to Table 9.4 in the Casebook, p. 1032.

Table 9.4A

**Asylum Applications Filed with INS, FY 2000
Leading Source Countries***

Rank	*Country*	*Number Received*	*Approval Rate for Cases Decided*
1.	China	6,476	54.8%
2.	Haiti	4,683	22.2%
3.	Mexico	3,936	7.9%
4.	Colombia	2,747	67.8%
5.	El Salvador	2,686	12.4%
6.	Somalia	2,415	74.1%
7.	Guatemala	2,084	20.1%
8.	India	1,615	49.6%
9.	Ethiopia	1,507	79.0%
10.	Liberia	1,082	58.5%
11.	Russia	946	50.7%
12.	Iran	934	70.5%
13.	Mauritania	847	25.8%
14.	Yugoslavia (incl. Croatia)	749	62.1%
15.	Burma	630	74.0%

* FY 2000 data are preliminary.

Source: Refugee Reports, Dec. 2000, at 6.

1099-1100: Internal Flight Alternative

Amendments to the asylum regulations promulgated in December 2000, 65 Fed.Reg. 76121 (2000), clarified the doctrine of internal flight alternatives and answered some of the questions posed in this section of the casebook. They now provide that the applicant lacks a well-founded fear if he or she "could avoid persecution by relocating to another part of the applicant's country of nationality * * *, if under all the circumstances it would be reasonable to expect the applicant to do so." 8 C.F.R. §§ 208.13(b)(2)(ii). In deciding on the reasonableness of relocation, the regulations specify that the adjudicator will consider whether the applicant would face "other serious harm" in that location, as well as, inter alia, the existence of civil strife and "social and cultural constraints, such as age, gender, health, and social and familial ties," although they state that such factors are not necessarily determinative. If the persecutor is the government, and the applicant has been persecuted in the past, the regulations establish a presumption that internal relocation is not reasonable – essentially that the persecution is nationwide in scope – unless INS rebuts that presumption by a preponderance of the evidence. Id. § 208.13(b)(3). If there is no proof of past persecution, the applicant bears the burden of establishing that a reasonable possibility of harm exists throughout the country of origin.

For a thorough proposal advocating new ways of looking at the internal flight alternative concept, see Hathaway, *International Refugee Law: The Michigan Guidelines on the Internal Protection Alternative,* 21 Mich. J. Int'l L. 131 (1999).

1119: Notes: Membership in a Particular Social Group (add at end of note 1)

The *Sanchez-Trujillo* requirement of a "voluntary associational relationship" received wide attention but has been rejected by most courts that have considered it, both in the United States and abroad, in favor of the *Acosta* "unchangeable characteristic" approach. In *Hernandez-Montiel v. INS,* 225 F.3d 1084 (9th Cir.2000), the Ninth Circuit surveyed the case law and reconsidered its own earlier holding. The court reasoned that because *Sanchez-Trujillo* had described a family as a prototypical example of a "particular social group," even though family relationships are not necessarily voluntary, that opinion itself recognized that other criteria could also be applied. Without overruling the earlier case, *Hernandez-Montiel* therefore held that a particular social group is "one united by a voluntary association, including a former association, *or* by an innate characteristic that is so fundamental to the identities or consciences of its members that members either cannot or should not be required to change it." *Id.* at 1093. The court went on to vacate the BIA's denial of asylum and withholding to a claimant who belonged to the particular social group of "gay men in Mexico with female sexual identities" and who had suffered harassment and physical abuse, including by Mexican police officers, because of this affiliation. *See also Aguirre-Cervantes v. INS,* 242 F.3d 1169 (9th Cir.2001) (applying *Hernandez-Montiel,* the court determined that the asylum claim, based on domestic violence meted out frequently by the father, met the refugee definition, as persecution on account of membership in a particular social group consisting of the immediate family). Consider also how proposed rules to amend the asylum regulations, which the Department of Justice published for notice and comment in December 2000, would deal with these issues. (Excerpts from the proposed rules are set forth below, material for p. 1140 *infra*, following *Matter of S-A-*.)

1121: Past Persecution (add at end of note 3)

The Department of Justice amended the asylum regulations in December 2000, 65 Fed.Reg. 76121 (2000), in major part to clarify the grounds on which the INS might rebut the presumption of future persecution when past persecution is established, and also to clarify when a person could obtain asylum based on past persecution even if there were no qualifying risk of future persecution. With regard to overcoming the evidentiary presumption, the previous regulations referred only to proof of changed country conditions. The BIA and several courts read that factor as the only possible ground for rebuttal under the regulations as then written. *See Matter of C-Y-Z-,* Int.Dec. 3319 (BIA 1997). The new regulations clarify that any "fundamental change of circumstances" -- in the home country or in the applicant's own situation, such as a change of religious belief – can be used to rebut. Most importantly, they also add as a ground of rebuttal a showing by INS that the applicant could avoid persecution by relocating to another part of the home country and that, under all the circumstances, "it would be reasonable to expect the applicant to do so." 8 C.F.R. §§ 208.13(b)(1)(i). Similar amendments were made to the regulation governing withholding of removal under INA § 241(b)(3). 8 C.F.R. § 208.16(b)(1).

INS was also concerned that *Matter of H-* could be read as broadly allowing discretionary grants of asylum in the absence of a future risk, based not only on compelling reasons arising out of the severity of the past persecution, as the earlier regulations specified, but also on general "humanitarian factors." The new regulations retain the "compelling reasons" language, but then specify one further additional basis for a grant to a past victim who lacks a future risk of persecution: when there is a "reasonable possibility that he or she may suffer other serious harm upon removal to that country." 8 C.F.R. § 208.13(b)(1)(iii). The supplementary material published with the new regulations at the proposal stage, 63 Fed.Reg. 31945-50 (1998), stated that this clause refers to harm as severe as persecution, but harm not inflicted on the basis of one of the five grounds. It does not include mere economic disadvantage or the inability to practice one's profession.

1141: Gender-based or Gender-related Asylum Claims (add at end of section)

Domestic Abuse

In recent years, considerable legal and policy debate has centered on asylum claims based on family violence or domestic abuse. *See* Musalo & Knight, *Gender-Based Asylum: An Analysis of Recent Trends,* 77 Interp.Rel. 1533 (2000) . In a case that drew considerable attention in 1999, a divided Board, sitting *en banc,* ruled against an asylum claim based on severe spousal abuse that had gone unremedied by the authorities in the woman's home country, Guatemala. *Matter of R-A-,* Int.Dec. 3403 (BIA 1999) . But a few months later, a three-member panel granted asylum to a woman severely abused by her father in Morocco because she had not followed the precepts of his understanding of the Muslim religion. It ruled that his actions amounted to persecution on account of religion. *Matter of S-A-,* Int.Dec. 3433 (BIA 2000) . The latter decision was designated as a precedent in June 2000, at INS's urging, while the Justice Department wrestled with its ultimate response to *R-A-.* In December 2000, the Department published proposed amendments to the asylum regulations, including new definitions of "persecution," "on account of," and "membership in a particular social group." The changes were intended, in part, to make the doctrine more amenable to domestic violence claims, although the published rules show signs of considerable internal differences within the Justice Department on how to handle such matters. Finally, in one of her last acts in office, Attorney General Janet Reno vacated the BIA decision in *Matter of R-A-*. Reno directed the Board to wait until the new asylum regulations were final and then to reconsider the case in light of those regulations. 78 Interp.Rel. 256, 335 (2001). The Bush Administration has not signaled its views on these issues nor whether it will try to turn the proposed regulations into final regulations.

Edited versions of these decisions and the proposed regulations follow.

MATTER OF R-A-
Board of Immigration Appeals (*en banc*), 1999.
Int.Dec. 3403.

FILPPU, BOARD MEMBER:

* * *

The question before us is whether the respondent qualifies as a "refugee" as a result of the heinous abuse she suffered and still fears from her husband in Guatemala. Specifically, we address whether the repeated spouse abuse inflicted on the respondent makes her eligible for asylum as an alien who has been persecuted on account of her membership in a particular social group or her political opinion. We find that the group identified by the Immigration Judge has not adequately been shown to be a "particular social group" for asylum purposes. We further find that the respondent has failed to show that her husband was motivated to harm her, even in part, because of her membership in a particular social group or because of an actual or imputed political opinion.

* * *

The respondent is a native and citizen of Guatemala. She married at age 16. Her husband was then 21 years old. He currently resides in Guatemala, as do their two children. Immediately after their marriage, the respondent and her husband moved to Guatemala City. From the beginning of the marriage, her husband engaged in acts of physical and sexual abuse against the respondent. He was domineering and violent. The respondent testified that her husband "always mistreated me from the moment we were married, he was always . . . aggressive."

> * * * As their marriage proceeded, the level and frequency of his rage increased concomitantly with the seeming senselessness and irrationality of his motives. He dislocated the respondent's jaw bone when her menstrual period was 15 days late. When she refused to abort her 3- to 4-month-old fetus, he kicked her violently in her spine. He would hit or kick the respondent "whenever he felt like it, wherever he happened to be: in the house, on the street, on the bus." The respondent stated that "[a]s time went on, he hit me for no reason at all."

The respondent's husband raped her repeatedly. He would beat her before and during the unwanted sex. When the respondent resisted, he would accuse her of seeing other men and threaten her with death. The rapes occurred "almost daily," and they caused her severe pain. He passed on a sexually transmitted disease to the respondent from his sexual relations outside their marriage. Once, he kicked the respondent in her genitalia, apparently for no reason, causing the respondent to bleed severely for 8 days. The respondent suffered the most severe pain when he forcefully sodomized her. When she protested, he responded, as he often did, "You're my woman, you do what I say."

* * *

When asked on cross-examination, the respondent at first indicated that she had no opinion of why her husband acted the way he did. She supposed, however, that it was because he had been mistreated when he was in the army and, as he had told her, he treated her the way he had been treated. The respondent believed he would abuse any woman who was his wife. She testified that he "was a repugnant man without any education," and that he saw her "as something that belonged to him and he could do anything he wanted" with her.

The respondent's pleas to Guatemalan police did not gain her protection. On three occasions, the police issued summons for her husband to appear, but he ignored them, and the police did not take further action. Twice, the respondent called the police, but they never responded. When the respondent appeared before a judge, he told her that he would not interfere in domestic disputes. Her husband told the respondent that, because of his former military service, calling the police would be futile as he was familiar with law enforcement officials. The respondent knew of no shelters or other organizations in Guatemala that could protect her. The abuse began "from the moment [they] were married," and continued until the respondent fled Guatemala in May 1995. One morning in May 1995, the respondent decided to leave permanently. With help, the respondent was able to flee Guatemala, and she arrived in Brownsville, Texas, 2 days later.

A witness, testifying for the respondent, stated that she learned through the respondent's sister that the respondent's husband was "going to hunt her down and kill her if she comes back to Guatemala."

We struggle to describe how deplorable we find the husband's conduct to have been.

* * *

Dr. Doris Bersing testified that spouse abuse is common in Latin American countries and that she was not aware of social or legal resources for battered women in Guatemala. Women in Guatemala, according to Dr. Bersing, have other problems related to general conditions in that country, and she suggested that such women could leave abusive partners but that they would face other problems such as poverty. Dr. Bersing further testified that the respondent was different from other battered women she had seen in that the respondent possessed an extraordinary fear of her husband and her abuse had been extremely severe.

Dr. Bersing noted that spouse abuse was a problem in many countries throughout the world, but she said it was a particular problem in Latin America, especially in Guatemala and Nicaragua. As we understand her testimony, its roots lie in such things as the Latin American patriarchal culture, the militaristic and violent nature of societies undergoing civil war, alcoholism, and sexual abuse in general. Nevertheless, she testified that husbands are supposed to honor, respect, and take care of their wives, and that spouse abuse is something that is present "underground" or "underneath in the culture." But if a woman chooses the wrong husband her options are few in countries such as Guatemala, which lack effective methods for dealing with the problem.

The Department of State issued an advisory opinion as to the respondent's asylum request. The opinion states that the respondent's alleged mistreatment could have occurred given its understanding of country conditions in Guatemala. The opinion further indicates:

> [S]pousal abuse complaints by husbands have increased from 30 to 120 a month due to increased nationwide educational programs, which have encouraged women to seek assistance. Family court judges may issue injunctions against abusive spouses, which police are charged with enforcing. The [Human Rights Ombudsman] women's rights department and various non-governmental organizations provide medical and legal assistance.

The respondent has submitted numerous articles and reports regarding violence against women in Guatemala and other Latin American countries. * * *

III. IMMIGRATION JUDGE'S DECISION

The Immigration Judge found the respondent to be credible, and she concluded that the respondent suffered harm that rose to the level of past persecution. The Immigration Judge also held that the Guatemalan Government was either unwilling or unable to control the respondent's husband. The balance of her decision addressed the issue of whether the respondent's harm was on account of a protected ground.

The Immigration Judge first concluded that the respondent was persecuted because of her membership in the particular social group of "Guatemalan women who have been involved intimately with Guatemalan male companions, who believe that women are to live under male domination." She found that such a group was cognizable and cohesive, as members shared the common and immutable characteristics of gender and the experience of having been intimately involved with a male companion who practices male domination through violence. The Immigration Judge then held that members of such a group are targeted for persecution by the men who seek to dominate and control them.

The Immigration Judge further found that, through the respondent's resistance to his acts of violence, her husband imputed to the respondent the political opinion that women should not be dominated by men, and he was motivated to commit the abuse because of the political opinion he believed her to hold.

* * *

[W]e find no definitive answer in the language of the statute [to the question whether spouse abuse may qualify a female applicant as a "refugee."] Congress envisioned that the spouse of an alien granted asylum would ordinarily be accorded derivative asylee status, if he or she was not independently eligible. Congress provided for that derivative status, if the spouse were "accompanying, or following to join," the principal applicant. *See* section 208(c) of the Act (1994). Subsequent to enactment of the basic asylum provisions of current law in 1980, Congress has created specific forms of relief, outside our refugee laws, for some women living in or escaping from abusive marriages. *See, e.g.,* section 240A(b)(2) of the Act, 8 U.S.C. § 1229b(b)(2) (Supp. II 1996) (cancellation of removal for spouses battered by a permanent resident or United States citizen); section 244(a)(3) of the Act, 8 U.S.C. § 1254(a)(3) (1994) (suspension of deportation for spouses battered by a permanent resident or United States citizen). No changes relative to battered spouses were made in the refugee definition or the asylum statute at the time of enactment of the battered spouse provisions.

The existence of derivative refugee status for spouses, as well as these nonrefugee provisions for battered spouses, raises the question whether Congress intended or expected that our immigration laws, even in the refugee and asylum context, would cover battered spouses who are leaving marriages to aliens having no ties to the United States. But we do not read the literal language of the statute actually to foreclose a construction that would accord refugee status to a battered spouse. In this case, we look principally to the facts to resolve both the "political opinion" and "social group" claims, and we do not intend any categorical rulings as to analogous social group claims arising under any other conceivable set of circumstances. Nevertheless, in reaching our decision, we find significant guidance in assessing the operation of the "particular social group" category by looking to the way in which the other grounds in the statute's "on account of" clause operate.

* * *

VI. ANALYSIS

As noted above, we agree with the Immigration Judge that the severe injuries sustained by the respondent rise to the level of harm sufficient (and more than sufficient) to constitute "persecution." We also credit the respondent's testimony in general and specifically her account of being unsuccessful in obtaining meaningful assistance from the authorities in Guatemala. Accordingly, we find that she has adequately established on this record that she was unable to avail herself of the protection of the Government of Guatemala in connection with the abuse inflicted by her husband. The determinative issue, as correctly identified by the Immigration Judge, is whether the harm experienced by the respondent was, or in the future may be, inflicted "on account of" a statutorily protected ground.

It is not possible to review this record without having great sympathy for the respondent and extreme contempt for the actions of her husband. The questions before us, however, are not whether some equitable or prosecutorial authority ought to be invoked to prevent the respondent's deportation to Guatemala. Indeed, the Service has adequate authority in the form of "deferred action" to accomplish that result if it deems it appropriate. Rather, the questions before us concern the respondent's eligibility for relief under our refugee and asylum laws. And, as explained below, we do not agree with the Immigration Judge that the respondent was harmed on account of either actual or imputed political opinion or membership in a particular social group.

A. Imputed Political Opinion

The record indicates that the respondent's husband harmed the respondent regardless of what she actually believed or what he thought she believed.

* * *

[U]nder *Elias-Zacarias*, the victim also must offer some evidence, direct or circumstantial, that it was the victim's political opinion that motivated the persecutor. The respondent's husband, it seems, must have had some reason or reasons for treating the respondent as he did. And it is possible that his own view of men and women played a role in his brutality, as may have been the case with the brutality that he himself experienced and witnessed. What we find lacking in this respondent's showing, however, is any meaningful evidence that her husband's behavior was influenced at all by his perception of the respondent's opinion.

The respondent argues that, given the nature of domestic violence and sexual assaults, her husband necessarily imputed to her the view that she believed women should not be controlled and dominated by men. Even accepting the premise that he might have believed that the respondent disagreed with his views of women, it does not necessarily follow that he harmed the respondent *because* of those beliefs, rather than because of his own personal or psychological makeup coupled with his troubled perception of her actions at times. *See id.* at 482; *Sangha v. INS*, 103 F.3d 1482, 1487 (9th Cir.1997) ("[T]he petitioner must prove something more than violence plus disparity of views.").

The Immigration Judge found, and the respondent argues, that her husband imputed a hostile opinion to her from her acts of resistance to his violence, and that he then punished her for that hostile opinion. The Court's ruling in *Elias-Zacarias,* however, establishes that the existence of a political opinion held by a persecutor, and actions by a victim that conflict with the demands of the persecutor, are not sufficient to require a conclusion that the persecutor seeks to harm the victim because of a contrary political opinion attributed to the victim. Both the respondent's argument and the "male domination" reasoning of *Lazo-Majano* [813 F.2d 1432 (9th Cir.1987)] seem to us to be akin to the analysis which the Supreme Court later did not accept as conclusive of political opinion persecution.

As we understand the respondent's rationale, it would seem that virtually any victim of repeated violence who offers some resistance could qualify for asylum, particularly where the government did not control the assailant. Under this approach, the perpetrator is presumed to impute to the victim a political opinion, in opposition to the perpetrator's authority, stemming simply from an act of resistance. Then, notwithstanding any other motivation for the original violence, the imputed political opinion becomes the assumed basis for the infliction of more harm.

It is certainly logical and only human to presume that no victim of violence desires to be such a victim and will resist in some manner. But it is another matter to presume that the perpetrator of the violence inflicts it *because* the perpetrator believes the victim opposes either the abuse or the authority of the abuser. We do not find that the second proposition necessarily follows from the first. Moreover, it seems to us that this approach ignores the question of what motivated the abuse at the outset, and it necessarily assumes that the original motivation is no longer the basis, at least not by itself, for the subsequent harm. We are unwilling to accept a string of presumptions or assumptions as a substitute for our own assessment of the evidence in this record, particularly when the reliability of these presumptions as genuine reflections of human behavior has not been established.

As for the record here, there has been no showing that the respondent's husband targeted any other women in Guatemala, even though we may reasonably presume that they, too, did not all share his view of male domination.
* * *

B. Particular Social Group

1. Cognizableness

Initially, we find that "Guatemalan women who have been involved intimately with Guatemalan male companions, who believe that women are to live under male domination" is not a particular social group. Absent from this group's makeup is "a voluntary associational relationship" that is of "central concern" in the Ninth Circuit [citing *Sanchez- Trujillo v. INS* and related cases].

Moreover, regardless of Ninth Circuit law, we find that the respondent's claimed social group fails under our own independent assessment of what constitutes a qualifying social group. We find it questionable that the social group adopted by the Immigration Judge appears to have been defined principally, if not exclusively, for purposes of this asylum case, and without regard to the question of whether anyone in Guatemala perceives this group to exist in any form whatsoever. The respondent fits within the proposed group. But the group is defined largely in the abstract. It seems to bear little or no relation to the way in which Guatemalans might identify subdivisions within their own society or otherwise might perceive individuals either to possess or to lack an important characteristic or trait. The proposed group may satisfy the basic requirement of containing an immutable or fundamental individual characteristic. But, for the group to be viable for asylum purposes, we believe there must also be some showing of how the characteristic is understood in the alien's society, such that we in turn may understand that the potential persecutors in fact see persons sharing the characteristic as warranting suppression or the infliction of harm.

Our administrative precedents do not require a voluntary associational relationship as a social group attribute. But we have ruled that the term "particular social group" is to be construed in keeping with the other four statutory characteristics that are the focus of persecution: race, religion, nationality, and political opinion. *Matter of Acosta, supra.* These other four characteristics are ones that typically separate various factions within countries. They frequently are recognized groupings in a particular society. The members of the group generally understand their own affiliation with the grouping, as do other persons in the particular society.

In the present case, the respondent has shown that women living with abusive partners face a variety of legal and practical problems in obtaining protection or in leaving the abusive relationship. But the respondent has not shown that "Guatemalan women who have been involved intimately with Guatemalan male companions, who believe that women are to live under male domination" is a group that is recognized and understood to be a societal faction, or is otherwise a recognized segment of the population, within Guatemala. The respondent has shown neither that the victims of spouse abuse view themselves as members of this group, nor, most importantly, that their male oppressors see their victimized companions as part of this group.

The lack of a showing in this respect makes it much less likely that we will recognize the alleged group as a particular social group for asylum purposes, or that the respondent will be able to establish that it was her group characteristic which motivated her abuser's actions. Indeed, if the alleged persecutor is not even aware of the group's existence, it becomes harder to understand how the persecutor may have been motivated by the victim's "membership" in the group to inflict the harm on the victim.

The respondent's showing fails in another respect, one that is noteworthy in terms of our ruling in *Matter of Kasinga*. She has not shown that spouse abuse is itself an important societal attribute, or, in other words, that the characteristic of being abused is one that is important within Guatemalan society. The respondent has shown official tolerance of her husband's cruelty toward her. But, for "social group" purposes, she has not shown that women are expected by society to be abused, or that there are any adverse societal consequences to women or their husbands if the women are not abused. While not determinative, the prominence or importance of a characteristic within a society is another factor bearing on whether we will recognize that factor as part of a "particular social group" under our refugee provisions. If a characteristic is important in a given society, it is more likely that distinctions will be drawn within that society between those who share and those who do not share the characteristic.

Here, the respondent has proposed a social group definition that may amount to a legally crafted description of some attributes of her tragic personal circumstances. It may also be true that this description fits many other victims of spouse abuse.

In our opinion, however, the mere existence of shared descriptive characteristics is insufficient to qualify those possessing the common characteristics as members of a particular social group. The existence of shared attributes is certainly relevant, and indeed important, to a "social group" assessment. Our past case law points out the critical role that is played in "social group" analysis by common characteristics which potential persecutors identify as a basis for the infliction of harm. *Matter of Kasinga, supra; Matter of H-, supra*. But the social group concept would virtually swallow the entire refugee definition if common characteristics, coupled with a meaningful level of harm, were all that need be shown.

The starting point for "social group" analysis remains the existence of an immutable or fundamental individual characteristic in accordance with *Matter of Acosta, supra*. We never declared, however, that the starting point for assessing social group claims articulated in *Acosta* was also the ending point. The factors we look to in this case, beyond *Acosta*'s "immutableness" test, are not prerequisites, and we do not rule out the use of additional considerations that may properly bear on whether a social group should be recognized in an individual case. But these factors are consistent with the operation of the other four grounds for asylum and are therefore appropriate, in our judgment, for consideration in the "particular social group" context.

On the record before us, we find that the respondent has not adequately established that we should recognize, under our law, the particular social group identified by the Immigration Judge.[1]

2. Nexus

Further, we cannot agree with the Immigration Judge's nexus analysis. In analyzing "particular social group" claims, our decisions, as well as those of the Ninth Circuit, in which this case arises, require that the persecution or well-founded fear of persecution be on account of, or, in other words, because of, the alien's membership in that particular social group. This is reinforced by the Supreme Court's ruling in *INS v. Elias-Zacarias*.

In this case, even if we were to accept as a particular social group "Guatemalan women who have been involved intimately with Guatemalan male companions, who believe that women are to live under male domination," the respondent has not established that her husband has targeted and harmed the respondent because he perceived her to be a member of this particular social group. The record indicates that he has targeted only the respondent. The respondent's husband has not shown an interest in any member of this group other than the respondent herself. The respondent fails to show how other members of the group may be at risk of harm from him. If group membership were the motivation behind his abuse, one would expect to see some evidence of it manifested in actions toward other members of the same group.

* * *

The Immigration Judge nevertheless found, and the respondent argues on appeal, that her various possible group memberships account for her plight, in large measure because the social climate and the Government of Guatemala afford her no protection from her husband's abuse. Societal attitudes and the concomitant effectiveness (or lack thereof) of governmental intervention very well may have contributed to the ability of the respondent's husband to carry out his abusive actions over a period of many years. But this argument takes us away from looking at the motivation of the husband and focuses instead on the failure of the government to offer protection.

---

[1] Other "social group" definitions potentially covering the respondent were suggested below or in the appeal briefs, such as "Guatemalan women" and "battered spouses." We need not now address whether there are any circumstances under which the various alternative proposals might qualify as a "particular social group," as each of them fails on this record under the "on account of," or nexus, requirement of the statute, for the reasons we identify below with regard to the group adopted by the Immigration Judge. * * *

Focusing on societal attitudes and a particular government's response to the infliction of injury is frequently appropriate in the adjudication of asylum cases. It is most warranted when the harm is being inflicted by elements within the government or by private organizations that target minority factions within a society. But governmental inaction is not a reliable indicator of the motivations behind the actions of private parties. And this is not a case in which it has been shown that the Government of Guatemala encourages its male citizens to abuse its female citizens, nor in which the Government has suddenly and unreasonably withdrawn protection from a segment of the population in the expectation that a third party will inflict harm and thereby indirectly achieve a governmental objective.

The record in this case reflects that the views of society and of many governmental institutions in Guatemala can result in the tolerance of spouse abuse at levels we find appalling. But the record also shows that abusive marriages are not viewed as desirable, that spouse abuse is recognized as a problem, and that some measures have been pursued in an attempt to respond to this acknowledged problem. In this context, we are not convinced that the absence of an effective governmental reaction to the respondent's abuse translates into a finding that her husband inflicted the abuse because she was a member of a particular social group. The record does not support such a conclusion, as a matter of fact, when the husband's own behavior is examined. And Guatemala's societal and governmental attitudes and actions do not warrant our declaring this to be the case as a matter of law.

* * *

The adequacy of state protection is obviously an essential inquiry in asylum cases. But its bearing on the "on account of" test for refugee status depends on the facts of the case and the context in which it arises. In this case, the independent actions of the respondent's husband may have been tolerated. But, as previously explained, this record does not show that his actions represent desired behavior within Guatemala or that the Guatemalan Government encourages domestic abuse.

Importantly, construing private acts of violence to be qualifying governmental persecution, by virtue of the inadequacy of protection, would obviate, perhaps entirely, the "on account of" requirement in the statute. We understand the "on account of" test to direct an inquiry into the motives of the entity actually inflicting the harm. *See INS v. Elias-Zacarias, supra.* Further, the adoption of such an approach would represent a fundamental change in the analysis of refugee claims. We see no principled basis for restricting such an approach to cases involving violence against women. The absence of adequate governmental protection, it would seem, should equally translate into refugee status for other categories of persons unable to protect themselves.

A focus on the adequacy of governmental protection would also shift the analysis in cases of refugee claims arising from civil war, as well as any other circumstance in which a government lacked the ability effectively to police all segments of society. This is not to say that the outcome of such an analysis would necessarily yield different results. The point, however, is that the existing statutory formula for assessing refugee claims would be altered. Instead of assessing the motivation of the actual persecutor, we might, for example, be focusing on the motivation or justification of the government for not intervening and affording real protection.

We reject the approach advocated by the respondent in view of the existing statutory language and the body of case law construing it. Consequently, the respondent must show more than a lack of protection or the existence of societal attitudes favoring male domination. She must make a showing from which it is reasonable to conclude that her husband was motivated to harm her, at least in part, by her asserted group membership.

* * *

3. The *Kasinga* Decision

Our decision in *Matter of Kasinga,* does not prescribe a different result. *

* *

In contrast to our ruling in *Matter of Kasinga, supra*, the Immigration Judge in the instant case has not articulated a viable social group. The common characteristic of not having undergone FGM was one that was identified by Kasinga's tribe, and motivated both her family and the tribe to enforce the practice on Kasinga and other young women. Indeed, the tribe expected or required FGM of women prior to marriage, signifying the importance of the practice within that tribal society. The record in *Kasinga* indicated that African women faced threats or acts of violence or social ostracization for either refusing the practice or attempting to protect female children from FGM. Moreover, although the source of Kasinga's fear of physical harm was limited to her aunt and husband, she established that FGM was so pervasive that her tribal society targeted "young women of the Tchamba-Kunsuntu Tribe who have not had FGM, as practiced by that tribe, and who oppose the practice."

The respondent in this case has not demonstrated that domestic violence is as pervasive in Guatemala as FGM is among the Tchamba-Kunsuntu Tribe, or, more importantly, that domestic violence is a practice encouraged and viewed as societally important in Guatemala. She has not shown that women are expected to undergo abuse from their husbands, or that husbands who do not abuse their wives, or the nonabused wives themselves, face social ostracization or other threats to make them conform to a societal expectation of abuse. While the respondent here found no source of official protection in Guatemala, the young woman in *Kasinga* testified that the police in Togo were looking for her and would return her to her family to undergo FGM.

We recognize that the respondent's situation is similar to that in *Kasinga*, in part, because the person actually inflicting the harm or feared harm is a family member of the victim. While the cases bear some similarities in this regard, we do not find this to be a factor that *supports* the claim of group recognition. Rather, it is a factor to be overcome if the group is to be accepted.

* * *

4. The Dissent

* * *

[T]he dissent's arguments for a political or social group motivation seem artificial. In our judgment, asylum law is not simply about the construction of various presumptions and inferences for bringing inarguably atrocious human action within one of the five grounds for which relief may be granted, particularly when those presumed or inferred motivations are undetected by both the abuser and the victim. For example, the perpetrators and victims of persecution because of race, religion, and political opinion typically understand and can explain the societal hatreds that lead to the harm or feared harm. We find it very difficult to accept the proposition that a persecutor targets persons who qualify as refugees for reasons that neither the persecutor nor the victims have been shown to understand as playing any role in the persecution.

In *Matter of S-P-,* for example, we found that it was reasonable to believe that imputed political opinion played a role in the harm suffered by a person captured during a military operation and suspected of being a member of an armed opposition force in a civil war context. The political aspects of the conflict itself were readily apparent, and the participants on both sides well understood the conflict to have a significant political dimension. We were not required to presume the existence of a motivating factor that escaped recognition by any of the parties to the civil war. Our inquiry was simply to determine whether it was reasonable to believe that a known motivating factor in the existing conflict had actually contributed to the particular prisoner's torture.

In the case now before us, it simply has not been shown that political opinion or social group membership can reasonably be understood as the motivation behind the spouse abuse.* * *

The dissent also relies on the impunity with which the respondent's husband acted as support for its "on account of" conclusions. In this regard, it draws on the opinion of Lord Hoffman in *Islam (A.P.) v. Secretary of State for the Home Dep't,* App. Cas. (Mar. 25, 1999), *available in* <http://www.parliament.the-stationery-office.co.uk/pa/ld9899/ldjudgmt/jd990325/ islamp1.htm>, which argues that a Jewish businessman attacked by an Aryan competitor in Nazi Germany would be a victim of persecution on account of race because of the failure of the authorities to provide protection, even though the competitor was personally motivated only by business rivalry. But the very point of this example was to shift the focus away from the motivation of the entity causing the harm and to focus instead on governmental discrimination as satisfying the causation or nexus element for refugee status. Indeed, it does not appear that Lord Hoffman's nexus argument would be any different if the business competitor inflicting the harm had also been Jewish. The dissent's argument, consequently, is a variant of the respondent's claim that she should be accorded refugee status simply because she was not adequately protected by her government. We are not persuaded by this argument in the context of this case for the reasons we set forth earlier in addressing the respondent's contention.

We do agree with the dissent that the reasons set forth by the respondent's husband obviously do not in any way justify the abuse. But we find the lack of legitimate motives, an unconscionable level of harm, the escalation of the harm over time, and even the very incomprehensibleness of the abuse to be an inadequate basis from which to infer a statutorily qualifying motive. It is the respondent who bears the burden of proof. The dissent's approach, however, would seem effectively to shift the burden to the Service, as it would presume the existence of a qualifying case arising from serious harm and the absence of any apparently legitimate motive.

* * *

The respondent in this case has been terribly abused and has a genuine and reasonable fear of returning to Guatemala. Whether the district director may, at his discretion, grant the respondent relief upon humanitarian grounds—relief beyond the jurisdiction of the Immigration Judge and this Board—is a matter the parties can explore outside the present proceedings. We further note that Congress has legislated various forms of relief for abused spouses and children. The issue of whether our asylum laws (or some other legislative provision) should be amended to include additional protection for abused women, such as this respondent, is a matter to be addressed by Congress. In our judgment, however, Congress did not intend the "social group" category to be an all-encompassing residual category for persons facing genuine social ills that governments do not remedy. The solution to the respondent's plight does not lie in our asylum laws as they are currently formulated.

* * *

GUENDELSBERGER, BOARD MEMBER, dissenting [joined by four other Board Members]:

I respectfully dissent. I agree with the thorough and well-reasoned decision of the Immigration Judge that the respondent has demonstrated past persecution and a well-founded fear of future persecution based on her membership in a particular social group and upon her express and imputed political opinion.

* * *

This is not merely a case of domestic violence involving criminal conduct. The respondent's husband engaged in a prolonged and persistent pattern of abuse designed to dominate the respondent and to overcome any effort on her part to assert her independence or to resist his abuse. His mistreatment and persecution of her in private and in public was founded, as the majority states, on his view that it was his right to treat his wife as "his property to do as he pleased." He acted with the knowledge that no one would interfere. His horrific conduct, both initially and in response to her opposition to it, was not that of an individual acting at variance with societal norms, but one who recognized that he was acting in accordance with them.

The harm to the respondent occurred in the context of egregious governmental acquiescence. When the respondent sought the aid and assistance of government officials and institutions, she was told that they could do nothing for her. This is not a case in which the government tried, but failed, to afford protection. Here the government made no effort and showed no interest in protecting the respondent from her abusive spouse. Thus, when the respondent went to the police or to the court to seek relief from threats, physical violence, broken bones, rape, and sodomy inflicted by her husband, Guatemalan police officials and the judge refused to intervene.

The record confirms the Immigration Judge's finding that in Guatemala there are "institutional biases against women that prevent female victims of domestic violence from receiving protection from their male companions or spouses." The Immigration Judge found that these institutional biases "appear to stem from a pervasive belief, common in patriarchal societies, that a man should be able to control a wife or female companion by any means he sees fit: including rape, torture, and beatings." Because of the principle that men should control women with whom they are intimately involved and the belief that domestic abuse is a family matter in which others must not intervene, women are not protected when they complain of domestic violence, and men who inflict such violence are not prosecuted. The respondent's husband told her that because of his connections to the military, the police and courts would not support her against him, and consistent with his threats, when she sought governmental intervention, her pleas fell on deaf ears and she was told she could not divorce him because her husband's consent was needed. No one, neither society nor the government, was able or willing to protect the respondent from her husband.

* * *

III. PERSECUTION ON ACCOUNT OF MEMBERSHIP IN A PARTICULAR SOCIAL GROUP

The respondent has been harmed in the past and possesses a well-founded fear of harm in the future "on account of . . . membership in a particular social group." The majority proposes a laundry list of hurdles to be cleared before she may demonstrate membership in a particular social group. This stringent approach to asylum law disregards decisions of tribunals, both domestic and foreign, which extend asylum protection to women who flee human rights abuses within their own homes. It also ignores international human rights developments and the guiding principle of the Charter of the United Nations, the Universal Declaration of Human Rights, and the 1951 Convention Relating to the Status of Refugees, "that human beings shall enjoy fundamental rights and freedoms without discrimination." United Nations Convention Relating to the Status of Refugees, preamble, *adopted* July 28, 1951, 189 U.N.T.S. 150 (entered into force Apr. 22, 1954) ("Convention"). The respondent has a fundamental right to protection from abuse based on gender. When domestic abuse based on gender occurs, as here, with state acquiescence, the respondent should be afforded the protection of asylum law.

A. The Immigration Judge's Finding of a Particular Social Group is Consistent with Board Precedent

The Immigration Judge found that the respondent was a member of a social group comprised of "Guatemalan women, who have been involved intimately with Guatemalan male companions, who believe that women are to live under male domination." In so finding, she carefully analyzed the facts of the case and correctly applied the law as set forth in *Matter of Acosta*, 19 I&N Dec. 211 (BIA 1985), *modified on other grounds, Matter of Mogharrabi*, 19 I&N Dec. 439 (BIA 1987), and, most recently, in *Matter of Kasinga,* Int.Dec. 3278 (BIA 1996).

* * *

Under *Acosta,* * * * immutability is of the essence. In a number of decisions, we have applied the *Acosta* immutability standard to recognize particular social groups. In each case, we recognized an immutable trait or past experience shared by the members of the social group. The shared past experience of former members of the national police force in El Salvador, for example, has been recognized as an immutable characteristic which makes such individuals members of a particular social group for asylum purposes. *Matter of Fuentes*, 19 I&N Dec. 658 (BIA 1988). Similarly, gay men and lesbians in Cuba have been found to constitute a particular social group. *Matter of Toboso-Alfonso*, 20 I&N Dec. 819 (BIA 1990). * * *

The Immigration Judge decided the case before her consistent with our precedent decision in *Kasinga.* In both cases, the social group was defined by reference to gender in combination with one or more additional factors. In *Kasinga,* the social group was defined by gender, ethnic affiliation, and opposition to female genital mutilation ("FGM"). In the instant case, the social group is based on gender, relationship to an abusive partner, and opposition to domestic violence. As the Immigration Judge below correctly observed, the respondent's relationship to, and association with, her husband is something she cannot change. It is an immutable characteristic under the *Acosta* guidelines, which we affirmed in *Kasinga.*

* * *

In attempting to distinguish this case from *Kasinga*, the majority contends that domestic violence in Guatemala, unlike FGM in Togo, is not so pervasive or "societally important" that the respondent will face "social ostracization" for refusing to submit to the harm. The majority's distinction is flawed. The facts of *Kasinga* did not suggest that Kasinga would face severe social ostracization for her refusal to submit to FGM; rather, as a member of a social group defined by her unique circumstances, she faced harm only because she lost the protection of her father. In *Kasinga*, a family member, Kasinga's aunt, targeted her after the death of her father who, as the primary authority figure in her family, had previously protected her from FGM. In other words, the practice was not so pervasive in Togo that her father, also a member of the ethnic group which had targeted her, had been unable to identify the practice as harmful. Some persons within Togo viewed FGM as an acceptable practice; other persons, even those within the same ethnic group (such as Kasinga's father, mother, and sister), did not. We extended asylum protection to Kasinga not because she faced societal ostracization, but because she demonstrated a well-founded fear of harm on account of her membership in a group composed of persons sharing her specific circumstances.

In the end, there are no meaningful distinctions that justify recognizing the social group claim in *Kasinga* while refusing to recognize such a social group claim in the instant case. The gender-based characteristics shared by the members of each group are immutable, the form of abuse resisted in both cases was considered culturally normative and was broadly sanctioned by the community, and the persecution imposed occurred without possibility of state protection.

B. The Instant Case Involves More Than Mere Membership in a Statistical Group

* * *

Social groups may be defined more or less broadly depending upon the level of generality of the defining characteristics. In the instant case, the Immigration Judge used a fairly precise and narrow focus. She could have legitimately broadened the perspective to include all Guatemalan women or, possibly, all married Guatemalan women as the particular social group. See, in this regard, the discussion in *Islam (A.P.) v. Secretary of State for the Home Dep't,* — App. Cas. — (Mar. 25, 1999), *available in* <http://www.parliament.the-stationery-office.co.uk/pa/ld9899/ldjudgmt/jd990325/islam01.htm>, (opinion of Lord Steyn, recognizing a particular social group consisting of all Pakistani women and, in the alternative, a particular social group consisting of women suspected by their husbands of adultery who would be unprotected by the Government of Pakistan). Whether defined broadly or narrowly, an independent contextual evaluation of the respondent's claim in the instant case demonstrates a particular social group.

C. Gender-Related Social Group Claims, Like Those Involving Race, Religion, Nationality, and Political Opinion, Implicate Fundamental Human Rights

The international community has recognized that gender-based violence, such as domestic violence, is not merely a random crime or a private matter; rather, such violence is a violation of fundamental human rights. In recognition of the special issues confronting female victims of violence, international bodies have responded accordingly. *See, e.g., Declaration on the Elimination of Violence Against Women,* G.A. Res. 48/104, U.N. GAOR, 48th Sess., Agenda Item 111, U.N. Doc. A/Res/48/104 (1994) (recognizing violence against women as human rights violation); *Conclusions on the International Protection of Refugees,* U.N. High Commissioner for Refugees, 36th Sess., No. 39(k) (1985) (recognizing that women in certain situations qualify for asylum based on membership in gender-based social groups).

* * *

More recently, in conjoined appeals involving women seeking asylum protection in the United Kingdom for domestic violence in Pakistan, the House of Lords found "women in Pakistan" to constitute a particular social group under the Convention's refugee definition, *Islam (A.P.) v. Secretary of State for the Home Dep't, supra.* Lord Steyn found "women in Pakistan" to be a "logical application of the seminal reasoning" of *Acosta.* Lord Hoffman recognized the importance of *context* in deciding whether a social group has been identified: "While persecutory conduct cannot define the social group, the actions of the persecutors may serve to identify or even cause the creation of a particular social group." *Id.* Citing the example of a Jew whose business was destroyed by a competitor in Nazi Germany, Lord Hoffman recognized that a persecutor's knowledge that he could act with impunity "for reasons of" (i.e., "on account of") his victim's religion went to the heart of the analysis of why the harm occurred. *Id.*

D. The Respondent Was Harmed and Has a Well-Founded Fear of Harm on Account of Membership in a Particular Social Group

Once a particular social group has been recognized, the asylum applicant must present at least "some evidence" of motive on the part of the persecutor, either direct or circumstantial, from which it is reasonable to believe that the harm was motivated, at least in part, by an actual or imputed protected ground. *INS v. Elias- Zacarias*, 502 U.S. 478, 483 (1992); *Ratnam v. INS,* 154 F.3d 990 (9th Cir.1998); *Singh v. Ilchert*, 63 F.3d 1501 (9th Cir.1995) (finding that persecutory conduct may have more than one motive); *Matter of S-P-*, Int.Dec. 3287 (BIA 1996). In identifying persecutorial motive, a number of factors may be taken into consideration. *Matter of S-P-, supra.*

First, to assess motivation, it is appropriate to consider the factual circumstances surrounding the violence. The factual record reflects quite clearly that the severe beatings were directed at the respondent by her husband to dominate and subdue her, precisely because of her gender, as he inflicted his harm directly on her vagina, sought to abort her pregnancy, and raped her.

Second, the very incomprehensibleness of the husband's motives supports the respondent's claim that the harm is "on account of" a protected ground. This is not a case of simple assault. Nor is this a case where the factors motivating the harm arguably are limited only to some comprehensible criminal motive. *Cf. Matter of V-T-S-, supra* (holding that evidence that perpetrators were motivated by their victim's wealth, in the absence of evidence to suggest other motivations, will not support a finding of persecution within the meaning of the Act). Rather, this is a case where the respondent's husband treated her merely as his property, to do with as he pleased. Under these circumstances, to place undue emphasis on the respondent's explanations for her husband's motives misses the obvious point that *no good reason* could exist for such behavior.

Illegitimate motives can give rise to an inference that the harm has occurred on account of a statutorily protected characteristic which, in this case, is the respondent's membership in a particular social group and her actual or imputed political opinion. * * *

Third, we should attempt to identify why such horrific violence occurs at all. In *Kasinga*, we determined that FGM exists as a means of controlling women's sexuality. So too does domestic violence exist as a means by which men may systematically destroy the power of women, a form of violence rooted in the economic, social, and cultural subordination of women. * * * Moreover, it is well established in the record before us that Guatemalan society is especially oppressive of women generally. The materials submitted reveal that extreme patriarchal notions are firmly entrenched in Guatemalan society.

Finally, as has been advanced by the House of Lords in *Islam (A.P.) v. Secretary of State for the Home Dep't, supra,* the level of impunity with which a persecutor acts is relevant to an "on account of" determination. Like the persecutor who targets the Jewish shopkeeper because he knows he can act with impunity owing to his victim's religion, the respondent's husband knows he can commit his atrocities with impunity because of the respondent's gender and their relationship. The respondent testified that her husband repeatedly expressed that it would be "useless" for her to contact the authorities, especially given his connections with members of the police. The respondent's husband was not a simple criminal, acting outside societal norms; rather, he knew that, as a woman subject to his subordination, the respondent would receive no protection from the authorities if she resisted his abuse and persecution.

It is reasonable to believe, on the basis of the record before us, that the husband was motivated, at least in part, "on account of" the respondent's membership in a particular social group that is defined by her gender, her relationship to him, and her opposition to domestic violence.

IV. PERSECUTION ON ACCOUNT OF ACTUAL OR IMPUTED OPINION OPPOSING DOMESTIC ABUSE AND VIOLENCE AGAINST WOMEN

Although they represent distinct bases for asylum and withholding of deportation, claims of persecution inflicted on account of membership in a particular social group and of persecution inflicted on account of actual or imputed political opinion may share certain attributes. * * *

Opposition to male domination and violence against women, and support for gender equity, constitutes a political opinion. *See Fatin v. INS, supra*, at 1242 (acknowledging that there is "little doubt that feminism qualifies as a political opinion within the meaning of the relevant statutes"). Congress' enactment of the Violence Against Women Act of 1994, 42 U.S.C. § 13981 (1994) ("VAWA"), which addresses crimes of violence "due, at least in part, to an animus based on the victim's gender," reflects a political point of view that finds domestic violence abhorrent and intolerable. Such opposition is not restricted to those who have not been victims of domestic violence, but constitutes a political opinion that may also be held by victims of domestic violence themselves. Both the respondent's status as a battered spouse in an intimate relationship with a man who imposes such domination and her actual or perceived opinion opposing domestic violence trigger continuing abuse from the persecutor who seeks to dominate her.

* * *

The majority insists that the respondent's husband persecuted her regardless of what she believed or what he thought she believed, claiming that the record does not reflect he was motivated by gender animus generally. The majority contends that the abuser was not, even in part, motivated by the respondent's resistance to his domination, even though he had told her he viewed women as property to be treated brutally in order to sustain his domination. This is contrary to fact, law, and logic. To reach such a conclusion, the majority must ignore entirely the mixed motive doctrine, which not only constitutes a well- established basis for asylum in cases arising before the Ninth Circuit, but also constitutes a basis for asylum in claims made before this Board. Furthermore, as we stated in conjunction with our consideration of the respondent as a member of a particular social group, illegitimate motives triggering persecution raise an inference that the harm has occurred on account of a statutorily enumerated ground.

* * *

Had the respondent been subjected to such heinous abuse due to political opposition to communism, imputed as a result of her family's economic class or political activities, the majority would recognize her situation as one of persecution on account of political opinion. She is not less eligible or entitled to protection on account of her political opinion opposing male domination expressed through the abuse of women by their husbands, or the political opinion attributed to her, than were the comparably qualifying applicants to whom we have granted asylum.

* * *

MATTER OF S-A-
Board of Immigration Appeals, 2000.
Int.Dec. 3433.

HURWITZ, BOARD MEMBER:

[The immigration judge found the respondent inadmissible and denied her application for asylum and withholding of removal.]

* * *

I. BACKGROUND

The respondent is a native and citizen of Morocco, who is either 20 or 21 years old. She testified that she was schooled for 3 years and knows how to write her name, but she is otherwise illiterate.

The respondent claims that in Morocco she was a victim of her father's escalating physical and emotional abuse. According to the respondent, the abuse arose primarily out of religious differences between her and her father, i.e., the father's orthodox Muslim beliefs, particularly pertaining to women, and her liberal Muslim views. Her father beat her a minimum of once a week using his hands, his feet, or a belt. She notes that her father did not mistreat her two brothers.

The respondent related that when she was about 14 years old, her maternal aunt, who is a United States citizen and resides in this country, sent her a somewhat short skirt. On one occasion the respondent wore the skirt outside her home. Upon returning home, her father verbally reprimanded her, heated a straight razor, and burned those portions of her thighs that had been exposed while she was wearing the skirt. He told her that he was taking this action to scar her thighs so that, in the future, she would not be tempted to wear what he considered improper attire. The respondent stated that she and her mother were afraid to go to the hospital after the incident, so her mother went to the local pharmacy and procured an ointment to treat the burns.

[She also testified to other incidents of severe violence at the hands of her father and to his orders that she remain in the house and have no casual contact with strangers.]

* * *

The respondent stated that she did not consider requesting police protection or seeking any other kind of governmental intervention because her mother's previous efforts in that regard had proven unproductive. According to the respondent, she twice attempted to commit suicide in Morocco, and on two other occasions she attempted to run away in an effort to escape her circumstances. After at least one of the suicide attempts, she had her stomach pumped in a hospital and was unconscious for 3 days.

* * *

The respondent's maternal aunt testified on her behalf at the hearing. The aunt stated that she has weekly telephonic contact with her sister, the respondent's mother, and that she visits Morocco once a year. She testified that the respondent's father is

> very strict, he's Muslim . . . [and he] is very tough when it comes to the religion, so he wants [the respondent] to . . . wear . . . the long robe to cover her face with the veil and when she . . . doesn't listen to him, . . . he abuse her, he beat her up . . . because he said that his daughter, he want her to be Muslim girl, like to follow the Islam.

* * *

II. CREDIBILITY
* * *

We find particularly significant the evidence of record regarding the respondent's fear of seeking governmental protection from her father's abuse. Both the respondent and her aunt testified that, in Moroccan society, such action would be not only unproductive but potentially dangerous. The report of the United States Department of State that is contained in the record confirms that "few women report abuse to authorities" because the judicial procedure is skewed against them, as even medical documentation is considered insufficient evidence of physical abuse, and women who do not prevail in court are returned to the abusive home. Committees on International Relations and Foreign Relations, 105th Cong., 2d Sess., *Country Reports on Human Rights Practices for 1997* 1538 (Joint Comm. Print 1998) [hereinafter 1997 Country Reports].

Finally, we find that, in addition to corroborating the respondent's testimony concerning the futility and perils of seeking governmental protection, the 1997 *Country Reports* corroborate other dimensions of the testimony offered by the respondent and her aunt. The report states that, in Morocco, domestic violence is commonplace and legal remedies are generally unavailable to women. *Id.* at 1538. The report also indicates that "[g]irls are much less likely to be sent to school than are boys" and notes that the illiteracy rate for women is 67 percent. *Id.* at 1539.

We conclude that the respondent presented credible testimony in support of her asylum claim. We must therefore decide whether the respondent merits the relief that she has requested. * * *

III. ASYLUM AND WITHHOLDING OF REMOVAL

[After finding that the respondent had suffered past persecution, that if she returned she "would likely face severe, possibly fatal, persecution," and that she had no genuine recourse to the governmental authorities in Morocco, the Board turned to the issue of nexus.]

* * *

E. "On Account of"

An alien must also demonstrate that the persecution alleged was inflicted or would be inflicted on account of race, religion, nationality, membership in a particular social group, or political opinion. Sections 101(a)(42)(A), 208(a) of the Act. An asylum applicant is not obliged, however, to show conclusively why persecution has occurred or may occur. *See, e.g., Matter of S-P-, supra.*

The jurisprudence relevant to the respondent's allegations includes decisions granting relief to those persecuted on the basis of their religious beliefs. Both this Board and the federal circuit courts of appeals have found merit to the claims of aliens asserting that they were persecuted on account of their religion. *See, e.g., Kossov v. INS,* 132 F.3d 405, 409 (7th Cir.1998) (finding past persecution where a woman applicant was beaten and taunted because of her religious beliefs and eventually suffered a miscarriage); *Fisher v. INS,* 79 F.3d 955 (9th Cir.1996) (holding that dress and conduct rules pertaining to women may amount to persecution if a woman's refusal to comply is on account of her religious or political views); *Matter of Chen, supra,* at 19-20 (granting relief to the son of a Christian minister who was subjected to atrocious persecution, including burns to his body, house arrest, and a prohibition on school attendance).

> We find that the persecution suffered by the respondent was on account of her religious beliefs, as they differed from those of her father concerning the proper role of women in Moroccan society.
> The record clearly establishes that, because of his orthodox Muslim beliefs regarding women and his daughter's refusal to share or submit to his religion-inspired restrictions and demands, the respondent's father treated her differently from her brothers. * * *

Because the persecution suffered by the respondent was on account of her religious beliefs, we find this case distinguishable on the facts from circuit court decisions holding that persecution on account of gender alone does not constitute persecution on account of membership in a particular social group. *See, e.g., Gomez v. INS,* 947 F.2d 660 (2d Cir.1991). We also find that because of the religious element in this case, the domestic abuse suffered by the respondent is different from that described in *Matter of R-A-,* Int.Dec. 3403 (BIA 1999).

* * *

ORDER: The respondent's appeal from the denial of her asylum application is sustained. The respondent is granted asylum and is admitted to the United States as an asylee.

Proposed Amendments to the Asylum Regulations

On December 7, 2000, the Department of Justice published proposed amendments to the asylum regulations, acting in part in response to the decision in *Matter of R-A-, supra* . 65 Fed.Reg. 76588-98 (2000). The proposal, which has not been finally acted on, includes these new definitions of key terms not previously defined by regulation:

> (a) *Persecution.* Persecution is the infliction of objectively serious harm or suffering that is subjectively experienced as serious harm or suffering by the applicant, regardless of whether the persecutor intends to cause harm. Inherent in the meaning of the term persecution is that the serious harm or suffering that an applicant experienced or fears must be inflicted by the government of the country of persecution or by a person or group that government is

unwilling or unable to control. In evaluating whether a government is unwilling or unable to control the infliction of harm or suffering, the immigration judge or asylum officer should consider whether the government takes reasonable steps to control the infliction of harm or suffering and whether the applicant has reasonable access to the state protection that exists. Evidence of the following are pertinent and may be considered: Government complicity with respect to the infliction of harm or suffering at issue; attempts by the applicant, if any, to obtain protection from government officials and the government's response to these attempts; official action that is perfunctory; a pattern of government unresponsiveness; general country conditions and the government's denial of services; the nature of the government's policies with respect to the harm or suffering at issue; and any steps the government has taken to prevent infliction of such harm or suffering.

(b) *On account of the applicant's protected characteristic.* An asylum applicant must establish that the persecutor acted, or that there is a reasonable possibility that the persecutor would act, against the applicant on account of the applicant's race, religion, nationality, membership in a particular social group, or political opinion, or on account of what the persecutor perceives to be the applicant's race, religion, nationality, membership in a particular social group, or political opinion. In cases involving a persecutor with mixed motivations, the applicant must establish that the applicant's protected characteristic is central to the persecutor's motivation to act against the applicant. Both direct and circumstantial evidence may be relevant to the inquiry. Evidence that the persecutor seeks to act against other individuals who share the applicant's protected characteristic is relevant and may be considered but shall not be required.

(c) *Membership in a particular social group.*
(1) A particular social group is composed of members who share a common, immutable characteristic, such as sex, color, kinship ties, or past experience, that a member either cannot change or that is so fundamental to the identity or conscience of the member that he or she should not be required to change it. The group must exist independently of the fact of persecution. In determining whether an applicant cannot change, or should not be expected to change, the shared characteristic, all relevant evidence should be considered, including the applicant's individual circumstances and information country conditions information about the applicant's society.
(2) When past experience defines a particular social group, the past experience must be an experience that, at the time it occurred, the member either could not have changed or was so fundamental to his or her identity or conscience that he or she should not have been required to change it.

(3) Factors that may be considered in addition to the required factors set forth in paragraph (b)(2)(i) of this section, but are not necessarily determinative, in deciding whether a particular social group exists include whether:

(i) The members of the group are closely affiliated with each other;

(ii) The members are driven by a common motive or interest;

(iii) A voluntary associational relationship exists among the members;

(iv) The group is recognized to be a societal faction or is otherwise a recognized segment of the population in the country in question;

(v) Members view themselves as members of the group; and

(vi) The society in which the group exists distinguishes members of the group for different treatment or status than is accorded to other members of the society.

How would these three new definitions, taken together, change the existing treatment of asylum applications involving domestic violence? How would they affect applications based on other threatened harms? In particular, how would they affect consideration of the broader issues regarding "particular social group" considered in the casebook? Should such changes be made? (The Bush Administration has not yet signaled its plans with regard to this set of proposed rules nor its stance toward asylum applications based on domestic violence.)

Note

For judicial consideration of asylum and related claims involving domestic violence, see, *e.g., Ali v. Reno*, 237 F.3d 591 (6th Cir.2001) (denying a claim to protection under the Torture Convention, because domestic law enforcement authorities had not acquiesced in the family violence; dictum states that such a claim might be valid if authorities ignored or consented to the abuse); *Aguirre-Cervantes v. INS*, 242 F.3d 1169 (9th Cir.2001) (finding eligible for asylum a 19-year-old Mexican woman based on severe abuse committed by her father, who was judged to have persecuted on the basis of membership in the particular social group constituted by his immediate family). *See generally* Gilbert, *Family Violence and U.S. Immigration Law: New Developments*, Immigration Briefings, Mar. 2001, at 24-33.

Children's Asylum Claims and the Elián González Case

In December 1998, INS issued Guidelines for Children's Asylum Claims, designedly "similar in approach" to the Gender Guidelines issued in 1995 and discussed at Casebook p. 1130. They are reprinted at 76 Interp.Rel. 5 (1999). Noting the unique vulnerability of minors, the guidelines offer several considerations that should be taken into account in adjudicating such claims, especially when a child applies independently, and not simply as a dependent included on the application of an accompanying parent. The guidelines are particularly useful in discussing age-sensitive interview techniques that might be appropriate for younger children.

Certain elements of the guidelines attracted unexpectedly intense attention in early 2000, in connection with the case of Elián González, which was covered intensely by the media. Elián was a Cuban child found tied to an inner tube at sea in November 1999 after his mother and most of the other adult passengers attempting to cross from Cuba to Florida perished in the sinking of their boat. He was brought by the Coast Guard to a Miami hospital and was released shortly thereafter by INS to his great-uncle, Lázaro González, a Cuban expatriate living in Miami, pending completion of his immigration processing. The poignancy of his rescue made the case a *cause célèbre* on both sides of the Florida strait, because his mother had taken him on the trip without the knowledge or consent of his father, Juan Miguel González, from whom his mother had been divorced. The father demanded his return to Cuba and stated that no asylum application— or any other application—should be considered on his behalf. The Cuban government, and Fidel Castro personally, became deeply involved in public rallies and other efforts supporting his return. Meantime Elián also became a symbol for much of the Cuban-American community in the United States, who believed passionately that he should not return to Cuba. Lázaro's home in Miami became the scene of rallies and round-the-clock vigils. His arrival also coincided with the beginning of the presidential primary season, which heightened the level of political interest in his case. Several members of Congress, which was in a long recess when he arrived, vowed to pass a bill granting him U.S. citizenship.

After interviewing the father in Cuba and the great-uncle in Miami, INS decided on January 5, 2000 to honor the father's wishes, and therefore not to consider asylum claims that had been filed in Elián's name. Lázaro's lawyers asserted that the Guidelines mandated consideration of the asylum claim on its merits, rather than a refusal at the threshold. They pointed to a passage in the Guidelines providing that "Asylum Officers should not assume that a child cannot have an asylum claim independent of the parents." *Id.* at 19. INS concluded, however, that it would not consider the claim in these circumstances, because Elián and his father had had a close relationship, Juan Miguel was judged to be asserting his true will in insisting on Elián's return, and the purported asylum claims did not "present an objective basis for ignoring the parents' wishes." The INS decision concluded that "there is no divergence of interest between the father and child with respect to Elián's asylum application which warrants interference with the father's parental authority."

The great-uncle, as next friend, challenged the decision in federal court, and also initiated a separate action for custody in state court. Both courts rejected his claims. The federal court decisions are published as *González ex rel. González v. Reno,* 212 F.3d 1338 (11th Cir.2000), *affirming* 86 F.Supp.2d 1167 (S.D.Fla.2000), *rehearing and rehearing en banc denied with opinion,* 215 F.3d 1243 (11th Cir.2000), *cert. denied,* 530 U.S. 1270, 120 S.Ct. 2737, 147 L.Ed.2d 1001 (2000). For the final state court decision, see *In re González,* 2000 WL 492102 (Fla.Cir.Ct. Apr. 13, 2000) (NO. 00-00479-FC-28). (The federal case attracted amicus briefs from several human rights organizations, who did not take a position on the particular controversy, but who worried that INS' approach might undermine the Guidelines.)

In the meantime, Juan Miguel came to the United States in April 2000, intending to resume custody while the legal battles were concluded. The Miami family refused to turn over Elián on terms that Juan Miguel could accept, even after negotiating sessions in Miami directly between them and Attorney General Reno. Elián was ultimately extracted by force from the home in a swift pre-dawn raid on April 22. The controversy over the raid was intense, but public opinion shifted strongly in favor of Elián's reunion with his father. Promised congressional hearings on the raid were never held, and no legislation on Elián ever reached the floor. Elián and his father returned to Cuba a few hours after the Supreme Court denied certiorari.

Those who wish to consider the Elián González case in more detail will find a useful collection of key documents on the INS website (http://www.ins.usdoj.gov/graphics/publicaffairs/ElianG.htm). Worth especially close attention are the INS's January 5, 2000, decision and the various court rulings. For wider musings on this unique case, see Motomura, *The Year is 2020: Looking Back on the Elián González Case (A Fantasy)*, 77 Interp.Rel. 853 (2000).

1142-45: The Exception Clauses

In *INS v. Aguirre-Aguirre*, 526 U.S. 415, 119 S.Ct. 1439, 143 L.Ed.2d 590 (1999), the Supreme Court considered the withholding exception clause that applies when "there are serious reasons for considering that the alien has committed a serious nonpolitical crime outside the United States" (now INA § 241(b)(3)(B)(iii)). The Court described the facts and the BIA's ruling as follows (526 U.S. at 421-23, 119 S.Ct. at 1444, citations omitted):

> According to the official hearing record, respondent testified that he and his fellow members would "strike" [in support of their political objectives] by "burning buses, breaking windows or just attacking the police, police cars." Respondent estimated that he participated in setting about 10 buses on fire, after dousing them with gasoline. Before setting fire to the buses, he and his group would order passengers to leave the bus. Passengers who refused were stoned, hit with sticks, or bound with ropes. In addition, respondent testified that he and his group "would break the windows of . . . stores," "t[ake] the people out of the stores that were there," and "throw everything on the floor."
>
> * * *
>
> In addressing the definition of a serious nonpolitical crime, the BIA applied the interpretation it first set forth in *Matter of McMullen*, 19 I. & N. Dec., at 97-98: "In evaluating the political nature of a crime, we consider it important that the political aspect of the offense outweigh its common-law character. This would not be the case if the crime is grossly out of proportion to the political objective or if it involves acts of an atrocious nature." In the instant case, the BIA found, "the criminal nature of the respondent's acts

outweigh their political nature." The BIA acknowledged respondent's dissatisfaction with the Guatemalan government's "seeming inaction in the investigation of student deaths and in its raising of student bus fares." It said, however: "The ire of the ES [Aguirre's student organization] manifested itself disproportionately in the destruction of property and assaults on civilians. Although the ES had a political agenda, those goals were outweighed by their criminal strategy of strikes . . . ." The BIA further concluded respondent should not be granted discretionary asylum relief in light of "the nature of his acts against innocent Guatemalans."

The Ninth Circuit had reversed the BIA on three grounds. First, relying on the UNHCR Handbook, it held that the BIA was required to balance the seriousness of the offense against the gravity of the persecution risked upon return. Second, the BIA had not sufficiently considered whether Aguirre's acts were of an atrocious nature. And finally, the BIA "should have considered the political necessity and success of Aguirre's methods."

The Supreme Court ruled unanimously that all three rulings were erroneous. The first holding presented the clearest error. The BIA's interpretation, separating the assessment of the seriousness of the offense from the judgment about persecution, is consistent with the plain language of the exception clause. The UNHCR Handbook, although a useful interpretative aid, is not binding. A finding that the offense is particularly serious can therefore bar withholding no matter what persecution risk the alien faces. Second, atrociousness is not required for a finding that the criminal element of an offense outweighs its political aspect. As to the third issue, the BIA determined that the exception clause applied because of the lack of proportion between his criminal acts and his political objectives. No more was required.

The Supreme Court underscored the deference that should be given to the BIA's statutory interpretation, under *Chevron U.S.A. Inc. v. Natural Resources Defense Council, Inc.*, 467 U.S. 837, 842, 104 S.Ct. 2778, 81 L.Ed.2d 694 (1984). Other reasons also call for deference here (526 U.S. at 425, 119 S.Ct. at 1445):

> [W]e have recognized that judicial deference to the Executive Branch is especially appropriate in the immigration context where officials "exercise especially sensitive political functions that implicate questions of foreign relations." *INS v. Abudu*, 485 U.S. 94, 110, 108 S.Ct. 904, 99 L.Ed.2d 90 (1988). A decision by the Attorney General to deem certain violent offenses committed in another country as political in nature, and to allow the perpetrators to remain in the United States, may affect our relations with that country or its neighbors. The judiciary is not well positioned to shoulder primary responsibility for assessing the likelihood and importance of such diplomatic repercussions.

Aguirre addresses the exception to protection based on criminal acts outside the United States. In separate cases involving Laotian nationals who had originally been admitted to the United States as refugees under INA § 207, the

BIA provided guidance in a related but somewhat different setting: asylum claimants with criminal convictions in the United States. Under INA § 241(b)(3)(B)(ii), withholding of removal is barred for an alien who, "having been convicted by a final judgment of a particularly serious crime, is a danger to the community of the United States." An aggravated felony (or felonies) for which the alien was sentenced to at least five years of imprisonment in the aggregate is considered *per se* a particularly serious crime, under an amendment enacted in the 1996 Act. But if the sentence falls below that threshold, the BIA held, there is no presumption that the crime is particularly serious, even if it fits the definition of an aggravated felony. Instead, a careful a case-by-case inquiry into the facts and circumstances of the offense must be undertaken. *Matter of L-S-,* Int.Dec. 3386 (BIA 1999) (alien convicted of bringing an undocumented alien into the U.S. and sentenced to 3½ months, held not barred from withholding); *Matter of S-S-,* Int.Dec. 3374 (BIA 1999) (alien convicted of robbery in the first degree while armed with a handgun and sentenced to 55 months in prison, held barred).

1145-46: The Convention Against Torture (add at end)

As part of the Foreign Affairs Reform and Restructuring Act of 1998, Div. G., Pub.L. 105-277, 112 Stat. 2681, Congress enacted a provision executing Article 3 of the Torture Convention (with respect to both removal and extradition) and mandated that the affected agencies issue implementing regulations within 120 days. *Id., § 2242* (reprinted in the statutory supplement). INS's regulations, published at 64 Fed.Reg. 8478 (1999), took effect on March 22, 1999, and are incorporated into the asylum regulations printed in the Statutory Supplement (8 C.F.R. Part 208). The major changes appear in revised §§ 208.16-.18 and 208.30-.31. The regulations generally incorporate the determination of Torture Convention protection into existing procedures before the immigration judges, who may grant withholding of removal under the Torture Convention, with effect essentially like that of withholding under § 241(b)(3). Torture Convention protection will generally be considered only if the person fails to qualify for asylum or regular withholding. Consideration of torture claims is also incorporated into the credible fear determinations made as part of expedited removal. An alien found there to have a credible fear of torture will ordinarily be placed in full removal proceedings before an immigration judge to have the claim determined. Those who fail to meet the credible fear threshold may be summarily removed.

Aliens subject to the special removal procedures known as administrative removal (INA § 238(b), applicable to non-LPR aggravated felons) or reinstatement (INA § 241(a)(5), allowing swift repatriation under prior removal orders), who request either Torture Convention protection or standard withholding of removal under § 241(b)(3) are referred to an asylum officer for screening. (Such aliens are statutorily ineligible for asylum.) The process is similar to credible fear screening in expedited removal, but the threshold is more demanding. This process is known as "reasonable fear" screening, and one who passes will be referred to an immigration judge for a proceeding that addresses only the withholding claim. If no "reasonable fear" is shown, the alien remains subject to speedy expulsion. Aliens who qualify, in any of the above procedures, for protection under the Torture Convention, but who are covered by a bar in INA § 241(b)(3)(B) (for example, serious criminals) will receive only "deferral of removal," and they may be held in detention. Deferral of removal is a status that is more easily terminated than either asylum or withholding,

For the BIA's first case construing the Torture Convention's protection against *refoulement, see Matter of S-V-,* Int.Dec. 3430 (BIA 2000) (protection denied; government's inability to control Colombian guerrillas who would allegedly torture the claimant is not sufficient to meet the treaty requirement that torture occur with the acquiescence of government officials). *See also Ali v. Reno,* 237 F.3d 591 (6th Cir.2001) (construing the requirement of "acquiescence" by government officials that appears in the Convention's definition of torture, in context of a claim of threatened domestic violence).

1150: The Factfinding Challenge (add at end of paragraph following block quote)

A somewhat similar revelation of an apparent false claim occurred in 2001. The case of *Abankwah v. INS,* 185 F.3d 18 (2d Cir.1999), had gained considerable global notoriety. There the court reversed the BIA's denial of asylum to a woman who claimed that she would be subjected to female genital mutilation as a punishment for premarital sex, if returned to her village in Ghana. In December 2000, however, the *Washington Post* carried a story that the claimant had stolen identity papers belonging to the real Adelaide Abankwah, who was residing illegally in the United States and at first was reluctant to come forward and expose the fraud. An INS investigation and the newspaper's own inquiries in her home village in Ghana indicated that she had fabricated the underlying story about the tribe's threat to her. *See* Branigin & Farah, *Asylum Seeker is Impostor, INS Says: Woman's Plea Had Powerful Support*, Wash. Post, Dec. 20, 2000, at A1.

1155: The Factfinding Challenge (add at end of part 7)

Another 1998 decision by the BIA regarding the evaluation of facts has come to play a major role in asylum cases. Under its doctrine, immigration judges now typically impose a greater burden of corroboration on asylum seekers. *Matter of M-D-,* Int.Dec. 3339 (BIA 1998). The Board stated that it was implementing *Matter of S-M-J-,* Int.Dec. 3303 (BIA 1997) (discussed in the Casebook at p. 1154), but it laid considerable stress on this passage from that earlier decision: *"where it is reasonable to expect* corroborating evidence for certain alleged facts pertaining to the specifics of an applicant's claim, such evidence should be provided . . . [or] an explanation should be given as to why such information was not presented." *Matter of M-D-, supra,* at 4, (emphasis and ellipsis added by the *M-D-* opinion). The claimant in *M-D-* was a Mauritanian who said he had spent 11 months in a refugee camp in Senegal. The Board rejected his claim, holding that it would have been reasonable to expect him to provide greater evidence of identity and of his stay in the refugee camp, possibly through a letter from his sister who, he testified, lives in Senegal outside the refugee camp, or from his family still in the camp.

On judicial review, the Court of Appeals for the Second Circuit reversed and remanded for further proceedings. *Diallo v. INS,* 232 F.3d 279 (2d Cir.2000). Diallo had argued that the BIA's doctrine requiring corroboration was fundamentally inconsistent with treaty standards and the governing regulations. The regulations provide: "The testimony of the applicant, if credible, may be sufficient to sustain the burden of proof without corroboration." 8 C.F.R. §§ 208.13(a), 208.16(b). The court disagreed with this part of Diallo's argument. The regulation is permissive and was "apparently drafted to ensure that lack of corroboration would not necessarily defeat an asylum claim, * * * not to excuse the requirement of corroboration in all cases in which an applicant's testimony is credible." 232 F.3d at 286. The BIA's basic rule requiring corroboration where it can be reasonably expected, or else an explanation for why corroboration cannot be provided, is entirely consistent with the governing regulations and with international standards, as reflected in the UNHCR Handbook. The court explicitly rejected the contrary rule in the Ninth Circuit, "a blanket holding that credible testimony is automatically sufficient and renders corroborating evidence unnecessary," citing *Cordon-Garcia v. INS,* 204 F.3d 985, 992 (9th Cir.2000).

Nonetheless, the *Diallo* court found "fatal flaws" in the BIA's application of the rule in this case, primarily because it failed to rule explicitly on Diallo's credibility and also failed to explain adequately why it found his limited corroboration and proffered explanation insufficient. *See also Abdulai v. Ashcroft,* 239 F.3d 542 (3d Cir.2001) (similarly approving the BIA's general corroboration requirement but finding its application too severe in the particular case and remanding for further consideration and explanation).

The Ninth Circuit reaffirmed and elaborated its own doctrine in *Ladha v. INS,* 215 F.3d 889 (9th Cir.2000). In defending the *M-D-* approach, the INS had there relied on earlier circuit cases indicating that credible testimony alone would be sufficient *if* corroborative evidence is unavailable. The *Ladha* decision rejected such an interpretation of its earlier rulings; "this circuit assumes evidence corroborating testimony found to be credible is 'unavailable' if not presented." *Id.* at 900. A footnote, however, appeared to limit the full impact of this doctrine: "We do not address if or when it is proper to consider the 'availability' of corroborating evidence as a basis for an adverse credibility finding; we are concerned only with the body of cases addressing corroboration *after* a finding that an applicant is credible." *Id.* at 900 n.11. In *Sidhu v. INS,* 220 F.3d 1085, 1090 n.2 (9th Cir.2000), the court applied this doctrine in affirming the BIA's authority to make an adverse credibility finding when the applicant failed to produce his father to corroborate his story. The father lived in a nearby suburb in the United States and had been a witness to the central events in India. Nonetheless, later Ninth Circuit cases have returned to the theme that the BIA may not require corroboration in the absence of an adequately grounded adverse credibility finding. *See, e.g., Kataria v. INS,* 232 F.3d 1107, 1114 (9th Cir.2000).

1167-70: From TPS to NACARA

Final regulations implementing § 202 of NACARA (the amnesty for Nicaraguans and Cubans) were published at 65 Fed.Reg. 15846-57 (2000). Interim regulations governing § 203 (special rules for suspension of deportation for Guatemalans and Salvadorans) were published at 64 Fed.Reg. 27856-82 (1999). In a significant move, and in an effort to bring greater parity to the treatment of the respective groups under the different sections of NACARA, the Clinton administration added to the latter regulations a presumption that should ease the approval of nearly all time-eligible Guatemalans and Salvadorans. Under the presumption, *ABC* class members will be presumed to have established extreme hardship for suspension or cancellation purposes if they submit a completed application form responding to basic questions regarding extreme hardship. The INS may challenge the presumption and seek to rebut the hardship showing, but such challenges are expected to be rare. For a thorough analysis, see Silverman & Joaquin, *NACARA for Guatemalans, Salvadorans and Former Soviet Bloc Nationals: An Update*, 76 Interp.Rel. 1141 (1999). Proposals in the 106th Congress to bring complete parity to all the Central American groups, and also to extend coverage to long-resident Hondurans, were not enacted. *See* 76 Interp.Rel. 793, 1249, 1606 (1999); 77 *id.* 1083, 1121, 1373, 1562 (2000).

1170-71: TPS in Practice

As of June 2001, the designations of TPS for Montserrat and Somalia, mentioned in the casebook, have been extended at least into the latter half of 2001, with the same cut-off dates originally used (the date by which the person had to be present in the United States in order to benefit from TPS). TPS for Bosnia was allowed to lapse as of February 10, 2001. Liberia was redesignated a second time, moving up the cut-off date to Sept. 29, 1998, but effective only for a year. Thereafter, covered Liberians have benefited from DED ordered by the President, currently authorized through Sept. 29, 2001. Burundi, Sierra Leone and Sudan were redesignated, moving up the cut-off date to November 9, 1999, and TPS will last at least into November 2001. The Attorney General added Guinea-Bissau to the list in March 1999, effective only to September 10, 2000, and not renewed. Angola was designated on March 29, 2000, and then redesignated one year later for a further 12-month period. The Attorney General also provided 18 months of TPS for nationals of Nicaragua and Honduras in January 1999, based on the destruction caused by Hurricane Mitch in November 1998. This TPS period was later extended to July 5, 2002. The Administration decided not to heed calls to grant TPS also to aliens from El Salvador and Guatemala as a result of Hurricane Mitch, judging that the natural disaster had been less severe in those countries. But it did provide a less formal stay of removal to those two countries' nationals through early March 1999. 76 Interp.Rel. 1, 47 (1999). An earthquake in El Salvador in early 2001 led to a formal 18-month designation of TPS for Salvadorans, commencing March 9, 2001. Persons from the Kosovo province of Yugoslavia received TPS in June 1998, and the class was redesignated and expanded in June 1999, with effect until December 8, 2000. 77 Interp.Rel. 696 (2000). It was not further extended.

The information in this paragraph is drawn from Interpreter Releases and the comprehensive TPS chart showing dates and Federal Register citations, on the INS website at http://www.ins.usdoj.gov/graphics/services/tps_inter.htm.

The President's grant of DED to Haitians in December 1997 eventually led to the result the Administration sought. In late 1998 Congress enacted the Haitian Refugee Immigration Fairness Act of 1998, Pub.L. 105-277, Div. A., Title IX, 112 Stat. 2681. It provides adjustment of status for what the proponents estimated would be 50,000 Haitians, on terms similar to those applied to Nicaraguans and Cubans under the *de facto* amnesty provided by § 202 of NACARA. The benefit is available to Haitian nationals physically present since December 31, 1995 who filed for asylum or were paroled before that date, plus certain unaccompanied, orphaned or abandoned Haitian children. INS published final regulations implementing the Act at 65 Fed.Reg. 15835 (2000). *See* Jacklin, *The Haitian Refugee Immigration Fairness Act ("HRIFA")*, Immigration Briefings, Sept. 1999.

For a thorough study of TPS, with thoughtful recommendations for reforms, see S. Martin, Schoenholtz, & Meyers, *Temporary Protection: Towards a New Regional and Domestic Framework*. 12 Geo. Immig. L.J. 543 (1998).